The Thi
on the Ap

The Things You Find on the Appalachian Trail

A Memoir of Discovery, Endurance and a Lazy Dog

KEVIN RUNOLFSON

McFarland & Company, Inc., Publishers
Jefferson, North Carolina, and London

All photographs are from the author's collection.

Library of Congress Cataloguing-in-Publication Data

Runolfson, Kevin, 1973–
    The things you find on the Appalachian Trail : a memoir of discovery, endurance and a lazy dog / by Kevin Runolfson.
       p.   cm.
    Includes index.

    ISBN 978-0-7864-4767-1
    softcover : 50# alkaline paper ∞

    1. Appalachian Trail—Description and travel.   2. Runolfson, Kevin, 1973– —Travel—Appalachian Trail.   3. Hiking—Appalachian Trail.   4. Runolfson, Kevin, 1973– —Relations with women.   5. Man-woman relationships—Appalachian Trail.   6. Dogs—Appalachian Trail.   7. Human-animal relationships—Appalachian Trail.   I. Title.
F106.R88   2010
917.404′43—dc22   2009051645

British Library cataloguing data are available

©2010 Kevin Runolfson. All rights reserved

No part of this book may be reproduced or transmitted in any form or by any means, electronic or mechanical, including photocopying or recording, or by any information storage and retrieval system, without permission in writing from the publisher.

On the cover: Rufus, taking a much needed break on the Appalachian Trail (2001); background ©2010 shutterstock

Manufactured in the United States of America

McFarland & Company, Inc., Publishers
  Box 611, Jefferson, North Carolina 28640
    www.mcfarlandpub.com

Table of Contents

Preface   1

1. The Beginning of a Long Trip   3
2. Rufus, Rangers and Rain   30
3. Thinning of the Herd   51
4. Carnivorous Death Cows   68
5. Virginia Is for Lovers   91
6. Baking with New Friends   112
7. Tribulations of New York–New Jersey   130
8. Hot and Hotter Still   147
9. The Greens and the Whites   162
10. New Hampshire Brings Dad, but Takes Rufus   185
11. Mainly Beautiful   208

Epilogue   220
Index   221

Preface

After four years in the Marine Corps and three years of an angry marriage, I am done with both. I'm leaving everything behind and hiking the Appalachian Trail, a 2167-mile footpath that extends from Georgia to Maine along the Appalachian Mountains. The only things I am taking with me are a backpack full of gear and my newly adopted dog, Rufus, a one-year-old Shar Pei–Chocolate Lab mix. Together, Rufus and I set off into the mountains.

I expect a long, quiet walk in the woods occasionally interrupted by a fellow hiker, but instead I discover an entire hiker community where everyone is loosely related by the common goal of reaching Maine. Almost every day I meet someone new. I receive trail magic, the name for random acts of kindness bestowed onto hikers, and meet trail angels, people who perform such acts.

Hiking with Rufus becomes an adventure on its own. I adopted him as stalwart companion, but it turns out I have acquired a lazy bundle of fear wrapped in fur. I quickly learn that Rufus is afraid of bridges, fire, rain, thunder, lightning and most wildlife. He also doesn't like to walk when it's too hot, too cold, too early, too late, daytime or nighttime. A rock would make a better hiking partner.

I meet a beautiful hiker named Teresa, and after bumping into each other for several hundred miles, we become hiking partners. The trail takes us through towns, over mountains, and across 14 different states as I encounter weeks of rain, record breaking heat, bears, snakes and killer cows. I grow as a person, my relationship with Teresa becomes romantic, and Rufus evolves into an unstoppable hiking machine (unless, of course, he encounters rain, heat, cold, wildlife, or pretty much anything else). The end of the trail nears, but does that mean my relationship with Teresa must end with it? Only Maine will tell.

I wrote this book a couple of years after completing the trail. I kept a nightly journal while hiking, and the journal proved invaluable in writing the story. I also carried a camera, and some of those photographs are in this book. Let it be known, however, that the pictures don't adequately capture trail life. Most of my pictures show happy hikers under blue skies. They don't show the miserable days, or the week of constant rain. Truth be told, it was usually only on the nice days that anyone had the energy to break out a camera.

Hiking the trail was one of the best experiences of my life, and in this book I hope to share that experience with anyone willing to listen.

1

The Beginning of a Long Trip

I can't believe it! Here I am at Amicalola Falls State Park in northern Georgia, ready to embark on my dream adventure: hiking the Appalachian Trail. My ride is driving away, red taillights disappearing into the black night, and I am left with only my faithful dog, Rufus, for company. The visitor center has been closed for hours, its yellow security lights emitting a soft glow across the deserted parking lot. The forest makes its own sound: a soft wind moving through the tree limbs, the scurrying of tiny nocturnal feet, and an occasional hoot from an owl. My guidebook says there is a shelter a couple hundred yards up the Appalachian Trail, so I throw on my backpack and walk towards the visitor center, hoping to find a sign pointing the way. As I walk around to the back of the building I see a single brush stroke of blue paint on a wooden post. Only four inches wide by eight inches tall, roughly the size of my hand, this simple blaze of paint marks the beginning of my six-month hike. Guided by the glow of my headlamp and the lights from the building, I head towards the faint silhouette of a stone arch beyond the wooden post. I take my first step through the eight-foot-tall portal and begin my journey.

The Appalachian Trail, commonly known as the A.T. or simply "the trail," begins in Georgia and is a continuous footpath that stretches for 2,167 miles over mountains and meadows, crossing rivers and streams, through towns and along ridges before finally ending on the summit of Mt. Katahdin in northern Maine.

I first heard about the trail around 1998 while stationed at Marine Corps Air Base El Toro near Los Angeles. I lived the first twenty-two years of my life in Spokane, Washington, and had never heard of the A.T. One day the travel section of the local newspaper, *The Orange County Register*, had a three-page article about the A.T. complete with a map depicting the trail as it crossed through fourteen different states. I read the article twice, engrossed in the author's account of climbing over mountains, making friends with fellow hikers, and conversing with the locals as he hiked towards Maine. It grasped something in my soul, a sense of adventure, and I knew I wanted to hike it.

After I finished my four-year tour in the Marine Corps, I didn't have a job, and my rocky three-year marriage had finally gone over the cliff. Luckily, we didn't have any kids, but it still was a messy, bitter divorce. While separated from my wife during the last year of our marriage, I saved meticulously for this trip. Once out of the Corps, I moved back to Spokane and stayed with my parents for a few months. I read everything I could about the trail, taking some advice and leaving the rest, and ultimately planned to hike it my own way. Come March, I had the money, the time, the knowledge, and a dog willing to follow me anywhere. I was ready.

"C'mon, Rufus," I say as we step through the shadowy arch. I make a mental note to come back in the morning and preserve my start with some photographs. Right now I need to find the shelter and get some sleep. Ahead of me the path begins to climb and the woods quickly absorb the faint light coming from the visitor center. I start up the trail, plunging into the darkness with nothing but my dim headlamp to show me the way.

I've been walking less than ten minutes when a voice booms out, "What're you looking for?" The unexpected noise shatters the silence, and I almost have a heart attack. Visions of inbred mountain men with no teeth race through my mind, and my first instinct is to get the hell out of here fast, but I've waited too long and worked to hard to back out now.

"I'm looking for the shelter!" I yell back to the dark woods.

A tiny light appears in the darkness to my left, and the voice, in a lower, gentler tone, calls out, "It's right here. Come on over."

I follow the voice and one hundred feet down a small worn path is the shelter, a simple four-sided wood box with a roof. I walk over and introduce myself to the man who called out.

"Thanks for the help. My name's Kevin, and this is Rufus," I say.

"Come on in and sit down, Kevin. Name's Loren," he answers. "I take it you're hiking the trail?" I nod my head yes. "Me too, I've been here since yesterday though. Trying to get some rest before I start hiking."

Since yesterday? I've been on the trail for five minutes, and if it were not 11 P.M. and pitch black out, I would be hiking. Once inside the shelter, however, I am able to get a good look at Loren and his statement begins to make more sense. He is a tall, thin, sixty-year-old man with the worst sunburned nose I have ever seen. Small blisters ooze droplets of pus, and looks like a good sneeze will blow it clean off his face. The nose isn't his only physical ailment, though. He looks exhausted, like he hasn't eaten or slept in a week. Every movement is slow and deliberate, sending a grimace of pain across his face. I don't know what he did to put him in such a condition, but I sure hope it was more than the quarter-mile walk from the visitor center to here.

"Did ya see the bike down by the visitor center?" he asks, noticing me staring at his nose. I shake my head no. "Good, then maybe someone took it. Anyway, I just rode that bike from Ohio to here; took me two weeks. I threw on my pack and pedaled until I got here."

My jaw drops and my respect for this man soars as I now understand the cause of his pain. Most people wouldn't bike to the end of their driveway, but this man rode over 500 miles to start a 2,100-mile hike.

"You biked from Ohio to here?" I ask, making sure I heard him right.

"Yup, burnt my nose pretty bad too. The ride took more out of me than I thought, so I'm going to spend another day here before hiking out. Pretty crappy bike too. Bought it for fifty bucks at a garage sale. It didn't ride real good, but I wanted something I could throw away once I got here. Happy to get rid of that bike, the front wheel's been wobbly since Pennsylvania," he says, then looks at Rufus. "Hey, how did you get here? It's too late for buses, and I thought cabs didn't take dogs."

"Just some guy I met on the Internet," I reply. "I was surfing the Internet for shuttles from the Atlanta airport to here, and I came across his name on a hiking website. Most shuttles charge close to $100, but his post said no charge. I called him and he stated he wanted to hike the trail someday, so every now and then he shuttles hikers from Atlanta to here for free. Something about building good karma."

"Well, Kevin, first day on the A.T. and you've already met a trail angel."

"A trail angel?" I ask, unfamiliar with the term.

"A trail angel. It's a person who helps a hiker purely out of kindness and doesn't want anything in return except a thanks." Loren climbs into his sleeping back and turns off his headlamp.

I spread my sleeping bag out on a cot and look around. The shelter is about twelve feet by twelve feet, and contains eight metal cots and nothing else. Two other hikers are in the cots next to mine, but they don't talk much. They are a couple of teenagers from Quebec and speak very little English. I speak great English, I just don't know any French. Needless to say, we don't have an enlightened conversation.

With no one left to share my excitement of starting the trail, I crawl into my sleeping bag and roll out Rufus' sleeping pad. As I settle down to sleep I ask myself if I really know what I have set out to do. When I was a kid, my parents took my brother and me out camping several times a year, but that always involved a trailer full of the comforts of home. In college I developed a taste for hiking, and in the Marine Corps I hiked all over Southern California, but my longest trip was only three days. I have never attempted something as daunting as six months in the woods.

Eventually sleep overcomes anxiety and I drift off, while Rufus sits up listening to every little sound. Rufus is a one-year-old Shar Pei–Chocolate Lab mix that I picked up from the Humane Society four months ago. He has the brown coat and body of a chocolate lab, the head and wrinkles of a Shar Pei, and the disposition and energy of a sack of flour. My dog is lazy, and I am hoping this walk will energize him.

I wake up with the sun to the sound of chattering teeth. Not mine, my dog's. It dropped well below freezing last night and Rufus isn't used to it. His extremely short fur isn't designed for these temperatures. I didn't realize how cold it got here in March, and I tell myself I'm not going to be the first person to hike the trail with a Popsicle dog. I will have to work harder at keeping Rufus warm. We get out of the shelter and into the sunshine, warming up with a walk down to the visitor center to take some pictures.

It is a beautifully clear day, and I have the park to myself as the visitor center doesn't open for another hour. I entertain the thought of hiking over to Amicalola Falls but quickly give up that idea. I already have a full day of hiking in front of me, considering Amicalola Falls State Park isn't even the southern end the trail, though this is where 99 percent of all hikers start or finish. Correctly said, Amicalola Falls is the start of the approach trail to get to the Appalachian Trail. Springer Mountain, the official start of the trail, is a distant 8.8 miles away. The only ways to get to Springer are to hike from here or take a long, bumpy logging road that passes within a mile of the summit. As most hikers arrive by cab or bus, not too many can take advantage of the shortcut. So, it's almost nine miles to get to the starting point of a 2,100-mile hike!

March 26, 2001. 2167 miles to Kahtadin. Rufus and I at Amicolola Falls State Park.

Wanting to enjoy the morning sun before entering the cold woods, I wander around outside the visitor center. There are several signs and even a box of pamphlets explaining the Appalachian Trail, the brainchild of environmentalist Benton MacKaye. Ninety years ago MacKaye envisioned a trail running from Mt. Washington, New Hampshire (the highest peak in New England), to Mt. Mitchell, North Carolina (the highest peak east of the Mississippi). Local hiking clubs had already built and maintained trails throughout the Appalachian Mountains, so MacKaye wanted to connect the trails into one grand path that traversed the length of the Appalachians.

In 1921, MacKaye wrote the article "An Appalachian Trail: A Project in Regional Planning" that outlined this concept. One idea was that the trail could be broken up into sections that the local hiking groups would maintain. True to MacKaye's vision, there are now thirty-one different hiking clubs along the trail doing everything from cutting away fallen trees that block the path to rebuilding shelters and digging new wells. Each club has only what their membership can handle, from a 7.2-mile section in Pennsylvania maintained by the York Hiking Club to the entire 266-mile section in Maine cared for by the Maine Appalachian Trail Club. Without these volunteers spending countless hours in the woods, the trail would quickly become nothing more than an overgrown footpath.

In 1925, Benton MacKaye, along with members of both the National Park Service and the U.S. Forest Service, founded the Appalachian Trail Conference (ATC), the governing body of the A.T. That year, with a mere one hundred volunteers, work on the trail began. By 1937, thousands of volunteers had worked on the trail and the last mile was finished, completing a tremendous undertaking that created a continuous footpath running the distance from Mt. Katahdin, Maine, to Mt. Oglethorpe, Georgia (later moved 15 miles north to Springer Mountain.) Its fame was short-lived, though, as World War II took away the attention and manpower once devoted to the trail. It slowly fell into disrepair and nature moved back in. However, in 1948 the Appalachian Trail regained its national recognition when a brave young man took on the challenge of being the first person to thru-hike the entire trail. Earl Shaffer, fresh out of the military, set out on the journey. Much of the trail was unmarked and obliterated, but Shaffer hiked from Georgia to Maine in less than five months. Stories of his exploits were heard in hiking groups across America. The local hiking clubs, restocked with men coming back from the war, once again took on the tremendous project of maintaining the trail.

Even though the trail was reclaimed, it was still far from perfect. Much of it ran along roads or on private property. One year the trail would wind through an open meadow, and the next year a housing development would be built there, forcing the local hiking club to build a new path. In 1968 Congress recognized the Appalachian Trail as a National Scenic Trail and set aside money to purchase land. With funding from Congress and the help of local clubs, the

ATC starting buying property so the entire trail could be permanently routed through protected state or federal land. It has been a long process, but now over 99 percent of the trail is protected by a buffer zone that prohibits a ski resort or a Wal-Mart from being built on it. This buffer zone is anywhere from 100 to 1,000 feet wide and protects the trail, as well as the shelters along it and the streams, rivers, meadows, plants, and animals beside it.

Warmed by the walk around the park, Rufus and I head back into the woods. The first mile follows an incredibly steep dirt road that goes straight up the side of a mountain, and it kicks my butt. I have been running four miles a day for the last two years and consider myself in good shape, but I'm not prepared for this. A mile uphill doesn't sound so tough, but a mile uphill over rocks and roots, lugging a fifty-pound backpack, is a different story. The trail finally leaves the road and continues up and down more hills, Rufus and I staggering over every one. Rufus doesn't run around and sniff everything as he has his own fifteen-pound pack to struggle with. He is carrying a bright red dogpack that fits over his back and shoulders. It has two large pockets, one on each side, that contain his food and his water bowl, two eight-foot lengths of rope that serve as leashes, and a small square sleeping pad.

The trail, though physically hard, is very easy to follow with a blue blaze painted on a tree or rock every couple hundred yards. The actual A.T. is marked by white blazes of the same size and shape. The blue blazes mark side trails to water, shelters and the different paths that cross the trail, including this one.

For six long, grueling hours Rufus and I follow the blue blazes over continuous mountains when I finally I see it, my first white blaze. I've reached the summit of Springer Mountain! Drenched in sweat and barely able to breathe, I can officially start hiking the Appalachian Trail. I stand tall on the 3,782-foot summit for the view I've worked so hard to attain: a 320-degree panoramic view of trees. The summit is heavily forested, and only a tiny opening faces out west where I am able to look out upon the Georgia mountains. As I enjoy my petite view, another hiker comes trudging up the trail.

"Yup, that's it. All the way up this mountain for that little tiny view," says the hiker, a man in his mid-fifties. "I take it you're hiking the trail?"

"Yes, with my dog," I reply, still looking out at the rolling mountains.

"Then get used to this. The trail marches right up a tree-covered mountain with no view, drops down the other side, and repeats the process."

"I take it you've hiked the trail before?" I ask.

"Well, almost. Last year I made it to Connecticut before I sprained my ankle and had to get off the trail. I'm going to try it all again this year. My name's Arkon, by the way. That's Greek for 'old man.' You have a trail name yet?"

"No, should I have one?"

"Don't worry about it, you'll get one."

1. The Beginning of a Long Trip

Trail names are a tradition out here, much like nicknames in college. The tradition started in the mid-seventies when the number of hikers began to increase exponentially. Some people name themselves, but most are named by fellow hikers, and by the end of the first month almost everyone will have a trail name. It is a lot easier to remember someone by his or her trail name. There may be five Steves hiking the trail, but there is only one Arkon.

"It is beautiful today, isn't it?" Arkon says as he sits down and pulls out a candy bar from his pack. "Last year the clouds were pissing on me here. It was a miserable day, cold and wet. Where are you planning on staying tonight?"

"I don't really know. Wherever I find that looks good," I say.

"Well, if you don't mind hiking a few more miles there's a nice shelter with a great stream behind it at the base of the mountain. That's where I'm heading."

He shoves his candy wrapper in his pack and heads down the other side of the mountain. I follow him to the shelter and we each claim a spot. The Amicalola shelter was an anomaly with its four walls and a door. This shelter, like most on the trail, is a simple three-sided structure with one side open to the elements. There aren't any cots, just room for six to eight to sleep side by side on the plywood floor, and the only amenity is a privy (trail term for outhouse) fifty yards behind it.

I lay out my sleeping bag and Rufus immediately plops down on it. I dump some food into his bowl, and after cooking a dinner of mac and cheese, I lie down next to Rufus and throw the sleeping bag over us like a blanket. It's the last week of March and daylight savings time isn't for another week. As the sun sets, the temperature quickly plummets, but with both Rufus and me under my sleeping bag we are quite warm. It's too early to sleep, but too cold to do anything other than lie here and look outside at the fading light. I look around the shelter and see several strange contraptions hanging from the ceiling. Long strings hang down from the rafters, and on the end of each one is a four-inch stick tied perpendicular to the string. Most of them have an empty tuna can suspended on a knot several inches above the stick.

"What are those things, Arkon?" I ask.

"Mouse hangers. You hang your food bag on the stick there."

"You're kidding me."

"No, really, that's what they are. The mice will climb down the string but are unable to get past the tuna can. One night, though, I did see a mouse climb down an empty string, shift his body back and forth until the string started swinging, then launch himself towards a food bag suspended two feet away," he says, swinging one of the hangers to illustrate his story. "The poor sucker almost made it, but he caught his foot on the tuna can and went spinning out of control, landing on the floor. He hightailed it on out of the shelter. Most shelters have these mouse-hangers in them, but some don't. You can make one out of your bear-bag string. You have bear-bag string, right?"

"In my pack," I say, pointing towards my pack beside me. "Big problem with bears getting food?"

"Bears? No. The shelters that do have bear problems usually have a cable system set up to secure your food. The biggest threats to food are mice, raccoons, and squirrels. All you really need to do is hang your food high enough off the ground to keep those guys away from it."

I crawl out of my warm sleeping bag and quickly hang my food bag on one of the hangers. I have found a mentor and I want to extract all the knowledge I can from Arkon. Last year he pushed too hard trying to complete the trail and injured himself, but this year he has a new plan. Hike slow, enjoy the trip, and make it as far as he can before winter sets in. Arkon and I talk for another hour until we see a headlamp bobbing down the trail.

"Over here, man! The shelter's over here!" Arkon yells out to the stranger. A few minutes later Loren's face appears and he crawls in. He still looks exhausted, and within ten minutes Loren is fast asleep. I explain Loren's situation to Arkon, then try to get some sleep myself. It's only 7:00 P.M., but it's dark and cold, and there's nothing else to do but talk or sleep.

The next day I wake with the sun. It is my first full day on the Appalachian Trail and I am almost giddy. Rufus is still curled up beside me under the sleeping bag, and he is as warm as toast. For a wake up call I yank off the sleeping bag, exposing him to the cold morning air. Rufus wakes with a jump and a snarl, and gives me a dirty look before hopping out of the shelter to find a place to relieve himself. Some dogs have no sense of humor.

Arkon and Loren have already packed up and are leaving, so I begin what will be a daily ritual for the next six months. I feed Rufus, then start my white gas stove, and as the water heats to a boil, I pack up Rufus' stuff and mine. When the water is hot I make a bowl of instant oatmeal and have my own breakfast. After breakfast is the mundane task of brushing my teeth, refilling my water bottle (using a small hand-pump water filter) and double checking to make sure I don't leave anything.

I saddle up Rufus with his pack, something he neither enjoys nor fights but simply accepts, then put on my own pack and start walking. It takes half a mile to work out the soreness from yesterday's exertion but soon I am in a rhythm, and within a couple hours I come upon Arkon and Loren taking a break.

"Damn young kids," Arkon says to me as I approach. "I get up an hour earlier than you, but you catch up without a problem. I wish I had hiked this thing when I was younger and my body didn't fight me every step. Where are you headed tonight?"

I shrug my shoulders and he opens up his guidebook. I carry the same book. It's called the Data Book, printed by the ATC, and is almost a necessity for all hikers. It is a small book that breaks the trail into eleven sections. It then lists the shelters, towns, water sources, major mountains and best camping spots, along with the corresponding mileage from the start of that particular section. I have a second book called the Thru-Hiker's Companion, but it is more of a luxury than a necessity. It is a lot thicker and heavier than the Data Book, and while it doesn't list every single item like the Data Book, it contains a lot of background information about shelters, parks and interesting sites, and most importantly, has rough maps of the towns and lists the services available in them.

I am also carrying a set of maps for the A.T. Each hiking club is responsible for mapping its section and the ATC prints the maps. The maps are not really needed since the trail is so well marked, and at $120 for the set of fifty maps I was hesitant to buy them. I asked my older brother for his advice, and he asked me a very simple question: "Have you ever even considered hiking through the back country for a weekend without some type of map?" I responded, "No." He then asked me why I would consider hiking 2,100 miles in completely unknown terrain without one. I bought the whole set. As the whole set weighs close to ten pounds I have only the Georgia map with me; the rest are in my mail drops. I pull out the map and sit down next to Arkon.

"Justus Creek is a great place to stay tonight," Arkon says, pointing to a blue squiggly line on my map. "No shelter, but there's a lot of flat places to camp along the creek, and it is a beautiful spot. It'll make for a twelve-mile day today, shouldn't be too hard."

Loren shakes his head as he looks at his Data Book. I don't know if he will be able to walk twelve miles today, but Rufus and I can. I hike with Arkon and Loren for a few minutes, but they both move too slowly for me. I tell them I'll see them tonight and easily outpace the older men.

I'm still excited to be on the trail, but the actual task of walking is tedious when alone. I talk to Rufus to pass the time but he ignores me; he must still be angry for the wakeup call this morning. I walk all day in silence, and at last come over the crest of the hill descending towards Justus Creek. I see a tent, then another, and another. It looks like a homeless camp. Numerous tents in varying degrees of completion run up and down both sides of the creek. Clothes hang from every available protrusion — tops of tents, tree branches, rocks — and are even on the ground. Half a dozen campfires burn along the banks with a handful of hikers sitting around each one. A couple brave souls are bathing in Justus Creek, learning about the wonderful effects of hypothermia. And here I brought Rufus for company thinking this would be a solitary endeavor!

This side is packed, but there is a wooden bridge spanning the creek. I cross the sturdy bridge when I hear a whining emanating from the camp. Great: not only do I get to spend the night with twenty of my closest hobos, I get to sleep next to a daycare center. I look back to see who brought the kid, only to see Rufus on the far side of the bridge, one paw tentatively touching the first plank while he scans the flowing creek three feet below. He's the one whining! I can't believe it. My dog is afraid of bridges. I have never met a dog afraid of bridges, and I'm not sure how to get him to deal with his fears and cross the creek. Intense counseling with a trained psychologist might help, but so would a catapult. Unfortunately, I have neither. After ten minutes of coaxing and pleading he still hasn't moved, so I throw on his leash and drag him. Rufus finally moves, hunkering low and testing every plank before setting his full weight on it. It's going to be a long trip.

The evening turns out to be as cold as the last couple of nights, and across the creek there is a group of hikers sitting around an inviting fire. Among the group is one of the most beautiful women I have ever seen, with curly brown hair framing her face. After setting up my tent I head over to the fire, bringing my irresistibly cute dog with me. Not wanting to waste any flirting time struggling with Rufus on the bridge, I pick him up and carry him. I set Rufus down where he can enjoy the warmth and work my way over to where this dream girl sits. She looks up at me with her big brown eyes and says in a musical voice, "Where's your dog going?"

"Huh, what?" I romantically reply, unfamiliar with this new pickup line.

"Your dog, the one you just carried over here. He got up and left. Where's he going?"

I look back in time to see a brown rump and tail crossing the crest of the hill we had come down to get here; Rufus is heading back towards Springer Mountain!

"Ahhhh, save my spot. I'll be back," I reply. I'm off at a dead run up the hill, intent on catching my dog before he makes it all the way back to the parking lot. My saving grace is that Rufus, though built like an ox, stands to just below my knee and runs with all the speed and grace of a hemorrhoidic sloth. Catching up to him is easy; stopping this sixty-five pound block of muscle is a bit tougher.

"Rufus, stop!" "Halt, you mangy mutt!" "Please stop, pretty please?" Nothing works, so I grab him by the collar and hang on for the ride until he stops. Now I'm panting as hard as Rufus and it's getting dark, so I put Rufus on his leash and we quickly hike the half mile back to camp.

Frustrated, but not done flirting, I am walking towards the fire when my arm is almost ripped out of its socket from behind. I turn around to see the end of the leash attached to a furry, brown anchor. The fire is twenty feet away, and Rufus has firmly planted himself. I pull on the leash to no avail; Rufus doesn't budge. Okay, my dog is afraid of both bridges and fire. No problem. I tie him to a tree and head to the fire myself. Again I work my way towards the woman and sit down on the log next to her with the plan of striking up a mesmerizing conversation. She has the first words, though.

"What's wrong with your dog?"

What could Rufus be doing now? Dragging the tree back towards Springer? Chewing off his feet so he doesn't have to hike anymore? I'm ready to throw him on the fire. Reluctantly, I turn around and look at Rufus, who is staring at me with cold eyes and shivering uncontrollably. A couple of minutes ago we were in a dead run, and I'm still sweating while he's already chilled. It's cold, but not that cold. It can't be below forty degrees. If nothing else, this dog is going to make my trip interesting. I walk back over to my tent, grab a couple of T-shirts and return, covering Rufus with them. Okay, Rufus has been exercised, fed, watered, tethered, and clothed. There is nothing more I can do for him. He has to be content while I do a little sweet-talking.

I sit back down as this lovely lady looks up at me and says, "Your dog's still cold, he's over there shaking."

Let the dog shake, shiver and freeze, I think. That's not what I say, though. I may not be Casanova, but I'm pretty sure that saying I plan to let my dog freeze to death won't get me high marks in the "sensitivity" column. Instead I reply, "Nah, he's just excited to be here. He'll be okay."

"No, he won't. He's freezing. I'll be right back," and she walks over to her tent, returning with a small green fleece blanket which she wraps around Rufus. "There, now he'll be warm. I'm Teresa."

I chat with Teresa and the other hikers around the fire. Teresa is hiking the trail with her grandpa, but already frustrated with his slow pace. It took them three days to get here from Springer, while I covered the same ground in two days. Also at the fire is an interesting couple named Texas Tortoise and Planting Flowers. They met while attempting a thru-hike two years ago and were married shortly after. They quit the trail after a couple hundred miles and are back this year to try to complete the whole thing.

The fire dies down and I am tired from the long day and chasing Rufus around, so I bid the group, and Teresa in particular, good night.

I carry Rufus back over the bridge to my tent, where another hiker is setting up his tent near mine. It's an enormous tent, easily big enough to fit Rufus, myself, and a Volkswagen Beetle. Being neighborly, I call out to him and whoever else he must be sharing the tent with.

"How are you guys doing tonight?" I ask. He turns and looks at me with a very confused, and wary, look. Hmmm, must be a local. I'm about to ask the question much slower when he answers.

"You guys? I'm the only one here. I am assuming you're talking to me, right?"

"I'm sorry," I reply. "I saw the huge tent and thought you must be with someone else. That's a lot of weight for one person to carry."

"Yeah, it is a little big for one person but it's the only tent I have. The name's Packman. Care for some fudge cake?" he says, holding out some type of food item.

I nod my head vigorously. I never turn down free food. Packman comes over and offers me a piece of the fudge cake, a dense, sticky type of fudge fruitcake. I rip a piece off the 12 × 12 brick and shove it in my mouth. Very delicious, but very heavy.

"Eat all you want," Packman says. "I've got twelve pounds of this stuff. It's my favorite thing to take canoeing, but I didn't realize it's so heavy."

Packman apparently didn't realize the weight of most of his items before heading into the woods. His tent alone is a whopping ten pounds, eight pounds heavier than my small one-man tent. He's a photographer so he brought his professional camera, several lenses, and a tripod. He also brought a full roll of duct tape, jeans, several jackets, full-size cook pots with a back-up set of metal utensils, a second pair of shoes and anything else that would fit in his pack. Turns out this is the first time he has ever gone backpacking. He tells me about his week-long canoe trips. He says he just brought everything with him that he took canoeing. His pack must weigh near 80 pounds, and the fact that Packman can carry it at all is amazing considering he stands no taller than 5'6" and can't weigh an ounce over 130.

With the fudge cake in my belly, I say goodnight to Packman and retire to my tent with Rufus beside me. I lie awake for a few minutes thinking about the woman I just met. I would like to hike with Teresa and talk to her more, but it sounds like I'm not going to get the chance as I don't want to hike any slower than I already am. I don't expect to see Teresa again.

In the morning I wake to the sound of rain hitting my tent. It is a brand new North Face Canyonlands that I purchased for this trip, and it proves to be worth every cent. Not a drop of water got through, and I am warm and dry. I try to wait out the rain because I hate packing up in it. No matter how hard I try, my stuff gets wet and muddy, and then I still have a waterlogged tent to deal with. I wait an hour, but the rain shows no sign of letting up so I wrap my tent up in a plastic garbage sack, stuff it in my pack, and get ready to head out. I notice that Packman had already left. So have Teresa and her grandfather. In fact, most everyone has left; just myself and a few scattered tents are all that remain at Justus Creek. I saddle up Rufus with his pack, don my own, and pass the tent inhabited by Texas Tortoise and Planting Flowers. As I walk by, Texas Tortoise pokes his head out.

"Still raining, I see," he observantly remarks.

"Yeah, you guys packing up soon and heading out?" I ask.

"No, we don't hike when it rains," Texas Tortoise replies, popping his head back into his shell and zipping up the door. They don't hike in the rain? The Southern Appalachians receive over 100 inches a rain a year, most of it in the spring. I wish them luck and head off.

It rains all day, sometimes sprinkling but usually pouring. A great way to test if something is waterproof is to walk in it all day in the rain. I just wish I hadn't waited until now to test my jacket. I purchased a lightweight Marmot Precip jacket for this trip as my other rain jackets are all heavy. This jacket is made of a single layer of waterproof nylon without any insulation to add weight.

It's supposed to be completely waterproof and breathable. The fabric is completely waterproof, but the problem is that somehow the water drips off the hood straight down into the inside of the jacket and onto my chest. No amount of playing with the hood or zipper can alleviate this problem, so while most of my upper body is dry, my chest is soaked. The only way to avoid the problem is to walk completely hunched over, but that's not feasible with a heavy backpack.

Walking in rain in fifty-degree temperatures with a wet shirt is not a lot of fun, but I'm wearing polypropylene long underwear, which holds in warmth even while wet, so while I am uncomfortable, I'm in no danger of freezing. In my pack are a wool hat, a fleece vest, several pairs of socks, a pair of pants with legs that zip off, and long underwear bottoms. If I have to I can put on all this clothing and stay warm even if the temperature drops below freezing, though I hope it doesn't.

While walking in the rain I learn something else about Rufus. He hates rain and is deathly afraid of thunder. Rufus is wearing a dog collar with two metal tags; one is a rabies vaccination tag, and the other has his name and my parents' phone number on it. While he walks these tags jingle like a cowbell so I always know where he is. As we walk, the rain goes from a downpour to a drizzle and back again, and every time it worsens the jingling stops, meaning Rufus has stopped. I turn around time after time to see Rufus hiding underneath any type of shelter he can find: a low-hanging branch, a bush, a leaf. Nothing helps, though. With this much rain coming down, nothing short of a solid roof will provide cover. Rufus tries his best to get out of the rain but he doesn't quite understand that he's still getting wet while huddled under a single oak leaf. I finally fashion a raincoat for him out of a plastic bag, cutting out a section for his head and tucking the corners in around his pack. It keeps most of the rain off his back, and Rufus resumes walking with me, until we come to our first blowdown.

A blowdown is a tree that has fallen across the trail, usually from wind or a heavy load of snow during the winter. Some are small enough to walk over, while others are so big that hikers are forced to create a path around the tree. Each trail club is responsible for clearing blowdowns, but this early in the season many of the clubs haven't had the time to clear them all as it involves hiking in with saws and axes. Some blowdowns, like this one, are a day's journey from any road and would take two volunteers two days to clear. This particular blowdown isn't a problem; it's a small tree with most of the branches broken off, so I step over it and keep hiking. A few seconds later I hear a very familiar whining sound. I look back and, surprise! No Rufus. Rufus is standing on the other side of the tree with one paw lifted onto it, expressing fear and confusion about how to get over this new obstacle of terror. I shout encouragement and he almost makes the jump, but he backs out at the last minute and lies down defeated. I walk back and lift my dog over the foot-high tree. This is going to be a really long trip.

The rain refuses to let up. It is three days into my dream hike and I am cold, wet, and tired from lifting Rufus over every blowdown, of which there are many. Late in the afternoon I look down off a ridge and see a farmhouse a quarter-mile away. I pray that someone will step out of the house and see Rufus and me shivering in the rain. Then they would open their home to us so we could spend a warm, dry night inside. I walk past the house trying to send telepathic messages to the homeowner, but no one comes out. Instead of lying down on a warm bed, I keep trudging along in the mud and rain towards the next shelter, which my guidebook says is thirteen miles from Justus Creek.

A few miles past the farmhouse I come to a paved, two-lane road cutting through the mountains. A hiker, wrapped in rain gear with his backpack at his feet, is standing by the road. I get closer and recognize the hooded figure.

"Hey, Arkon, what are you doing?" I ask.

"Hi, Kevin. I'm getting out of this blasted rain. I'm trying to hitch into Helen, a little town down the way, and rent a motel room. You want to come?" he says hopefully. It's very tempting, but I have only been in the woods for three days now, and I don't need to spend money in town yet.

"No thanks. I'm going to keep hiking and save my money. Where's Loren?" I ask.

"He's about half a day behind us. He's not moving real fast. I think he'll join me in Helen."

I leave Arkon at the road, reaching Wood's Hole Shelter as dusk arrives. The shelter only sleeps seven, and nine hikers are already packed inside. However, the roof extends out over a picnic table. I quickly claim a spot under the roof. By the end of the day fourteen hikers fill this little shelter. Teresa isn't here, and when I ask about her nobody knows who I am talking about. It's still too early to know many people, and right now everybody is concentrating on staying warm, dry and fed.

I awake to a fog-enshrouded world, but at least it isn't raining. After breakfast I check my clothes that I hung up to dry last night, but it is too cold and wet for anything to dry. I have only two sets of clothes, and with the threat of rain today, I don't want to get the dry clothes wet. That would leave me with nothing dry to wear tonight. Instead, I strip off my dry clothes and put on the damp ones, sending goose bumps across my body. I put on my pack, grab Rufus, and get out on the trail where I can warm up.

There's not much to do except think while hiking. Every tree looks the same and there aren't a lot of views, especially in this fog. Roots, rocks, and thorny vines appear out of nowhere to twist an ankle or stub a toe, forcing hikers spend the majority of the time looking down at their feet. So mile after mile of staring at my boots leaves me plenty of time to think about life.

Even though I'm wet and cold, I love this life. It's completely different than the one I left behind. Rent, traffic, bills, bosses and my ex-wife don't exist out here, and what once was taken for granted becomes all-important: food, water, and shelter. If I'm hungry, grabbing something out of the fridge is no longer an option. I have to ration what I have, and everything I want or need

1. The Beginning of a Long Trip

March 29, 2001. 26 miles from Springer, 2141 to Kahtadin. A short sun break at Wood's Hole Shelter, Georgia. Fourteen hikers crammed inside last night.

I have to carry. Water also becomes a precious commodity. If I run out, I have to continue to the next stream to fill up. Where I camp each night depends on where the water is. My priorities have changed, and I like it. It feels good to be free of the self-imposed stresses we create.

I hike through Slaughter Gap and up Blood Mountain, the site of a fierce battle 400 years ago between the Creek and Cherokee tribes. Legend has it that the ground ran red with blood from the dead and wounded Native American warriors. Since then the government has taken the land, given it to European settlers, and taken it back again, and now it is part of a National Forest. The 4,450-foot summit of Blood Mountain stands above the fog, giving way to magnificent views of rugged brown mountain-islands rising out of the low-lying clouds. It's still winter on the mountain tops, and the forests of deciduous trees are barren, not a speck of green to be seen.

A two-room stone shelter built in the 1930s adorns the summit. I take a peek inside and am glad I didn't spend the night in here. Fifty years ago this would have been an ideal place to stay: a summit cabin with large windows, a fireplace, and room for twenty people. Now it would take one hell of a storm for me to sleep in it. The dark interior is littered with garbage from weekend parties, the broken windows have been boarded over, and unseen creatures scurry across the floor. It's a depressing building and I don't feel like spending any time close to it.

I leave the summit and follow the trail as it drops straight back down into the wet fog. Several miles from Blood Mountain I reach Neels Gap, home of one of the most important spots on the whole trail: the Walasi-Yi Center, a sixty-year-old stone building that sits directly on the trail. A mere thirty miles from Springer Mountain, Walasi-Yi is the first re-supply point on the trail and has been catering to hikers for years. It offers hot showers, a laundromat, and postal services. Leaving Rufus outside with my pack, I walk through the large wood doors and into the warm building.

"Come on in," says a middle-aged man, stacking a shelf with individually wrapped Pop-tarts. "I'm Winston, the owner, and that over there is..." Winston looks around the store at the half dozen hikers milling about, but apparently doesn't see who he wants to see. He turns back to me and says, "Well, my wife Margie is around here somewhere. She's usually at the cash register. Anyway, we have a fair food selection and a decent gear shop, so feel free to browse as long as you want. If you have any questions on anything, feel free to ask."

March 29, 2001. Walking along the Georgia Mountains. It is too early in the season for any leaves on the trees.

1. The Beginning of a Long Trip

I wander the store, drooling over shelves stocked with bagels, Pop-tarts, noodles, granola bars and other foods, all individually packaged. The freezer is loaded with microwavable pizzas, burritos and pints of ice cream, all moderately priced. For the last four days I have been living off oatmeal, granola bars, and noodles. After deciding on a bowl of chili and a bag of Doritos, I wander over to the equipment side of the store. They have an incredible selection of quality gear. Because they are the only outfitter within fifty miles, they have a monopoly on much needed supplies. They can demand almost any price for the merchandise — but they don't. The jacket I bought at REI for $99 costs exactly the same here.

Margie returns to the cash register, so I pay for my food and pick up my first mail drop. Part of my preparation for hiking the A.T. was packing 25 boxes containing food, maps of the next section, traveler's checks, and replacement socks and T-shirts. They are stacked in my parents' basement, and my mom is mailing each box as I approach my next stop. Most of my boxes are being sent to post offices along the trail, but a few will be mailed to private businesses such as this one.

While researching the trail, I read numerous horror stories about hikers reaching a town to find the only grocer either closed for good or picked clean. Not wanting to have to hunt squirrels and chew on pine cones, I loaded up my boxes with enough food to last between stops. Now I see this place. If even the tiniest of stores along the way have a quarter of this selection, I have the feeling I will be throwing away much of my pre-packed food, as most of it is dehydrated stews and noodle dishes I concocted at home and failed to test out first. Several of my meals so far have been decent, like my lentil chili, but some have been downright awful. I'm throwing out every dehydrated beef stroganoff meal in my shipments. I'd rather eat cow pies.

"Here's your box," Margie says, handing me my cardboard container. "Make sure you sign the hiker register on the counter here. It's the only way we can keep track of how many hikers pass through here."

I pick up the notebook and leaf through it. Counting the number of names on a page, and the number of pages filled in, I guess that about 1,000 hikers have passed through here so far this year.

Margie tells me that about 3,000 hikers sign the register each year. Keeping track of the number of thru-hikers is a very inexact science. This is the first official register; the next one is at the ATC headquarters in West Virginia, and the last one is the ranger station at the base of Mt. Katahadin. The ATC estimates that only 15 to 20 percent of those who start the trail finish it, but since those numbers are simply based on these three journals, it is a rough guess.

With my mail drop in hand, I thank Margie and head out the door. My plan is to resupply here and keep hiking, but as I sort through my food, a shuttle from a place called Goose Creek Cabins arrives and most of the hikers here board it. An hour later the shuttle returns and the driver says it's the last one for the day, so I give in to peer pressure, load Rufus on the bus and twenty minutes later arrive at a small man-made catfish pond surrounded by old, but well cared for, cabins. A father and his two boys are trying their luck at the pond and have already landed a couple of flopping fish.

I pass the pond and step into the log cabin office. The place looks like a Merry Maids tornado ripped through it, leaving behind huge piles of organized clutter. The worn wood floor is spotless, but the walls are hidden behind piles of boxes and rows of tattered books balanced on wobbly shelves. An ancient, uneven pool table stands in one corner, adorned with a well-used hiker box. A hiker box is basically a grab bin for hikers, and almost every hostel along the trail will have one. Hikers leave unwanted food and gear in the box, and it's free for the taking. This way nothing is wasted. While I'm digging through bags of oatmeal and powdered milk, neither of which I need, Packman walks in.

"Hey, Packman," I say. "You're staying here too?"

"Yeah, I'm sharing a cabin with Jason, a hiker I met at Justus Creek. Got room for one more if you want to join us."

I jump at his offer and we head to the cabin where I meet Jason. He is about my age and as new to long-distance hiking as everyone else. I take my first shower in four days and give my dirty clothes to the front desk clerk, who charges five dollars to wash and dry a load of laundry. Rather spendy, but I'm willing to pay it. I'm not quite a mountain man yet and still like clean clothes. The cabin offers transportation to a restaurant in Blairsville for some real southern BBQ, and I board the shuttle with my two new friends, leaving a sleeping Rufus content on my bed.

Teresa is also on the shuttle along with eight other hikers. At the restaurant we all share one big table with myself, Packman, Jason and Teresa on one end. A retired man with a short white beard who calls himself Colonel Joe, a middle-aged woman named Debbie, and several hikers I don't know fill out the table. The waitress, in a perfect southern drawl, tells us the special is all-you-can-eat catfish. Thinking that it will be catfish fillets like fish-and-chips, I order the special. The waitress returns with my food, and I find myself face to face with an eight-inch fried catfish staring at me with its beady black eyes. The entire catfish is on my plate, head and all. Curious to see if they even bothered to clean it, I gingerly lift up the fish. Whew, at least the innards are gone. I get my money's worth, though, eating ten of the little bug-eyed bastards.

"So, Jason, I hear you have a trail name," Packman says as we sit around the table after dinner, waiting for the shuttle to return.

"I'm Achilles now, from the huge blisters I have on both of my heels. My boots suck. I have another pair at home and I'm going to have my dad mail 'em down."

"Where's home?" I ask.

"Maine, so basically I'm hiking home. Hey, I have a question for all of you. My girlfriend is in Maine and she wants to hike the end of the trail with me. I'm thinking about proposing to her on the summit of Mt. Katahdin. Do you think she'll like that, or is it not romantic enough?" Achilles asks, looking at all of us.

"That's very romantic," Teresa says. "She'll love that. Do you have a ring yet?"

"No, and I don't really have the money for one. All of my savings are going to this trip, but I'll think of something before then."

"She'll love whatever you get her, Jason," Teresa says, then turns to Packman. "So, Packman, what's your story?"

"Mine? I really don't have one. I'm taking a long break from work and my plan is to hike the trail as slowly as possible. In fact, I'm not even here yet," Packman says, sipping a soda.

"Not here yet? I'm looking right at you. Are you trying to be Confucius of the trail?" I ask.

"No, nothing that philosophical. I just haven't actually hiked to Neels Gap yet. I hitched here from a road just before Blood Mountain, and I'm going to return there in the morning to keep hiking. So far, between being out of shape and carrying way too much stuff, I have only hiked a handful of miles a day."

"So, what about you, Teresa?" I ask. "What happened to your grandpa? I saw him at the cabins, but why didn't he join us?"

"He's sleeping. The night at Justus Creek his tent leaked, and his sleeping bag got soaked. He had a cold and sleepless night. Guess it aggravated some old injuries so he hitched out on a road a couple miles past the creek to get here. I don't know if he's going to keep hiking ... hey, the shuttle's here!"

We board the shuttle and head back to the cabins. It's late and Teresa heads off to her cabin while Achilles, Packman, and I walk up to ours. A very excited Rufus greets me when I open the door. While petting him I notice that his skin is raw where his pack straps rub, so I apply some Neosporin from my little first-aid kit onto the chafing. Rufus isn't going to be able to carry his pack tomorrow, so I'll have to carry it. With the thought of that extra weight, I begin what will be an ongoing process of lightening my load. I remove an extra T-shirt, an extra pair of shorts, and a small set of binoculars from my pack to send home tomorrow. It's only a pound but it adds up mile after mile. It takes an estimated five million steps to walk the entire trail, and every ounce saved is thousands of accumulated pounds off my knees and back.

In the morning I tie Rufus' pack onto my own, bringing my load to sixty pounds, and start very slowly down the trail. Packman has left already in search of a ride, so Achilles and I take the shuttle back to Walasi-Yi. I mail my stuff home and call my folks to let them know I am alive, and ask my dad to mail out my hiking poles which I forgot. Achilles and I then start down the trail together, but my heavy pack slows me down and I tell Achilles to go ahead and not to wait for me. He bolts down the trail and once again it is just Rufus and I against these mountains.

I had no idea that the Southern Appalachians were so steep and rugged. I envisioned low rolling hills with gentle switchbacks up and down each side. Boy, was I wrong. Instead, the trail climbs straight up the sides of mountains so steep that mountain goats have to use ropes. The descent isn't any easier, and sometimes I swear curling into a ball and falling off the mountain would be faster.

My knees are taking a pounding on these mountains and walking is becoming increasingly painful. I resort to walking sideways on some of the steeper sections, and that helps a little. My dad is mailing my hiking poles to Hiawassee, a town about three days away. Until then it is a steady diet of hiker candy, known in the regular world as aspirin.

While struggling up a nearly vertical mountain with what feels like a tank on my back, I come to another small blowdown that Rufus refuses to cross. As I bend over to pick him up I hear a loud rip, and my pack slides off my right shoulder. Hmmm, strange: no pain. I would think my shoulder joint ripping in half would cause some type of discomfort, but nothing. I drop my pack to assess the damage, and my pack flops onto the ground with the right shoulder strap torn in half. I'm relieved that my shoulder is in one piece, but crap, it's a brand new pack. After ten minutes of cursing and whining, neither of which fixes my pack, I repair the strap with a piece of my bear-bag rope and continue on over the hills with a very uncomfortable, but functional, backpack.

After a long day of exhausting and painful hiking I reach a small clearing where Teresa, Achilles, Colonel Joe, and Debbie have already set up camp. The clearing is called the Cheese Factory Site, home to a dairy farm and cheese factory in the mid–1800s. Nothing is left of it now except the eroded remains of the old foundation. As much as I want to explore a little, I'm too tired to do anything but make a lentil chili meal and crawl into my tent. Now that the sun is down it is frigid out, but Rufus and I are quite warm. For such a compact dog he produces a heck of a lot of body heat, and on a cold night like tonight, having a furry brown heater next to me is worth every bit of discomfort he's caused so far.

Just as I am drifting off to sleep I here a faint voice call out, "Kevin, exactly how big is your tent?" My first thought is of Teresa, cold and alone in her tent, looking for a knight in shining armor to come to her rescue. I start looking for a white horse to prepare myself for the role of hero. The voice calls out again, and I realize the owner of the voice definitely has an Adam's apple. It's Achilles. Trying to save weight, he doesn't have a tent, just a tarp and a summer sleeping bag. Poor guy must be freezing.

"There's not much room. Rufus and I take up the whole tent. Sure is warm and toasty in here," I answer. "Why, are you cold out there?"

"I'm fucking freezing, Kevin! Stupid lightweight no tent idea! You sure there's no room in there?" Achilles says, forcing the words through his chattering teeth.

Being a friend, I have several options in front of me. The first is to ignore him and hope he falls asleep. I like this idea, except for the fact that if he freezes to death we'll have to drag his corpse until we reach town. Not a pleasant thought. My second option is to cram Achilles in with Rufus and me, but I have a long-standing rule against cuddling with members of my own sex and I see no reason to break it now. A third option is to swap sleeping bags with him for the night. My bag is rated to zero degrees and right now it's unzipped, lying across my dog and me like a blanket, and I'm still plenty warm.

"Achilles, there's not enough room in here for two, but tell you what, why don't you take my sleeping bag and I'll use yours. I'm warm in here with Rufus," I offer.

"I can't do that, you'll be cold," he replies.

"I'll still be warm. Here, you take my bag," I offer again.

"No, I can't put you out like that, I'll manage," Achilles says. We go back and forth a couple more times until my patience is gone.

"Just take the damn sleeping bag, man! Your teeth are chattering so hard it sounds like there's a lumberjack with a wood chipper beside me. Take the bag so I can get some sleep!" I yell, opening the tent door and tossing my bag at him.

He gives me his bag and I still sleep warm, even though I wake to a feathery layer of snow covering everything, including Achilles, who is snoring away oblivious to the chill. Teresa is already gone, and it's too cold sitting around waiting for Achilles to wake up, so with a couple of friendly kicks he's suddenly wide awake, allowing me to retrieve my bag.

After a breakfast of hot tea and instant oatmeal I check on Rufus. His sores have sufficiently healed, so I give him back his pack. He doesn't look thrilled to see it again, but I didn't bring him out here to be his mule. After Achilles bandages some blisters on his heels, we head out together. His blisters slow him down and soon I am walking by myself.

Around noon I run into Teresa, who has stopped to take a break. Finally I have a chance to talk to her.

"Hey, Teresa, where's your grandpa?" I ask. I need some kind of opening line, and "Do you come here often" or "Can I buy you a drink" sounds cheesy standing in the middle of the woods.

"He's all done with the trail. This has always been a dream of his, but he's half-blind, carried way too much weight, and is too stubborn to let me help him pack. Who needs five rolls of toilet paper anyway?" she says, shaking her head.

It's time to get to know this girl. I have her talking, and she has nowhere to run.

"So, you still plan on thru-hiking the trail? By yourself? Your grandpa isn't going to rejoin you?" Critical questions here.

"Nope, just me. I love him, but I can't hike with him. He moved way too slow for the pace I want to walk and I like being on my own, free to do whatever I want. I love this: no stress, no deadlines, nothing but walking day after day."

"I hear you there. Deciding to hike the trail has been the best decision of my life," I say, relieved that now I may actually be able to hike with her for a bit. "So what did you do before the trail?"

"I just finished up school at RIT. That's Rochester Institute of Technology in upstate New York. I received a degree in biology. I figured it's a general enough degree to let me do almost anything."

"What do you want to do with your degree?" I ask.

"I have no idea. That's why I'm out here. I graduated last fall with no idea what to do with my life, so I came out here. This is a soul-searching trip. I have to figure out what I want to do before reaching Katahdin. What about you?"

"I wanted an adventure," I say. "I spent four years in college getting a pre-law degree, then four years in the Marine Corps, and it was time to do something fun before embarking on a career."

We continue to talk while trudging up and down these never-ending mountains. Teresa is twenty-three years old, three years younger than I am, and is smart and independent. She had never backpacked before this trip but read numerous books, talked to other hikers through the Internet, and did extensive research before starting out. Her grandfather heard about her plans and decided to join Teresa, but he wasn't ready. She is determined and prepared. I have no doubts about her ability to make it to Maine.

After hiking all day we reach Dick's Creek Gap, where Highway 76 leads into the town of Hiawassee. Teresa plans on staying the night at the Blueberry Patch Hostel. It's a couple miles down the road so we agree on trying to hitchhike together, alleviating her apprehension of having to hitchhike alone. I get to play the hero again, but this time for a dashing damsel instead of a hairy hiker.

When I was young my parents, like all good parents, warned me about the dangers of hitchhiking and picking up hitchhikers. My mom told me about perverted old men ready to molest anyone they can lure into their cars, and my dad spun horror stories about hatchet-wielding maniacs prowling the highways looking for someone to chop up. The stories worked. I never hitchhiked until I was out on my own, and even then only out of necessity. But on the trail, hitching is a normal part of life because most towns are too far away to walk to. It would take me almost two full days to walk in and out of Hiawassee, eleven miles each way, and if I walked into town every week to resupply it would take an extra two months to hike the trail. By car it's a quick twenty minutes, so the only choice is to hitchhike. Luckily, many locals know about the trail and assume that the dirty-looking bearded guy carrying a backpack and sitting where the trail meets the road is most likely a hiker needing a lift.

Throwing my thumb in the air and caution to the wind, I stand on the side of the road hoping for a ride. The hardest part of hitching is watching dozens of cars and trucks whiz by, the drivers glancing at me and thinking exactly what my parents told me: all hitchhikers are maniacal axe murderers. I'm just a harmless hiker who wants a ride into town to get groceries, but its tough to convey this to people flying by at sixty miles an hour.

After fifteen minutes, however, a car does stop. Our trail angel is a middle aged man who drives by the trail every day and often stops for hikers. He drops Teresa off at the hostel and takes me to the post office in Hiawassee.

I thank him for the ride as I pull my pack out of the trunk. My plan is to get my hiking poles, catch a ride back to the trail, and find a place to camp. I walk in and ask the clerk for my package. He goes into the back and returns empty handed.

"Nope, no package for you. Maybe it'll come in tomorrow," he says.

Now what? My dad sent it three days ago using the so-called Priority Mail, guaranteed to get anywhere in the U.S. in two to three days. "You sure, can you check again? It was guaranteed to be here today," I ask again.

"Sure, I'll look," the clerk replies, returning a few minutes later. "Still no package. Might come in tomorrow."

"Well, is there any way to track it, to see if it will actually be here tomorrow so I'm not wasting my time in case it was sent to Texas? It was guaranteed to be here today."

"Nope, can't check it unless it was guaranteed. Don't have a way to do it."

"It was guaranteed," I reply, gritting my teeth together to keep from yelling.

"Might be here tomorrow" is all the clerk says, and he walks away into the back room.

I'm not sure what to do now because the Blueberry Patch Hostel doesn't take dogs, and I don't want to spend the money for a motel room. Hitching out to the trail tonight and coming back into town in the morning sounds like a lot of work, so I sit down in front of the post office to formulate a plan. A few minutes later a car pulls into a motel across the street, and Achilles gets out.

"Achilles, what are you doing here?" I yell, crossing the street to meet him.

"My blisters, I can't walk anymore. My boots have ripped the hell out of my feet and I need to take a few days off to let them heal," he says as he sits down, pulling off his boots and socks. He has silver dollar blisters on both heels, infected and oozing with pus. I'm amazed he's able to walk at all. The fourteen miles today must have been brutal. "What are you doing here, Kevin?" he asks.

"My hiking poles haven't arrived yet," I reply. "Einstein at the post office said they should be in tomorrow, so I'm stuck here."

"Since you're here, you up for splitting a room for the night?" Achilles asks, dabbing the last of the pus off his heels with his dirty sock.

We get a room and discover that no one delivers pizza in Hiawassee. We settle for a dinner of Subway sandwiches as a storm moves in. I wake up to rain and take a wet walk to the post office. Still no poles. The clerk tells me they might come in with the afternoon delivery, so I return to the motel room. At 4:00 P.M. I return to the post office, and the poles have finally arrived. It is still pouring, and instead of hiking out in the steady rain this late in the afternoon, I spend another night with Achilles. I hadn't planned on taking a zero-mileage day this early in the trip, but I'm in no rush to get back into the rain and the day off helps Rufus and me heal from a week of hard hiking. It also gives me time to sew some fleece padding onto Rufus' pack straps to keep them from rubbing. I don't want Rufus to end up with blisters like Achilles.

My original plan to camp out by the trail would have left me in a good position to hike with Teresa again, but by the time I get back on the trail I will be a full day behind her. Teresa is a strong hiker, and unless she slows down or takes a day off, I may not see her again. It's probably just as well. I came out here to forget about my ex-wife and my divorce. A day doesn't go by that I'm not filled with anger stemming from thoughts of that ruined relationship, and I don't need to meet another woman right now.

In the morning I gather up my gear and say goodbye to Achilles. He is going to take a few more days off to let his blisters heal. I step out into the persistent rain and hitchhike back to the trail. A couple hours later I run into Debbie, Arkon and Colonel Joe, all wet but refreshed after taking a day off at the Blueberry Patch.

"Hey, Kevin, haven't seen you since Justus Creek. Glad to see you and that dog are still hiking," Arkon says.

"You too, old man," I say.

I haven't seen Arkon in four days and here he is again, appearing out of nowhere. That's how the trail works. Meeting other hikers is a random occurrence as everyone's pace is different. The best way to keep in touch is through the hiker's grapevine; word travels fast up and down the trail. Another way to keep track of people is through the informal shelter registers. The registers are simple spiral notebooks like the register at Walasi-Yi, where hikers can write notes, complaints, or occasionally, spiritual pick-me-ups. When the notebook is full it is carried into town and mailed to the hiker that originally left it (if there is an address on the front cover), and someone leaves a new one in its place.

I spend the morning hiking with Arkon, Debbie and Colonel Joe when we come upon a gnarly old oak tree right next to the trail. The tree marks my first state border, crossing out of Georgia and into North Carolina, meaning that I have only thirteen more states to cover. A couple quick photos mark my first milestone and I'm moving again.

I hike with this small group for a day, but Debbie, Colonel Joe and Arkon move too slow for me, so I say my good-byes and pick up my pace. North Carolina proves as rugged and steep as Georgia, but Rufus and I are getting our hiking legs under us and we plod along. I stop and laugh as I pass Chunky Gal

Trail (named after a trail maintainer's overweight girlfriend) and climb over the trail's first 5,000-foot mountain (Standing Indian). It has rained every day for the last three days, but now that I've spent ten days in the woods it doesn't bother me as much. It's part of the trail.

Four days out of Hiawassee, Rufus and I hike a hard, muddy and exhausting sixteen miles to Silver Bald Shelter, and I meet a hiker named Marcus and his dog, Shiggy. Marcus is a thirty-five-year-old Texan, but without the accent. Shiggy is a ten-year-old German Shepherd mix.

Rufus walks straight up to Shiggy and they immediately begin the traditional canine greeting of butt-smelling, then off Rufus and Shiggy go, barking and chasing each other around the shelter for an hour.

I wake to blue skies for the first time in over a week. An unseasonable heat wave has arrived, bringing with it unseasonable humidity. The trees are still bare from winter so there's nothing to block the sun's burning rays. The heat and humidity kick my butt, slowing my pace down to less than a mile an hour. Yesterday I was hiking in fifty-degree rain, and today I'm battling eighty-degree heat. Rufus' brown fur soaks in the sun and he quickly overheats, but for some reason he won't drink. He won't even step in water to cool off. He's been hiking in the rain for a week, but he won't cross a stream. I give him plenty of time to drink and even scoop the water up to his mouth, but he only stares at it. To avoid getting wet he jumps across the stream and collapses on the other side.

I carry his pack and dump water over him at every stream to keep him cool. It's all Rufus can do to keep up. The heat lasts for three days, slowing everyone down, and in the evening Rufus and Shiggy barely have enough energy to sniff each other, let alone run around. By noon of the third day of hot, humid weather I reach the appropriately named Rufus Morgan Shelter. This is home for the night, so Rufus will have the remainder of the day to rest.

A mile down the trail is Nantahala Outdoor Center (NOC), a hiker-friendly, whitewater rafting resort where I plan to resupply and hope to find a new backpack. Leaving Rufus in the shelter with plenty of food and water, I head down the trail towards NOC. The low rumble of the Nantahala River slowly increases to a roar, and numerous shouting voices mix with the noise as I get closer. I come around the last bend to see a roaring whitewater river awash in color. The colors come into focus as I come near: numerous red, yellow, orange, blue, and green kayaks training in the river. Ropes span the water, allowing a dozen kayakers to stay in one place while practicing techniques, and a two-lane wooden bridge allows access to the log buildings covering both banks. People are everywhere: hikers, kayakers, and families enjoying the beautiful day.

The sights and sounds overwhelm me. After a mere two weeks of hiking I've become accustomed to relative solitude and peacefulness. It's amazing how quiet the woods are. Now I'm surrounded by a cacophony of sounds and a myriad of colors among the throngs of people moving around, and I scurry into the outfitter to escape.

The outfitter, a trail term for an outdoor gear shop, is a huge building and has gear for every outdoor sport imaginable, from hiking to kayaking, rock climbing to bicycling. It also has a huge selection of backpacks. I pick up a Dana Design Terraplane, a backpack with very good reviews. When I try it on, it's like rubbing a magic lamp; out of nowhere a salesman materializes.

"Hi, I'm Jim. Can I help you with anything?" he asks.

"Just looking," I say. Gear salesmen do not impress me as I have discovered that most have no idea what they are talking about, and they often make up stuff. I purchased my heavy, expensive hiking boots because of a salesman. I went to the local REI in Spokane and told the shoe salesman I was hiking the A.T. and needed a pair of boots. The salesman told me how the beginning and end of the Appalachian Trail were very rough, and how I would need solid boots to make it. Well, I have been hiking in these boots for two weeks now and am starting to realize that lightweight hiking shoes would have worked fine, for half of the cost and weight. Another salesman told me I should have my sleeping bag 'winterized' to prepare for the trip, and a third tried to sell me a five pound first-aid kit because, as the salesman put it, "If you're ever mauled by a bear and bit by a rattlesnake in the same day, this is the kit you would want." If I'm mauled by a bear and bit by a rattler in the same day, I'm going to need a bottle of whiskey and a miracle, not a handful of bandages and some aspirin. Assuming Jim is a commission-based moron like the rest of them, I ignore him and continue looking at the packs.

"I see you're looking at the Terraplane pack. Now that is an excellent pack," he says, unsolicited. Here comes the sales pitch. "But I've found it fits some people perfect, while some people never feel comfortable in it. Before you buy any pack, let's load it up and see how it fits."

I'm stunned! Here is a salesman who stated that this might not be the pack for me, even though it is the most expensive one and he'll make the most commission selling it. Jim takes the pack from me and loads it up with forty pounds of weight, and I walk around the store with it on.

"Don't forget to walk up and down the stairs a few times. Feel free to take it outside and walk around the building. A pack shifts and feels different when walking up and down hills or crossing uneven terrain," Jim says. I walk up and down the stairs and the pack feels okay, but I don't think it will be comfortable after a full day of hiking and I tell Jim this.

"No problem. If it doesn't feel right, then it isn't the right pack for you. You don't want something you're not completely comfortable with. Let's look at another one." Jim picks an Osprey pack off the wall. "This is another excellent company and they make their contours a little different. It may fit better." He transfers the weight into the new pack, and once I have it on my back he helps adjust the straps, explaining the reasoning behind each one.

"Did you put less weight in this one?" I ask. It feels like a pillow is strapped to my back. Still, I don't trust Jim, thinking he might have put in less weight so the pack would be more "comfortable."

"No, I put the same weight into that one. You can take it off and check if you want." I do just that. Jim is telling the truth: it's loaded with the same weight but feels half as heavy. I walk up and down the stairs and around the store, not believing a pack could fit that well.

"That one feels better, huh? See, it's as simple as finding the right pack to fit your frame. You want to try a different one on?"

"Hell no! This pack feels like it's one with my spine."

I love this pack. The only problem is the $300 price tag for a canvas bag that straps to my back. It's either this, though, or my current pack held together with string. I hand Jim my credit card and purchase this wonderful item of antigravity. Now, however, I have my old pack to deal with. I explain this to Jim, and he tells me the post office is closed today, but if I leave him ten dollars and an address he'll see that it gets mailed out in the morning. (True to his word, two weeks later my old pack arrives at my parent's house.) I also purchase a pair of Teva sandals. By the end of the day I want to take my boots off to let my feet breathe, but my soles are too tender to walk around barefoot. Sandals are just the thing.

I load my new, luxurious backpack with groceries, throw on my sandals and walk back to the shelter to find Shiggy and Rufus running around with Marcus watching them. The one thing I wasn't able to find in NOC was dog food and I'm running low, but Marcus sees my paltry bag of kibbles and hands me a couple of days' worth out of Shiggy's food. I'm learning that this is how hikers are able to finish the trail. We help each other.

The next couple of days Rufus and I grind out the miles. I have never worn a pack so light and comfortable, and I am able to load some of Rufus' food into my pack, allowing him to keep up with me as we hike towards our next stop: Fontana Dam, the gateway to the Great Smoky Mountains.

2

Rufus, Rangers and Rain

The Great Smoky Mountains are the oldest mountains in the world. Estimated at 200–300 million years old, they are older than the Alps, Rockies, or Himalayas. They are thought to have once stood as high as 20,000 feet, but weather and erosion have taken their toll, reducing the highest peak, Clingmans Dome, to a mere 6,643 feet. The Great Smoky Mountains National Park encompasses 800 square miles of mountain range, almost all of which has returned to its natural state. A quarter of the park has never been logged and contains one of the largest stands of old-growth forest left in the United States. The Smokies are home to 66 species of mammals, the most famous being the American Black Bear with an estimated 600–800 living in the park. Roughly 200 varieties of birds, 50 species of native fish and over 80 types of reptiles and amphibians, including a species of lungless salamanders, call the Smokies home. When it comes to trees and shrubs, the Smokies have more species than all of Europe.

This extreme diversity is partially due to the last ice age 10,000 years ago. While the glaciers did not reach the Smokies, the towering walls of ice forced the migration of thousands of species south. The Smokies' unique ecosystem gave these "migrants" the comforts of home, as the valleys have a warm, humid climate common to the Southern Appalachians, while the climate of the higher peaks is equivalent to that of New Hampshire and Maine. This allowed the displaced animals to settle in climates comparable to their native beginnings.

The A.T. follows the crest of the Smokies, an unbroken ridge 5,000 feet above sea level that runs for thirty-six miles along the Tennessee–North Carolina border. This highland is dominated by spruce and fir forests, in sharp contrast to the deciduous forest of the lower hills and valleys, and is populated by many of the same species that are found a thousand miles to the north.

Drawn towards the majestic mountains looming above Fontana Reservoir, Rufus and I are attempting our longest day yet: 18 miles to Fontana Dam and the southern end of the park. Even though it's a bit cooler than the last few days, I take Rufus' pack so he can keep up. We reach the southern side of the reservoir as dusk approaches, and according to my map, the last mile should be an easy walk along the lake to the shelter. Looking forward to an evening saunter along the water, my high hopes are smashed down into anger and frustration. This "easy" mile finds a way to cross every hill and hump, often curving far to the left or right to find another hill to climb instead of simply bypassing it.

After a very long half hour of climbing five pointless ups and downs (also known as puds) I make it to the shelter nicknamed the Fontana Hilton. The Hilton, which sits on a peninsula jutting out into the reservoir, can accommodate twenty hikers and is surrounded by a lush, manicured lawn with several picnic tables and a water spigot. To make a good thing better, a quarter mile down the road is the visitor center with heated bathrooms and showers.

After stowing my stuff in the shelter, I walk in the cool night air down to the visitor center where I use the pay phone to call Ripplin' Water Kennels. Dogs are not allowed inside the park for some unknown reason. Nine million visitors a year are okay, but throw in a couple hundred dogs on leashes and, well, the ecosystem might collapse entirely, leaving nothing but a large void where the park once sat. I have seen the occasional inconsiderate owner who lets his dog run free to crap all over the place and chase wildlife, but those are exceptions. Just as many people let their kids run free, and those kids also chase wildlife and crap all over the place. I can't count the number of people I've seen trample on trails and meadows behind huge "Closed for Restoration" signs, throw rocks at birds and squirrels to get a reaction, or drop their garbage where they stand because walking 100 yards to the garbage can is too inconvenient.

What I really don't understand is that horses are allowed in the park. These 1,000-pound animals with their metal hooves cause extensive damage to the trail and destroy almost everything they walk on. When my dog craps on the trail I pick it up and bury it out of sight. I've never seen a horse owner do the same. Instead, portions of the trail are a foot thick in rotting horse shit, creating another obstacle for hikers to hurdle. Dogs should be the least of the park's worries.

Those are the rules though. Either I abide by them or I face a $5,000 fine, so I will kennel Rufus at the cost of $175 for a week while I hike the eighty miles of trail through the Smokies. I call the kennel owner from the visitor center, hoping he hasn't closed for the night. He answers the phone, but tells me he is not able to pick Rufus up until 5:00 P.M. tomorrow. Well, that makes it easy; tomorrow is a zero day.

In the morning, having nothing to do until evening, I put on my sandals and walk the mile into Fontana Village, a little resort that caters to masses of wealthy tourists heading to the park during the summer. Most of the shops are still closed because tourist season hasn't begun and thru-hikers generally don't have much money. The outfitter is open, though. I walk inside and find myself staring at frilly designer day packs being offered at twice market value.

I'm glad I purchased my pack in NOC or else I would be screwed here. However, I do need some new shoelaces, and even a store like this can't charge too much for those. I look around and realize I am the only customer in the store, and I am immediately spotted by a saleswoman wearing too much makeup and sporting one-inch manicured nails. This lady wouldn't know hiking if it was tattooed on her forehead, but she looks bored and rushes over to me.

"Hi, are you one of those hiker persons? How exciting!" she says. "My name is Kathy. Can I help you with anything today?"

"You carry any shoelaces?" I ask.

"Sure. What color are your boots?"

"Umm, brown," I say, rather perplexed.

"Of course they're brown. All hiking boots are brown. What shade of brown are they?"

"Umm, dark brown? Why?" I ask, now thoroughly confused on where this conversation is going.

"So we can match them up, of course! We don't need chestnut laces going with cinnamon boots, now do we?" Kathy says excitedly.

"Kathy, color isn't a real big concern of mine. All they have to do is lace up," I say, not meaning to be rude, but wanting to get what I need and get out of the store before I end up with matching hair ribbons and beard barrettes.

"That's okay, I'll pick them out for you. Now do you want the regular ones or the super-strength ones?" Kathy says, undaunted by my lack of interest in the art of color coordination.

"What's the difference?" I had not been aware there are "super-strength" shoelaces.

"I don't know, this one just says it's new and stronger than before," she says, reading from the package.

Just as I suspected, Kathy doesn't know her laces.

"Well, Kathy, which ones do you recommend?"

"The super-strength ones, of course! With all that walking, you'll surely want the stronger ones."

I can't argue with that logic, and since the "super-strength" laces are only fifty cents more, I quickly buy a pair of nutmeg brown, super-strength shoelaces and escape out into the village.

Fontana Village is a nice little resort, especially when you have it to yourself before the hordes of summer tourists descend. It's quiet and well maintained, with numerous small parks, shops, and various historical points of interest scattered about. Rufus and I spend the day together until it's time return to the visitor center to meet the kennel owner.

The owner is early and waiting when I arrive, leaving me very little time to say goodbye to Rufus. It's hard parting with him, even for a week. I'm going to miss my buddy. Rufus doesn't want to leave without me and refuses to get in the car. The owner lifts him into the backseat and shuts the door, then comes over to me.

"Okay son, remember to call me from Mountain Momma's Hostel at the other end of the park. If you can call around noon I can get Rufus to you that day, otherwise you might have to wait until the next day," he says before getting into the car. Rufus stares at me with his big brown sad eyes as he is taken away, not understanding why we are being separated. I know he could use the rest, but that doesn't make the walk back to the shelter any less lonely.

A group of hikers has arrived at the shelter: Derby, Dale, Rooster, Gypsy, Dig and Marcus (who knew a friend in the area who took Shiggy). The only person I know is Marcus, but the rest are a friendly group. The next morning we all rise early, and it's a beautiful day as I follow the painted blazes across the top of Fontana Dam. At 480 feet tall, it is the highest dam east of the Mississippi.

On the far side of the dam is a small wooden sign reading, "Entering Great Smoky Mountains National Park," and I attack the 3,000-foot climb that leads out of Fontana and onto the ridge line. The climb proves every bit as hard as it looked from the village, but I'm rewarded at the end with a view that extends for miles. To the north the whole expanse of the Smokies lies before me, and to the south are the steep and rugged Southern Appalachians. Below me is a familiar head of curly brown hair moving up the trail.

"Hey, Kevin! Where did you come from?" Teresa says in surprise when she sees me.

"Me? You were a full day in front of me, and I took a zero day at Fontana. How did you get behind me?" I ask, shocked but excited to see her again.

"You wouldn't believe it. I arrived at Fontana and spent the night at a small bed and breakfast owned by the nicest family. They invited me down to have dinner with them, and I was bored so I helped with the chores. They let me stay two more nights for free and treated me like I was part of their family. It was so much fun playing with their kids. I even did a little bit of gardening. Hey, where's Rufus?" Teresa asks, looking around.

"Dogs aren't allowed in the Smokies, so he's at a kennel for a week. It's weird, I miss him, but at the same time it's a relief not constantly having to worry about him. If I had my choice, though, he'd be here hiking with me."

"Well, I'm here! You can hike with me. And guess what? I have a trail name," she says, a smile spreading across her face.

"Well, what is it?"

"Phoenix! I have a big tattoo of a phoenix on my back. Rooster saw it so she named me."

We walk together along the ridge until we come upon a medieval-looking building. After further exploration we determine that it is a shelter. This monstrosity has three sides constructed of mortar and stone, and one open side enclosed by a chain-link fence that reaches from the ground to the roof. A chain-link door allows for access. The original idea behind this fortress design was to keep people and bears separated. That way, hikers could spill food, wipe greasy fingers onto sleeping bags, and toss crumbs out the gate in hopes of attracting a bear for a picture or two, all the while within the security of the cage.

The Park Service realized the sense of security the fence created eventually led to laziness and sloppiness among hikers, creating more problems than it solved. A full grown black bear, weighing up to 400 pounds, can bite through a tree as thick as a man's arm and remove a car door with its claws. It would have no problem tearing this fence apart as if it were papier-mâché. While no bear has actually stormed one of these shelters, the potential was always there.

The old stone shelters are now being replaced with the modern open shelters found along the A.T., with an emphasis on education. Each shelter in the Smokies now has a set of bear cables, a cable and pulley system where food bags are attached on one end of the cable and are hauled up before securing the other end so bears can't reach it. The easiest way to keep bears out of camp is to keep the food away from camp.

The open shelters made me nervous at first, with the realization that a bear can waltz right in and take his pick of hikers for breakfast. But actually, both black and grizzly bears have been unfairly portrayed in books and movies as violent killers just waiting for their next hiker meal to come walking up to the dinner table. There are 60,000 grizzly bears and 600,000 black bears in North America, and tens of millions of people visiting our parks and forests every year. This equation should result in hundreds of deaths a year, but it doesn't.

The truth is that bear attacks are very rare. In North America, 128 people have been killed by bears during the last one hundred years, 40 by black bears and the rest by grizzlies. That comes out to a little more than one death a year. In comparison, vehicle accidents kill 42,000 people a year, guns kill 35,000, deer colliding with automobiles kill 130 people, and man's best friend, the domestic dog, kills 18 people a year. Though bear attacks are increasing (27 deaths in the 1980s and 29 in the 1990s) this is because the wilderness is becoming increasingly accessible. People who shouldn't be allowed to own a goldfish are able to wander around forests populated with bears.

The reason attacks remain rare is that most bears avoid people, wanting nothing to do with us two-legged monstrosities. However, encounters do happen, and sometimes they turn fatal. In May 2000, the Great Smoky Mountains National Park had its first fatal mauling. Fifty-year-old Glenda Bradly, an experienced hiker, was hiking in the Little Creek area when she was attacked by a 115-pound female and her 50-pound cub. Because no one witnessed the attack, it will never be known exactly what happened, but it appears for some reason the bears decided Bradly was food. It was a poor year for berries, leaving the

April 12, 2001. 176 miles from Springer, 2000 to Katahdin. Thumper looking out of a Smoky Mountains bear-cage style shelter.

bears sick and malnourished, unable to catch smaller, faster prey. Evidently they decided to attack whatever animal they could catch, and they ended up fatally mauling and partially eating Bradly.

For every one of these tragic encounters there are dozens of incidents where a person should have been killed, but wasn't. Last year in the park, a tourist saw a 50-pound yearling attacking a fawn and decided that the bear shouldn't do that. He charged the bear, kicked it, and slammed it into the ground to save the deer. The startled bear brushed itself off and ran into the woods. In another incident a month later, several young men chased a bear around until it was tired so they could have their picture taken with it. The first brave young idiot tried to pick the bear up for the perfect photo opportunity. Not surprisingly, the bear didn't take kindly to this and bit the man. In a third encounter, a ranger came across a young bear trying to kill a fawn with a shocked crowd watching. Several members of the crowd decided to save Bambi and threw rocks at the bear, but it kept attacking the fawn. When that didn't work one man grabbed a stick and ran up to the bear, striking it several times before a ranger intervened. All three of these incidents occurred last year within the Great Smoky Mountains National Park. Many more encounters like these occurred all across the nation, from California to Maine. It's a wonder more humans aren't torn apart just for being stupid.

    Sitting outside the bear shelter, I pull out a mashed peanut butter sandwich for lunch while Teresa digs an apple out of her pack.
    "Kevin, you want an apple?" she asks, holding it out in her hand.
    "I can't do that. You eat it." Fresh fruit is rare on the trail. It is heavy and easily damaged bouncing inside a pack. She carried it this far, so she should be the one to eat the apple.
    "I have two of them," Teresa says, digging a second out of her pack. "I was going to eat one now and one tonight, but they are heavy. Here, help me lighten my pack." Teresa tosses me an apple and we eat, then hike on to Russel Field Shelter, another dungeon-shelter five miles away.
    On the way we cross a beautiful meadow with a small stream running through it, backdropped with panoramic views of the mountains. It would make a perfect place to camp, but the Smokies have very strict camping rules requiring that all hikers stay at the shelters. Weekenders (a term used for backpackers who are out for only a couple of days) are required to make reservations for the shelters and are not allowed to tent, so they have to stay in the shelters. Thru-hikers are required to sleep in the shelter if there is room, and can tent only if the shelter is full, and even then tenting is limited to a small designated area next to the shelter. The purpose behind the rules is to minimize damage to the environment by keeping everyone in one spot.
    The idea makes sense, with one major flaw. In an effort to cut costs, the Park Service skimped on one very important item: privies. There are "privy areas" with big new signs pointing the way, but no actual privy. These areas are littered with feces and toilet paper, because at this elevation in April the ground is still too frozen to allow us to dig and bury our waste. The Smokies are the most unsanitary section on the whole trail, and this problem could easily be avoided by adding a privy to each shelter.
    After sidestepping numerous land mines marked by little waifs of toilet paper, I do my business and head back to Russel Shelter. There are ten other thru-hikers here and we quickly fill the shelter. A pair of weekenders arrive with reservations, so the last two thru-hikers to arrive have to leave the shelter and camp outside. A couple in their late fifties named Homeless and Unemployed were the last ones in. Homeless and Unemployed, also known as Bob and MaryAnn, sold their house and quit their jobs to come hike the trail. Most trail names are distinctive and easy to remember, but the names Homeless and Unemployed seem interchangeable, so most of the time Bob and MaryAnn go by their real names to avoid confusion. They gather up their stuff and set up camp on a small rise behind the shelter, then come back in to socialize. That is, until a ranger comes passing through.

"Hey, whose tent is that set up behind the shelter?" the ranger asks when he sticks his head into the shelter.

"It's my wife's and mine," says Homeless, or Bob.

"Well, you can't sleep there. The tenting area is this open spot in front of the shelter. You need to move your tent," the ranger says, pointing to a spot outside.

Homeless looks out at where the ranger is pointing. "You mean the area used to tether horses and covered in a foot of shit? You can't be serious!"

"Oh, it's not that bad. We're trying to keep all the impact to one area. You'll have to move," the ranger says.

I look at the area. It *is* that bad: a depression in the ground beat down by horses and covered in filth. Still, not wanting to risk a fine, Homeless and Unemployed have no choice but to move.

That night it rains like I have never seen it rain before. I keep expecting Noah to wake me up and usher me to a large boat he built; instead it's Bob and his wife, MaryAnn, coming in to sleep on the shelter floor. The horse area flooded and turned their tent into a two-man dingy. If they could have camped on the rise where they first set up they would have been fine, but instead some power-happy ranger enforces the rules and ruins their night.

The rain continues into the morning. Teresa says she is going to sleep in and see if the storm passes, but I don't feel like waiting and head out with a hiker named Thumper, a guy a few years younger than me. Thumper earned his name from the way he walks, sounding like a herd of lead-footed bunny rabbits bouncing down the trail. By noon the rain stops and the clouds lift as we hike up Clingmans Dome, the highest point on the A.T. at 6,643 feet.

Clingmans Dome was once a revered challenge to climb. Now anyone can stand on the highest point in the Smokies via a paved road that ends at a parking lot half a mile and 500 vertical feet below the summit. Thumper and I climb the mountain the old-fashioned way and find that right on top of the summit, surrounded by pristine forest, is a 54-foot-high concrete observation tower that resembles a NASA launch pad, courtesy of the National Park Service. It's amazing that the Park Service can build and maintain this road and tower, but can't find the funds to build a dozen privies along the trail.

Thumper and I stash our packs in the trees and walk down the summit trail to the parking lot, where my guidebook says there are restrooms and tap water. As we descend the wide, paved trail I am ashamed of how overweight and out of shape Americans have become. Stone benches line the path every 100 yards, and one out of every three people walking the half-mile to the summit stops to rest. It's not just the older people having trouble either. Young adults and teenagers are out of breath 200 yards from the parking lot and have to take a break. I overhear one male teenager exclaim to his friends, "I walked a whole mile today!" and several others congratulate themselves on how they conquered Clingmans Dome. I don't mean to sound like an elitist, but walking half a mile along a paved path to the top of a 6,643-foot mountain is not conquering it. Disgusted with the display of obesity (and ironically disappointed that there are no candy or soda machines in the parking area), we start back towards the top.

Eight miles later we reach Newfoundland Gap along Highway 441, the only road that crosses through the Smokies, and appears to be the stopping point of most of the nine million yearly visitors. People are everywhere: driving fast, driving slow, walking, skipping, reading, sleeping, talking or eating. You name it, there's somebody doing it. I haven't seen so many people in one spot since the Atlanta airport. Thumper and I promptly find a suitable observation spot and began watching "hiker TV." As we watch, we notice a definite pattern among the tourists. Car after car pulls into the parking lot of one of the greatest parks in the United States, and most people's whole experience is to get out of the car (and sometimes not even that), walk a hundred feet, snap a dozen pictures, get back in their car and leave. This five-minute ritual is repeated hundreds of times in the two hours we watch. Only a few hearty souls actually get out and walk around, and just four times does someone throw on a backpack and disappear down a trail. One lady gets out of her car, walks fifty feet down the trail, turns around and walks back to her husband saying, "Now I can honestly say I've hiked the Appalachian Trail!" I can only shake my head. As we are people-watching, a family sees us with our packs and walks over.

"Hi y'all, whatcha doin' with them packs and all?" the father drawls.

"We're hiking the Appalachian Trail," I reply.

"Are ya now? Appalachian Trail? What's that?" Now this surprises me as the family just spent the last five minutes staring at a large sign with big bold letters reading "Appalachian Trail," complete with two paragraphs explaining the trail and a map of it.

"Well, it's a trail that goes from Georgia all the way up to Maine and it crosses through the Smokies. In fact, right now you're standing on it. We plan on hiking it all the way."

"Hmmm. So how far y'all plan on hiking, then?"

"Maine."

The whole family looks at us incredulously and breaks out in laughter. They walk away, the father muttering, "Maine! Those are fools, kids. Couldn't nobody walk to Maine from here."

Thumper and I look at each other, all elation of walking this far crushed. I've never had someone tell me this hike was impossible, especially now that I've already walked 200 miles. We no longer want to be part of this crowd. We leave the gap and hike towards Icewater Spring Shelter three miles away.

We quickly reach the shelter and find it full of weekenders with their stuff strewn everywhere. Several are already tapping a bottle of whiskey and singing drinking songs. Being only three miles from the road, this shelter attracts people who want a place to party, not sleep. I have no intentions of cramming into the shelter with that mess and set up my tent out front, rules be damned. Thumper, however, decides to sleep in the shelter. Teresa arrives an hour later, takes one look into the shelter, and sets up her tent next to mine.

Teresa tells me that most of the group we have been hiking with have hitch-hiked into town from Newfoundland Gap, so the only thru-hikers here are Teresa, Thumper and I. I am glad Teresa decided not to go. I enjoy hiking with her. We chat over dinner while some type of drinking song floats from the shelter.

Around 9:00 P.M. the coordination-challenged drinkers on the platform above Thumper spill their drinks. As gravity dictates, the whiskey flows through the cracks and down onto Thumper's sleeping bag. The partygoers issue a mumbled "sorry" before refilling their cups and starting a new song. Thumper gathers up his stuff and sets up his tent beside mine. The partygoers stay up for another hour, and finally pass out in a fit of silence. Finally I can get some sleep.

A little after sunrise I awake to Teresa's voice. "Kevin, are you awake?"

"I am now. Why, what's up?" Is a bear crawling through camp? Perhaps we can divert it towards the shelter.

"A huge storm is coming in. It's going to start pouring soon."

I poke my head out of my tent and see threatening black clouds overhead. I hate packing up in the rain; I'd rather deal with a bear. I'm out of bed in a flash, tearing down my tent and cramming everything into my backpack. I wake up Thumper, but he says he's sleeping in, tired from dealing with the drunks last night. I grab my pack and move into the shelter while Teresa simply gathers everything up in her arms and carries her stuff in.

"You need any help packing up?" I ask Teresa, hoping to hike out with her.

"No, I'm good. I'm going to make a hot breakfast and hike out after the storm passes. I don't feel like hiking in the rain today," she says. I look up and see that the sky is gray out to the horizon.

"I think it's going to rain all day today. We are going to get wet no matter what," I say.

"Maybe, but I'm going to try to wait it out. Don't wait for me, though. If you want to start hiking, go on ahead."

I throw on my pack and head out onto the trail. Within fifteen minutes the sky breaks loose and I am drenched. Maybe I should have waited for the worse of it to pass, but I keep trudging ahead in the rain. I just hope it doesn't bring thunder and lightning.

An hour later, as I cross an exposed, rocky ridge, my world turns white. Less than a second later thunder blasts the mountain, almost knocking me to my knees. A lightning storm erupts and I'm in the middle of it. I can't even see the bolts, just blinding flashes of light.

Every piece of advice I've ever read says that during a lightning storm you should stay off exposed ridges, avoid tall trees, and get to lower ground. Hmmm — those experts must never have hiked the A.T. through the Smokies, because right now there's nothing but exposed ridges followed by stands of tall trees, and no way to get off the damn mountain without a hang glider. I do the next best thing. I run. I speedwalk through the trees to the next exposed ridge, run as fast as I can across the wet rocks with a forty-pound pack bouncing on my back to the next stand of trees, and then speedwalk again until the next exposed section. I keep counting the time between the flash and boom, and slowly the interval increases. The flashes are beginning to look like lightning bolts again. After an hour, the lightning storm passes, but I keep moving, carried forward by adrenaline.

My last two days in the Smokies are nothing but fog and rain. I've been hiking during the day by myself, and at the shelters I meet up with Teresa, Thumper and Webb, a nineteen-year-old man who has had several brushes with the law and is out here to get his life in order.

The Smokies are nice, but I'm ready to leave the park. I want to get to Mountain Momma's Country Store and Hostel early enough to have a chance of getting Rufus, so on my last morning in the park I'm out of camp before anyone else is awake. Twelve miles later I reach Tennessee 32, a sparsely traveled highway on the park's northeastern boundary. I leave the A.T. and follow the highway until a dirt road branches off it. I take the dirt road with Rufus on my mind.

A mile down the winding road I come to Mountain Momma's Hostel, a one-story stone building about 80 years old. Hulks of rusting cars and pieces of worn-out farm machinery populate the land while chickens run free around half a dozen deteriorating cottages. The main bunkhouse, which costs $15 dollars a night and doesn't have a floor, is littered with trash and looks like a heavy raindrop might bring it down.

This isn't a place I want to stay tonight, but I might not have any choice. It's late afternoon already, and the kennel owner may not be able to make it out tonight. I call the kennel with my fingers crossed. The owner is there and just about to go pick up a dog. He tells me he can drop off Rufus around six tonight!

I go inside the small store and find that Mountain Momma makes a mean cheeseburger at a very reasonable price. Mountain Momma is a worn-out, sixty-year-old lady who runs both the small farm and store, and has been catering to hikers for the past ten years. She still loves what she does, but it is obvious she is getting too old to keep this place up on her own. I get my burger and take it outside to the front porch.

The front lawn is littered in hikers, with more coming in as I eat. I don't recognize any of them, and though a few are setting their packs in the bunkhouse, most look like they have no intention of staying the night here. I wonder where all these hikers are going to camp at tonight? It will be one busy place wherever it is.

While I am chomping on my second burger, three kids hike in. Each has a backpack, and they have the look and smell of hikers. I'll bet these three are the Outlaws. For the last several days I've heard rumors about them: a fifteen-year-old girl hiking the trail with her twelve-year-old sister and ten-year-old brother. The story is that they are home schooled and hiking a section of the A.T. for their physical education requirement. The eldest leads her little gang past me towards the store.

"Boo, here's money for three cheeseburgers. Go in and order those," she says to her brother before turning to her sister. "Mary, we need to get hats and gloves. It's supposed to snow the next couple days so let's see what they have here."

This is the first I've heard about an approaching snowstorm, but I still have my cold weather clothes so I'm not worried.

A few minutes later Boo returns to the porch with three cheeseburgers and is joined by the other two carrying hats, gloves, and food supplies. After they eat, the eldest helps the younger two pack up their supplies and leads them back up the road towards the trail. I'm amazed at her leadership and efficiency, not spending a penny more than she needed. She has more presence and strength than some of the Marine Corps officers I've worked with.

An hour after they leave, a National Park Service ranger drives up in his new 4 × 4 SUV, stepping out of the car with a smug look of arrogance and superiority.

"Hey everyone, listen up! I'm looking for three kids who are hiking the Appalachian Trail. I want to know if they passed through here," he shouts to the crowd of hikers. When he doesn't get an immediate response, Mr. Too Much Authority speaks even louder: "Hey, I'm asking a question here! Anyone see them?"

"What's wrong with them, they runaways or something?" an anonymous hiker calls out.

"Because they...," the ranger begins to say, then stops. He looks around for a minute and it's obvious he's trying to think up something to say other than the truth.

"While hiking through the park they camped away from the shelters a couple times. That's not allowed," he says, this time in a gentle voice. "Also, I don't think they are thru-hikers so they were supposed to have reservations for the shelters. I just want to make sure they are aware of the rules."

I can see the cow manure dripping out of his mouth. If the ranger expects cooperation, he has to offer honesty. The kids are out of the park and moving north. Why would the Park Service waste the time of a law enforcement ranger to inform them about the camping rules of a place they are no longer in? The ranger doesn't understand hikers. Even though no one knows the true story behind the Outlaws, we take care of our own and are not going to hand them over to a load of crap. They seem very capable and if they are running, that's their business. We need more than a phony story to rat them out.

"Nope, haven't seen 'em," a voice calls out.

"They may have come through, but I'm not sure," another says.

"Never heard of them, know their names?" says a third voice.

"Hmmm, don't remember any kids hiking the trail," answers a fourth.

After several more denials the defeated ranger drives away without so much as a thanks. The crowd slowly dissipates until I'm alone at Momma's waiting for my puppy.

It's a little before five when a car comes banging down the road. Maybe Rufus is early! The car stops, and instead of a four-legged slobber machine jumping out of the car, it's Teresa. She gets her pack from the back seat and tells the driver thanks before walking over to me.

"Hey, Kevin! Whatcha doing here?" she says.

"Waiting for Rufus. He should be here at six."

"Whee, Rufus is coming back! Hey, is the grill still open?" Just like a hiker. Quick pleasantries, then get down to business: food. Teresa walks into the store and comes back out a few minutes later with a burger.

"You're going to wait 'till six to get your dog? Then what are you going to do?" she asks.

"Well, I'm going to hike until I find a place to camp. I don't want to stay here."

"Hmmm, I'll wait with you for Rufus and then we can hike out together."

YES!!!! I was hoping for that, though I don't know if she's waiting to see Rufus, to be with me, or to pig out before the store closes. I don't care, though, because I'm glad to have her company. There's something about Teresa that I really like, but it's hard to pinpoint. Maybe it's her independence, hiking the trail completely on her own without really knowing what she was getting into. Some women I've dated couldn't go to the store by themselves, and here Teresa is on a six-month hike. She's easy to talk to, never condescending, and we are able to sit together in silence and be comfortable. That's a rare thing, not feeling like someone always has to be talking and entertaining the other.

A few minutes after six the kennel owner arrives and opens the back door. Rufus jumps out of the car and charges, jumping into my lap with his short stubby tail wagging vigorously. He looks great. He's a few pounds heavier and is now a buff hiking machine. We roll on the ground as he licks my face and I try to get him to wrestle, but he doesn't want to, and he ends up running over to Teresa for petting.

After Rufus is done getting his attention we pack up and are ready to hike when Webb comes half-jogging, half-walking down the road.

"Hi guys, no time to talk. Got to see if the grill's open, I'm starved!" he says, dropping his pack on the patio and rushing past us.

Unfortunately for him the grill is closed, but Mountain Momma does makes him a fresh turkey sandwich, and the three of us hike an easy two miles to State Line Branch, a strong-flowing creek with plenty of camping spots around it, most of them full. I now know where the horde of hikers from Mountain Momma's went. It looks like Justus Creek again. I go to sleep early with the idea of rising with the sun and getting ahead of all these hikers.

In the morning I am the only one up, and I'm heating water for oatmeal when Teresa sticks her head out of her tent.

"You're up early. What's the occasion?" she asks me, her curly hair frizzing about her head.

"I want to beat the crowd and put a little distance between myself and this group. You want to join me?"

"Since I'm awake, sure. I don't like hiking with enormous crowds either. I came out here for the serenity of the woods, not to hang out with thirty dirty hikers."

After breakfast we head up the mountain with a revitalized Rufus leading the way. It's cold and cloudy and our breath is visible as we walk.

"I have a question, Kevin," Teresa says as we huff our way up Snowbird Mountain. "What would be your idea of hell? I'm not talking about the fire-and-Satan hell in the Bible, but as a place you wouldn't want to live. A place where you could never be happy."

Wow, tough question! But this is what hikers do to pass the time: we talk.

"My hell would be being stuck in a relationship with an evil, vindictive person where you can't do anything right, and no matter how hard you try it will never be good enough. It sucks the life out of you. You dread going home because you know your night's going to end in an argument, usually about something trivial. I want to be able to enjoy life, not have it ripped from my soul," I answer. My marriage was like that. I think about all the things that went wrong in my marriage, what I did wrong and what she did wrong. Immediately after the divorce I truly hated my ex-wife. Now my feelings are abating; I still don't like her, but I no longer want her to be eaten alive by a rabid black bear.

"Now your turn. Same question," I say.

"That's easy," she beams. "My hell would be a world without sunshine or blue pens."

"Blue pens? Sunshine I understand, but blue pens? Is there something wrong with black?" I tentatively ask, not knowing if Teresa has a psychosis towards certain instruments of writing that she might become violent to defend.

"Black pens are so plain and boring. Blue has color, it's lively. All the shelters have black pens and I don't like it. If more people wrote with blue pens I think they would be happier. People need color in their lives, and a blue pen is just the thing to do it."

If all she needs is sunshine and a blue pen to make her happy, I can provide that. Well, at least the pen part of it. With our talk about sunshine, Mother Nature decides to show us who's boss. It starts snowing. I started out this morning in shorts, as I usually do, but it's really getting cold and I have to put more clothes on. After several hours of hiking in the snow, which is now almost three inches deep, we reach Groundhog Creek Shelter where we find the Outlaws holed up. The eldest is heating water on her stove as the other two shiver in their wet clothing.

"Mary! Boo! Didn't I tell you to get out of those wet clothes and into dry ones? Now do it and climb in your sleeping bags while I get some hot soup ready!" she says.

"Need any help?" I ask, though it looks like she is managing fine.

"No, we'll be all right. Even though we bought hats and gloves, it's still cold, though the storm is supposed to pass over tonight. We'll be fine, thanks."

I leave her alone to tend her siblings. She knows more about the weather than I do and seems prepared to get through the storm. I have no doubt she can handle her little group. After a hot lunch Teresa and I venture back into the storm, leaving the Outlaws huddled in their sleeping bags.

The snow abates but the wind kicks up as we climb Max Patch, a huge bald mountain. Twenty years ago the summit was cleared and used as a runway to supply a logging camp at the base of the mountain. The summit is

April 17, 2001. 248 miles from Springer, 1919 to Katahdin. Teresa heading up Max Patch in a snow storm.

2. Rufus, Rangers and Rain

April 17, 2001. 251 miles from Springer, 1910 to Katahdin. The summit of Max Patch, North Carolina. Yes, those are socks on my hands.

still treeless, and at 4,629 feet high, it supposedly offers one of the best 360-degree views in the south. Today we will have 360-degree views of blowing snow.

The wind intensifies to the point where the gusts knock me back a step, and it's so loud we can't talk to each other. In other words, it's a lot of fun. Teresa has never hiked in freezing, snowing, whiteout conditions before and loves it. Rufus sprints out from behind me and dives into the snow, trying to roll. The only problem is he's carrying his pack and ends up getting stuck on his back like a turtle. I take his pack and he runs again, sprinting twenty feet while scooping mouthfuls of snow on the run, then hits the ground and slides across the snow. He comes back to me with a smile from floppy ear to floppy ear before running off to do it again. This is one of the few times I have ever seen him play. It's good to see Rufus acting like a dog.

We walk through two-foot drifts of powdery snow and fight to gain ground against the punishing wind before finally reaching the summit. Teresa dances around the summit cairn and turns to me with the brightest, happiest smile I have ever seen. My world brightens from her smile, which all by itself will keep me warm the rest of the day.

I give Rufus back his pack as we start the frozen descent. On the way down we come to a snow-covered blowdown, and Rufus stops just short of it. He turns around and looks at me, turns back to the blowdown and leaps over it in a single jump, pack on and all, into the snow on the other side. I can't be more proud. My dog is growing up and I no longer have to lift him over the smaller blowdowns.

While we were climbing Max Patch we generated a lot of body heat, but now on the descent, the sweat on my skin is freezing. The novelty of ascending the mountain in a blizzard has worn off and my toes are starting to go numb. I can only imagine how Teresa's are; I'm wearing boots, but she's only wearing light hiking shoes. There isn't any place decent to set up camp so we continue on towards the shelter. We finally reach Roaring Fork Shelter, built to hold ten people, and there are already eight hikers inside. After walking nineteen miles today we have no intention of setting up our tents in the storm, so we cram ourselves inside.

At dusk Webb comes crashing through the makeshift blanket door one of the hikers put up.

"Damn, I'm freezing! I hope there's room for one more in here!" Webb says. The old shelter adage of "There's always room for one more" holds true, especially in conditions such as these.

"You bet man, come on in," says a hiker named Beer Master. "Hey, I just boiled up some water for tea. Here, you take it. I'll get some more going."

"Where'd you come from, Webb?" I ask, surprised to see him show up. Teresa and I are the only ones who made it here from State Line Branch this morning. The rest must be huddled with the Outlaws at the last shelter six miles back. Everyone here is a new face.

"I got up this morning and saw you guys had already left. I was hiking when it started raining, and then it started to snow! My sweater is frozen solid and it feels like I'm wearing an ice cube. Man, I just kept hiking so I could get here and out of these frozen clothes," Webb says, blue fingers wrapped around a mug of hot tea. Now I appreciate our early start. We never saw a drop of rain; thus we didn't have to deal with wet clothes turning to ice.

With all of us in the shelter, and the blanket over the door, it is fairly warm in here. It's a tight fit inside this small place and I have to use Rufus as a pillow, but it is better than being outside. I fall asleep listening to the wind whip around us.

In the morning I step out to snow on the ground and blue skies overhead. Teresa and Webb are still lying in their warm sleeping bags, so I head out with Rufus and follow the A.T. towards Hot Springs, a small trail town a few miles away. While walking, I write messages in the snow with my hiking poles, spelling out "fruit pie," "cheese," "beer," and "pizza" to motivate Teresa and Webb behind me. A couple hours from the shelter they catch up to me. My messages worked.

"So, Kevin, you like fruit pies?" Webb asks.

"They're okay. Why?"

Teresa and Webb look at each other and laugh. "We were talking, and Fruit Pie it is. You have been named," Webb says, slapping me on the back. Fruit Pie for a trail name? It could be worse, and tradition states I can't refuse any reasonable trail name placed upon me, so Fruit Pie I am.

We descend to Hot Springs, where the sun has melted away the snow, and the storm-covered summit of Max Patch seems a different world away. It's nice to be in a town again and not relegated to the services of a single hostel or shop. It's also nice not having to hitchhike into town. In this case, the A.T. proceeds through the center of town, following Main Street for a mile before heading back into the woods.

The trail travels through a dozen small towns and passes within five miles of two dozen more on its way to Maine. Most are like Hot Springs, small rural farming communities offering basic amenities. While a couple of the towns are fairly large, the biggest being Waynesboro in Virginia with almost 20,000 people, most have a population of less than 4,000. In these small towns, the locals know about the A.T. and are usually friendly to hikers. In return, hikers spend money at their businesses and for the most part don't make asses of themselves.

In town we meet a hiker named Larry, also known as Luwanda. No idea how he got that name, but I think it has something to do with women's dresses. Webb, Teresa and I plan on a zero day tomorrow, and Luwanda is staying the night here as well, so the four of us pool our resources to split a room.

Hot Springs only has five places to stay, so it's not real hard to pick one. The first two are motels, but they don't take dogs. The next options are two different hostels, and last choice is Hot Springs Campground that offers "cabins on the river with hot showers" for $40 a night. Well, if they are anything like the Goose Creek Cabins, it'll be well worth the money, so we head to the campground office, rent one, and walk over to it.

"This is it?" says Webb, staring at a wood structure no bigger than the shelters we've been sleeping in. The only difference is this one has a door.

"Maybe it's bigger on the inside," I add hopefully. It isn't. The entire cabin measures twelve feet by twelve feet, with plywood floors and no electricity. A bunk bed takes up a quarter of the room and a small loft extends over the tiny front porch. Neither the loft nor the bunk beds have mattresses, blankets, or pillows. It is indeed a shelter with a door.

Teresa, being the only girl, gets the privacy of the loft. Webb claims the upper bunk, which leaves Luwanda and me to share the lower bunk, and Rufus gets any portion of the floor he wants.

The shower is hot as promised, except it is part of the communal campground restrooms a hundred yards away, complete with rusty handles and a generous portion of green stuff growing in the corners. Considering my last shower was eight days ago at Fontana Dam, I'm not too picky.

"Now that we're all settled in, who's hungry?" I ask after I return from the shower. It's a rhetorical question as thru-hikers are always hungry. We've been hiking for three weeks and our metabolisms are catching up. I'm not a dietitian, but from talking to other hikers I've noticed a trend. During the first week on the trail, the appetite decreases as the body adjusts to different food and the strain of constant walking. The body burns a lot of fat during this time while the muscles harden. After that, the body realizes it's literally starving itself and needs more food. Appetites increase until our bodies are demanding and burning intense amounts of calories. Food becomes the main focus as the average hiker burns around 5,000 calories a day. Considering a pound of noodles contains 1,300 calories, it is nearly impossible to carry enough food to sustain a hiker, so we carry what we can and gorge ourselves when we get into town.

"Webb and I are planning on heading over to the Peddler's Pub for dinner. Want to join us?" Teresa asks.

"You bet. Luwanda, you coming?"

"No, you guys go ahead. I'm low on funds. I'm going to cook up some food here," Luwanda replies.

I leave Rufus in the cabin with Luwanda, and the three of us head to the pub. The Peddler's Pub overlooks a river and appears from the outside be a very trendy place. It is. We order $8.00 burgers (that don't even come with fries) and as an appetizer we order a plate of hot wings for $8.50. The waiter returns with the wings and I'm ready to dig in when he sets down the plate piled high with five wings, arranged in a cute little pentagon. We are not impressed.

"Um, excuse me, sir, did a couple chickens escape while you were bringing this to the table? I'm willing to go hunt them down and bring them back for you," Webb says, looking at the pathetic plate of wings.

"No, sir, I did not have any chickens run away. This is what you ordered," says the stuffy waiter, who obviously does not enjoy waiting on thru-hikers and would rather have his usual clientele of rich tourists.

"Go ahead and dig in, guys, I don't want to ruin my appetite," Webb says as the waiter starts to walk away, earning us a scalding look. The burger isn't much bigger, and after spending fifteen bucks each on meals that don't fill us up, we retire to our mansion on the water.

In the morning we try the other restaurant in town, Smoky Mountain Diner. This place has never heard of trend and hasn't changed in over forty years of operation. Our server, a middle-aged woman whistling happily at 9:00 in the morning, comes over with a steaming pot of coffee in her hand.

"Kin I take your order?" she asks in a thick accent.

Webb goes first. "I'll take the pancake breakfast with sausage, a side of potatoes, extra biscuits, and the egg and ham breakfast sandwich."

My turn. "I'll take much the same, except no sandwich, the ham omelet instead of the pancake breakfast, extra hash browns, side order of bacon, and gravy on my biscuits."

Now for Teresa. "I'm not like these pigs. I'll just have the waffle breakfast with juice."

"Y'all want coffee?" the waitress asks as she writes down our orders.

"Free refills?" I ask. The pub last night charged for refills of soda and iced tea.

"Where y'all from? O' course free fills," she says, and pours us three cups of coffee.

The food is very good, and my total cost? $4.25. Now, that is how a diner should be. This early in the trip, I've already spent more than I had planned because of the two days in Hiawassee and having to buy a new backpack. I need to start watching my money. While I don't have a car payment, a mortgage, insurance payments, or any of the other bills found in the working world, I also don't have an income. All I have is the money in my savings account, and that has to last until Maine.

Most hikers are on a tight budget as thru-hiking is not cheap; it costs roughly $3,000 to hike the trail, and that isn't including the upfront costs of gear and transportation. Food is by far the biggest expense. Most towns don't have a place where hikers can cook a real meal, so we usually eat out. Considering that I can eat a large pizza in a sitting and be hungry two hours later, it is very expensive to keep myself full. Coming straight out of the Marines, I don't have a lot of excess body fat to lose, so I have to constantly eat to prevent my body from devouring muscle-mass for energy.

After breakfast we decide that forty bucks for an overrated shelter isn't worth the money and we split up to find our own accommodations for tonight. Luwanda hikes out, while Webb and Teresa go to Elmer's Inn, an old Victorian house that has been converted into a hostel. Elmer, the owner and a 1976 thru-hiker, also makes breakfast and dinner for a modest price. Sounds perfect, except for one 65-pound problem: no dogs allowed.

We agree to meet tomorrow morning to hike out together, then I walk up the street to the inexpensive and dog-friendly Hiker Hostel. This place isn't quite a Victorian mansion — more like a Walton rambler. There are twenty bunk beds spread throughout the single floor, hot showers, a kitchen stocked with dishware, and several TVs with lots of movies. Randy, the owner, is a good man, and as in many hostels along the trail, the fee isn't to make money but simply to cover his expenses. Like Elmer, he does it because he enjoys helping hikers. I ask him about the possibility of a work-for-stay and he puts me to work spreading gravel on his driveway.

While I am working, another hiker walks by with a cold beer in his hand. It looks so good I head down to the store and buy a six-pack with the ten dollars I saved by spreading gravel. So much for saving money. I work in the hot sun and drink a cold beer, loving the simplicity of this life. Seven hikers show up for the night and we spend the evening drinking, eating, and telling stories while sitting around a campfire. When the fire burns down I claim a bunk bed inside and fall asleep, entirely buzzed and quite happy.

I wake up with a slight hangover, but otherwise feeling good. Rufus and I walk over to Elmer's to meet Teresa and Webb, and find Elmer in the kitchen preparing breakfast. When he tells me I can find Teresa and Webb in room #2, my heart drops. I didn't think they would be sharing a room. I knock on the door and Webb's groggy voice beckons me inside, with Webb and Teresa still in bed. I'm relieved to see they are in separate beds, but I can't help feeling a bit of jealousy. I would have loved to be in Webb's spot, to spend the night with Teresa, able to talk to her all night.

"You guys ready to go?" I ask, a little hurt. Neither one has packed up and they obviously aren't ready to go, but now I am.

"Not yet," Teresa says, pulling the covers around her. "This bed is so comfortable, I'm going to enjoy it a while longer."

"I don't think I'll be heading out today," Webb says. "I think I'm going to wait for Derby, Dale and Rooster. Go on, we'll catch up in a few days."

I say my good-byes, and with Rufus in tow, I begin my lonely journey out of Hot Springs. I was really starting to like Teresa, but it seems she isn't interested in me. I don't know if she's going to stay another night with Webb and I don't care; I need to hike. I came out here to hike, to forget about my destroyed marriage and to have fun. I told myself before starting out that I wasn't going to get involved on the trail, and I'm not going to let anything distract me from my goal of reaching Katahdin. With that mindset to protect my heart, I keep walking north, 280 miles down and only 1,888 left to go.

3

Thinning of the Herd

As always, the first miles out of town are straight uphill. The sadomasochist trail builders inevitably picked the hardest, highest, and steepest mountain to climb coming out of town. My pack is loaded down with food, my head hurts, and I'm dehydrated from drinking too much last night. I walk slowly and see only three other hikers today: Dan, Kingfish, and Travis. Dan and Kingfish are a couple of buddies hiking to Pennsylvania, and Travis is a young, fast kid that I've seen on and off over the last week.

I stop at Allen Gap for the night because the guidebook states there's a good spring at the gap and a convenience store half a mile down the road. In hopes of an ice cream bar, I hike half a mile down the road, where I find the shell of a store that hasn't been occupied in five years. I don't know if this is some sick joke from the author, luring hikers down this path only to laugh at their folly, but I'm not amused. Back at camp I search for this "good spring," but the best thing I come across is some mosquito-infested puddles covered by a brown mucus. I don't like this guidebook.

Tired, but in need of water, I set up my tent and tie Rufus to my half-full backpack. Rufus is unlike any other dog I have ever seen. He doesn't chew, so I could tie him up with a piece of licorice. He rarely barks, preferring to lie down and sleep until I get back. The best part about Rufus is that he doesn't realize he is stronger than a twenty-pound backpack. He just knows he's tied to something and leaves it at that.

With Rufus secure, I go in search of palatable water, and a hundred yards from camp I find a slow-moving stream that I'm able to filter water from. I am just about done when Rufus starts barking, and not just a woof or two. He sounds like he's in a fight! I drop my water and charge up the trail when a growling brown blur comes crashing through the bushes straight at me. Unable to think, I somehow manage to jump out of the way before this gruesome beast of terror rips into my flesh. To my surprise, and extreme jubilation, the animal ignores me and keeps running as it is being chased by a wild, green monster. The green monster jumps several feet in the air as it runs, tentacles of death whipping out from it.

I stand in fear and confusion as the adrenaline slowly seeps away and my vision clears. The brown thing is no beast, it's Rufus! He's being chased by ... my backpack? Rufus continues to run until he's caught up in some bushes. As I approach Rufus, I hear footsteps pounding down the trail, then someone shouting.

"Rufus! Stop, Rufus! It's just me," Travis yells as he comes running down the trail.

"Travis! What the hell's happening?" I'm not sure what is going on, but I'm relieved to see Travis running down the trail and not a 400-pound black bear. I'm even more relieved when he stops running. Apparently nothing is chasing him. He catches his breath, looks at me, and bursts into laughter.

"I'm so sorry, it's all my fault. I came hiking down the trail and must have startled Rufus, because when he saw me he jumped a foot in the air, dragging your pack. Well, he saw your pack move and that spooked him even more. He started barking and tried to run. Problem was, he was tied to the pack and the faster he ran, the faster the backpack followed, bouncing up and down off the ground and stuff flying out of it; clothes, food, water bottles, everything," Travis says, pausing to catch his breath. "Rufus would look behind him, see the pack jumping up and down chasing him, throwing things into the air, and he kept on running. I ran down the trail after him, yelling for him to stop. Now that I think about it, I don't think that helped. Is he okay?"

We walk over to Rufus, who is scared, shaking, and completely entangled in thorn bushes. We extricate him and my backpack. Neither has suffered a single cut or tear. Travis and I walk back up to camp, picking up my clothes and gear strewn along 200 yards of the trail. After calming Rufus down and tying him to a stout tree, I go get water again. Travis joins me.

"Hey, Travis, did you see Teresa or Webb today?" I ask, hoping Teresa had left town.

"Yeah man, saw Webb in Hot Springs. He said he was going to stay another day till some friends of his caught up. And I passed Teresa at the shelter a few miles back. She's staying there tonight."

I can't help breaking into a small smile. At least I know she's not still sharing a room with Webb.

In the morning, Travis and I head out together, but Travis, being a faster hiker, is soon out of sight. Once again it is just me and Rufus. The sun comes out and the day turns hot, leading me to experience what almost all hikers go through at one time or another—the dreaded chafing. Chafing occurs when sweaty skin continuously rubs on sweaty skin like sandpaper. A common place for chafing to occur in overweight hikers is between the upper thighs as they rub together while walking. This form is lovingly referred to as chub-rub and usually occurs on women.

Guys experience chafing in a different area, between the upper-inner thigh and the boys. Salty sweat only aggravates the chafing, and after a handful of miles it becomes downright painful to walk. After a twelve mile day I walk bow-legged into Jerry Cabin Shelter. There I'm able to wash myself in a cold stream to remove the salt and grime, which gives immediate respite to the burning sensation.

It's a full house at the shelter, and a few hours later Teresa shows up. We exchange smiles before she wanders off in search of a place to set up her tent. Travis isn't here; at his speed he'll be done in a couple of months. After dinner I help build a campfire and do what hikers do every night when there's no TV: we talk.

"Hey, you guys hear about Hawaii?" asks Kayak-Guy, a very thin hiker in his sixties. Obviously he has something good to say. I have no idea who Hawaii is, but trail-gossip is always new and exciting.

"No, what happened to him, or is it a her?" I ask.

"Hawaii's female, and after that hot bout of weather we had a few weeks ago she sent all her cold weather stuff home while at Fontana Dam, thinking spring had arrived for good. She got to Newfound Gap when it started snowing and ended up having to hitchhike into Gatlinburg. I heard she had to stay three days until it warmed up enough not to freeze her ass off."

"Who's heard about Powerbar?" asks another hiker. A couple of people tell him to go on with the story.

"He was some fitness fanatic dude who didn't want to carry a ton of food and a stove, so he came up with a great idea. He figured out how many calories he would burn a day and carried that many calories in Powerbars. After five days of eating fifteen Powerbars a day his bowels shut down. I heard he had to go to the hospital for constipation. What a crappy situation to be in."

"Who knows Davey Crock-of-shit?" a third hiker asks. "He thought he was some bad-ass mountain man who was going to live off the land for the entire hike. Dude, this guy couldn't even crawl into his sleeping bag without help. I loaned him a fork one night because he had planned to carve his own utensils, except he forgot his knife at home. Well, this guy thought he knew everything, and though I told him not to eat those berries, he did anyway. He turned green and puked for eight miles until he reached Hiawassee, and unlike Powerbar, his bowels had no problems letting loose. I haven't seen him since."

The talk continues as the fire burns down, and I learn that Loren has left the trail. Apparently he never recovered from his bicycle ride and was almost hospitalized for exhaustion. Maybe he'll try it again someday, and take a bus to Amicalola.

By morning my chafing is gone. It usually heals overnight because the skin has a chance to dry out. Breakfast is hot oatmeal again. I'm sick of it. I used to like the little packets of flavored oatmeal, but after a month of eating them every day I need a change.

"Just try what I do," Teresa says when I complain out loud. "Don't heat up the water. Pour cold water into the oatmeal and eat it."

Cold oatmeal? Does she think I'm some sort of savage? The idea sounds disgusting, but I can't stomach another bite of hot oatmeal, so I try it and find it delicious. Keep in mind that after a month of hiking in the woods, delicious is very relative. I would have preferred a large plate of steaming pancakes and eggs, but compared to hot oatmeal, the cold oatmeal is a very welcome switch.

Fueled by my new breakfast, I hike out with Teresa. For the most part we walk separately, running into each other during breaks and at the shelters. The next couple of days are very hot and tiring, and I take a lot of breaks for Rufus.

One afternoon while battling the blazing sun I come upon a very strange sight: a pair of headstones right next to the trail, eight miles from the closest road. The graves are for William and David Shelton, two family members who lived in North Carolina but fought for the Union during the Civil War. In the spring of 1863 they were returning to North Carolina to visit family when they were ambushed by Confederate forces. Here, deep in the North Carolina woods, is their final resting place.

A day out from Erwin, Tennessee, Teresa and I hike together all day. She sprained her ankle coming out of Hot Springs and caught it again on a rock today, so we take it slow. It is still unseasonably hot, but the trees are starting to sprout a canopy of leaves that provide scattered shade as we walk. Once again I take Rufus' pack so he can keep up, and the heat leaves me lost in my own thought with no energy for talking. Finally, we reach No Business Knob Shelter and stop for the night. Tired and thirsty, Teresa and I look for the spring that the guidebook says should be nearby.

"You find the water yet?" Teresa yells over to me as she searches the bushes behind the shelter.

"No, not yet. Wait — oh crap! A note on a tree here says the water source is the stream we crossed about a half-mile back. Would have been real nice if it was posted, say, at the stream!"

We walk back down the trail a half-mile to the small stream we had already passed, and I post the note on a tree next to it.

Once back at the shelter, I build a fire, and at the sight of the flames, Rufus immediately jumps into the shelter. I wrap him up in my sleeping bag and return to the fire. No one else arrives and it's just Teresa and I here. The trail is weird like that. For several days I can be hiking and camping with ten hikers, then suddenly everyone disappears and I'm by myself.

"So, do you know what you want to do after the hike?" Teresa asks as we sit by the fire.

"I think so. I want to get into law enforcement and would love to be a park ranger. When I'm done here that's what I'm going to look into. How about you?"

"I want to be a vet, a large one."

"Why would you want to gain weight?" I ask, confused. I've always been under the impression that women want to lose weight, not gain it.

3. Thinning of the Herd 55

"Not me being large, silly. I'm talking about the animals. I want to be a large animal vet. You know, horses and cows and those types of animals. My dream is to be a vet for a large zoo, taking care of all the big animals. It's so interesting. I took several classes at school where we worked with big animals, and I loved it. So that's what I want to do."

We talk until the fire burns down, then climb into the shelter. I have to wake up Rufus so I can climb into my sleeping bag. Rufus, not appreciating being bothered, walks over to Teresa and lies down next to her. Teresa goes to sleep, but I turn on my headlamp to write in my journal and occasionally steal glances of her lying in her sleeping bag curled up with Rufus. Her hair is down and tangled around her face. To be out here on her own and still remain feminine takes some courage. Many female hikers have cut off their hair and adopted a manly persona. Teresa hasn't changed who she is to be out here.

Next morning we rise early to hike the quick seven miles into Erwin. Unlike Hot Springs, the trail doesn't pass through the middle of Erwin, but instead runs along the edge of town. Where the trail meets the town stands Uncle Johnny's Hostel, owned and ran by John Shores. John, also known as Uncle Johnny, runs a very clean and professional hostel, but unlike Elmer's and Randy's, this is a business for John and he treats it as such. After a $2.00 shower and $3.00 load of laundry, I browse through the modest supply of equipment and food, all with inflated prices.

Kingfish walks in as I wait for my laundry to dry. He takes one look at the ten dollar phone cards selling for twelve dollars, and walks out empty-handed. Needing to resupply, Teresa and I talk to Uncle Johnny about getting a ride into town for a price of $2.00 a person. Just before I pull out my money, a car stops in front of the hostel with a young lady behind the wheel.

"Anybody need a ride into town?" she yells out the window. "I'm headed that way."

"How much?"

"Money? Hell no. Name's Murphy. I hiked the trail a couple of years ago and I'm returning favors. Anybody who wants a ride, jump in." Kingfish, Teresa, two other hikers and I take her up on the offer and pile into her car. Uncle Johnny doesn't say a word, but from the look on his face it's obvious he isn't happy about losing business. We zip into town and the first stop is Pizza Hut for a time honored hiker tradition: buffet!

"Hey, Kingfish, where's Dan?" I ask between massive bites of gooey cheese and hot pepperoni.

"You didn't hear? He was pissing fire and blood so he went to the hospital this morning. Turns out he's got a couple of kidney stones. Doctor told him to take a few days off to see if the stones will pass, but if they don't, nothing he can do but keep hiking. So if you hear a blood-curdling scream in the forest, be assured it's only Dan and his kidney stones. That reminds me. He just got a three-pound tub of peanut butter in his mail drop, and since he will staying here for a bit, he doesn't want it. Any of you guys want it?"

"I do. I'll take it," I say. I love peanut butter and jelly sandwiches. Out here, though, bread doesn't hold up well in a backpack; it inevitably gets squished. I found bagels are a great substitute — more calories and they don't squish as easily.

After lunch we hit the grocery store, where I buy a bag of bagels and a bottle of Extra-Strength Gold Bond Medicated Powder. I was told this stuff is a miracle for chafing, and supposedly a couple of splashes of powder a day will do it. Murphy gives us a ride back to Uncle Johnny's and I load up my pack. Teresa, however, pulls out a book and makes herself comfortable on the front porch.

"You heading out today, Teresa?" I ask her.

"No, I think I'm going to stay here tonight. I sprained my ankle again this morning. It's swollen and really hurts. I'm going to take it easy today and hope it heals a little," she says with worry in her voice. One of the greatest fears out here is injury as it is the only thing that can't be controlled. Money problems, loneliness, boredom, or lack of willpower can all be overcome, but an injury can stop a hike and there isn't anything that can be done about it except wait for it to heal.

Leaving Teresa behind, Rufus and I hike to Curly Maple Shelter. Travis is the sole occupant, sitting at the edge of the shelter reading a book. I'm surprised to see him here, but I am happy for the company.

The four mile hike from town to here stirred up my appetite, and even though I ate a large pizza a couple of hours ago, I'm hungry. I take out my stove and immediately realize I have made a big mistake.

"Um, shoot. Travis, I need a big favor. I forgot to get fuel. I only have enough for a day or two. Do you have any I can borrow?" I sheepishly ask, feeling quite stupid.

"Hey man, no problem. I've got plenty. Go ahead and use my stove tonight and save your gas. It's the least I can do after giving Rufus a heart attack."

"Thanks a lot. I don't understand why I keep running into you. You're a fast hiker. You should be a week ahead of me."

"I hike fast, but I also like to take a lot of breaks. I don't want to miss the trail because I'm moving too fast, so I'll hike through the boring parts, then spend two hours at a waterfall or an incredible viewpoint."

My water is soon boiling and I dig out a packet of noodles, when I realize I made another huge mistake: I didn't bring enough food! I miscalculated the distance to the next town and only brought three days of food instead of four. I'm going have to do some big days because I'm not going to ask Travis for some of his food. Fuel is one thing, but food is worth more than gold. Luckily, I have a ton of peanut butter.

3. Thinning of the Herd

After a breakfast of cold oatmeal, with some Grape-Nuts thrown in for variety, I step out into the cool sunshine. Rufus, for some unknown reason, is full of energy so I make good time climbing towards the 5,180-foot summit of Unaka Mountain. As I gain elevation the deciduous forest slowly gives way to red spruce trees, and when I reach the summit I'm in a huge red spruce forest unlike anything I have hiked through yet. This forest seems out of place, considering there isn't a single deciduous tree up here and the forest floor is clear and open, covered by a bed of spruce needles. Sunbeams break through the canopy, giving everything an eerie glow, and I wander around a forest that belongs in northern Maine, not Tennessee. I never knew something like this existed in the south.

After I explore the small, unique forest I head down the other side, and by the time I descend 1000 feet, the spruce trees have disappeared and I'm back in the maple and oak forests that I've been hiking through the last 350 miles.

After hiking seventeen miles today, I find a small meadow with a stream running through it. It's a perfect spot to spend the night and I set up my tent in the meadow. No one else comes hiking down the trail. I haven't seen another hiker all day, and I'm by myself here in my makeshift home. I came out expecting and wanting solitude but discovered the trail is full of people, and now that I am by myself, I'm lonely. Rufus curls up on my sleeping bag and falls asleep until I pour his dinner. He gets up, eats and promptly goes back to sleep. He's not real good company at night. There is the huge Mountain Momma's crowd no more than two days behind me, but that's too many people. I wouldn't mind traveling with a couple of people, one being Teresa. If she took a zero day at Erwin to let her ankle heal, Webb and his group will catch up to her and she'll hike with them, probably at a slower pace than I want to go since I want to keep ahead of the masses. Hopefully she'll catch up.

Today brings 6,285-foot Roan Mountain, the last 6,000-foot peak until Mt. Washington in New Hampshire. For the second day in a row Rufus is feeling strong and he leads the way up Roan Mountain into another spruce forest much like Unaka, except this one is not exclusively red spruce trees. Deciduous trees and small bushes intermix with the spruce, and the forest floor is covered with rambling plants. I reach the summit expecting a mixed conifer and deciduous forest, but instead I find a parking lot, half a dozen buildings, and a huge, obviously man-made clearing. I do some exploring and learn a little about this place.

Apparently, a 300-room hotel used to occupy this clearing, straddling the North Carolina–Tennessee border. The hotel, built in 1885 by wealthy Civil War general John T. Wilder, was a grand resort that attracted the affluent from all over the world, its luxury and remoteness making it an ideal vacation place for the wealthy. For thirty years the resort prospered, but then General Wilder began to feel the effects of age and retired from the business, leaving it in the

April 26, 2001. 263 miles from Springer, 1804 to Katahdin. North Carolina Appalachians, with Roan Mountain in the distance.

hands of caretakers who ran the hotel into the ground. Within a couple of years the hotel was bankrupt, abandoned, and left to looters.

Loggers quickly took over the unoccupied land, chopping down every tree on the mountain, while the extensive natural rhododendron plants were dug up and sold to local nurseries. After Wilder's death and the subsequent destruction of the mountain, his heirs sold the ravaged land to the U.S. Forest Service, who in turn gave the land to Tennessee to make Roan Mountain into a state park. The forest has returned, along with the rhododendrons. The flowers have blossomed into one of the largest natural rhododendron gardens in the world, and now 200,000 people a year visit Roan Mountain to see the impressive display of colors.

The flowers are still several months away from blooming and all the buildings are closed and locked until tourist season, so I keep hiking to Roan High Knob Shelter. This shelter was originally a fire-warden's cabin and has four sturdy sides, an actual door, and tons of garbage strewn about inside. It's amazing: I can walk for days in the woods and not see any trash, but come to a park and there is litter everywhere. Hikers, for whom every ounce counts, carry garbage for days to dispose of it properly. It's a different story in parks. People get out of their car, walk a mile or two on a trail carrying cans of soda and bags of food, yet lack the strength to pack the empties back out. I pick up litter as I hike, and I have witnessed other hikers doing the same, but there is too much to get it all. I hope someday everyone will understand that the wilderness is beautiful because it is wilderness, not a landfill.

After taking a quick break, and stuffing a Snickers wrapper lying on the ground into my garbage bag, Rufus and I hike on. We have walked twelve miles today but still have another seven to go because I want to camp on Little Hump Mountain. I pick up my pace and make it to the 5,449-foot summit of Little Hump just as the sun begins to set. There isn't a cloud in the sky, and I can see for miles across Little Hump and its big brother to the north, Hump Mountain.

The Humps are balds, meaning the summits are meadows, not forests. The Southern Appalachians have dozens of bald mountains. It is unknown why certain mountains are bald and others are forested as the tree line in the south is a theoretical 7,000 feet, and none of these mountains come close to that elevation. The taller Roan Mountain is forested, but this smaller mountain isn't. Theories for the balds range from forest fires to UFOs. All I know is the balds have magnificent 360-degree views.

I set up my tent and watch the sunset as I cook dinner. The sun shoots

April 27, 2001. Teresa and an unknown hiker with Little Hump and Roan Mountain behind them.

out rays of gold, purple and red, bathing the whole range in a pink light. Alone on top of the mountain, with the wind making the only noise, I experience one of the most peaceful moments I have ever known. I only wish Teresa were here to share it with me.

Sunrise proves to be every bit as good as the sunset, but a biting cold wind gets me moving. Rufus and I drop off the cold mountain into the warm valley between the humps, and by the time I'm standing on Hump Mountain the wind has died down, leaving only warm sunshine. I could spend the day on the summit if not for the fact that all I have left to eat is a pound of peanut butter and a couple of bagels, and I could eat those right now. Instead, I settle for half a bagel and save the rest for dinner tonight.

Hungrily, I leave the Humps and keep walking until I come to a small creek just past a dirt road. Sitting on the shore is a box of oranges with a small, handwritten sign reading, "Hikers, help yourself." Keeping cool in the creek are several six-packs of pop. I greedily devour three of the oranges and wash them down with two cans of Coke, wishing I could thank the unknown benefactor for this trail magic. Trail magic is the ultimate goodwill gesture, an unexpected show of kindness from strangers. It can be food, water, a ride, or a place to stay. The amazing thing about trail magic is that it seems to appear when needed most, like this food here.

With a satisfied belly, I leave North Carolina and cross into Tennessee at Highway 19E, leaving one of the best sections of the A.T. and entering one of the worst. The air is saturated with the thick, sweet stench of decaying flesh. Next to me on the side of the road is a rotting cow half-covered by a blue tarp. Swarms of flies buzz the putrid carcass and armies of maggots crawl though its body, enjoying the free buffet. It's a disgusting sight and I almost leave my breakfast next to the cow. Rufus doesn't want to be here either, so we quickly cross the road and into the woods.

The forest isn't much better. For a quarter of a mile the trail meanders along a small river polluted with bags, boxes, and piles of garbage. Almost half a mile from the road sit two sets of rusting washers and dryers, one still full of decaying clothes. I don't understand why anyone would want to destroy their own environment like this. Don't they know that this river is where they get their water?

The trail leaves the river of garbage and emerges into a pasture occupied by a dozen very large cows grazing and defecating on the trail. The cows turn to face us as we enter their domain. They watch me warily but take an instant dislike to Rufus. Two of them start advancing towards him, snorting and stomping their feet. Rufus immediately tries to hide between my legs, cowering and begging for help. I bang my hiking poles together and yell at the walking steaks until they back off a couple of feet, staring and still snorting. They make no effort to hide the fact that they don't like Rufus and me. I'm expecting the King

Cow to come out and lead his band of mighty mooers to battle against us as we tiptoe past the herd.

After avoiding the big bovines we continue through multiple pastures, with stealthy cow spies watching us from a distance. I've been hiking for five hours and am almost out of water. My guidebook says a small stream flows through the pastures and I find it, a fetid trickle of water flowing around piles of cow pies. I can imagine another dead cow hidden somewhere among the weeds, its rotten liquids oozing into the stream. I skip the water and Rufus refuses to touch it, so we push on for several more miles.

Well past the pastures of death I find a clear, fast-moving creek to get water and I eat my last bagel, using it like a knife to scrape away the remaining peanut butter in the jar; three pounds of peanut butter gone in three days. I haven't taken a crap in the last two days and visions of Powerbar float through my head. No more peanut butter for me for a while.

Two packets of cold oatmeal is all I have left for breakfast. That's the last of my food, but luckily it's only seven miles to Kincora Hostel and my next mail drop. The long days have caught up to Rufus, and a mile out from camp he's already fallen a hundred yards back. He doesn't seem to have any energy so I carry his pack, but he still keeps falling behind and I constantly wait for him. When we come to water, I take a long break so he can drink as much as he wants. He has finally learned to drink on his own and I no longer have to force water down his throat.

As the trail marches over endless puds (those pointless ups and downs with no view), Rufus walks slower and slower until he finally sits down and refuses to move. I feel bad for him, but there is nothing we can accomplish by sitting down in the middle of the trail. We have to keep moving, but Rufus doesn't understand this. After thirty minutes of prodding, pushing, and pulling I leave him sitting on the trail. I know he will follow me.

Several exhausting hours later I reach the road that leads to Kincora and sit down to wait for my dog. My legs are tight, my back hurts, and my shoulders are sore from the added weight of Rufus' pack. I stretch out to relieve the tightness, and an hour passes before a worn-out Rufus comes staggering down the trail. When he sees me, his droopy tail barely wags. He tries to break into a jog, which lasts for ten feet, before he slows in exhaustion. We both need a day off.

Rufus and I follow the road for a half a mile to Kincora Hostel. The hostel is a beautiful log cabin that the owner, Bob, built himself using timber from his land. Next to the hostel is an older but equally well-crafted log home that Bob and his wife live in. The hostel cabin has a full kitchen, a washer and dryer, hot showers, TV, a wood stove, and plenty of bunks, all for a $4.00 per day donation. Some hikers give more, while others take advantage of this hospitality and do not donate anything. Unlike Uncle Johnny's, Bob and Pat are not in it for the money; they just love to help hikers.

I walk up to the front porch and see a handful of hikers lounging around, none of whom I have ever met before. It's nice to be around people again. For the last three days I have had only Rufus to keep me company. I am glad to have human interaction again. I wouldn't make a good hermit.

After a hot shower, I sprawl out on the front porch while Rufus sleeps in the sunshine. I am contemplating what to do for dinner when Bob drives up in a truck and offers everyone a ride into town. He takes us to the post office, grocery store, and a restaurant before returning to the hostel, where I find Teresa cuddled up with Rufus on the front patio.

"I was hoping I'd find you here!" she says when she sees me, still lying next to Rufus. "I put in some long days to catch up." She pauses for a minute, thinking about what she said, and adds, "Partly to catch up to you. I also wanted to get away from a hiker named Flame."

"Who? I don't think I know him. Why did you want to get away from him?"

"I met Flame at Uncle Johnny's when I stayed the night there, and we hiked out together the next day and stayed at the same shelter that night. After that, he wouldn't leave my side, but luckily he's not a real fast hiker. He'd catch up to me during breaks, and yesterday he asked me if I wanted to split a motel room with him down the road. He didn't get the hint that I wasn't interested, so I put in some long days to lose him. Looks like I did."

I sit down on the front porch next to her. It's a warm night and we talk about the last couple of days. Her ankle felt better coming out of Erwin, and she was only five to eight miles behind me for the last three days. While I was watching the sunset on top of Little Hump, Teresa was watching the same sunset from Roan Mountain. If I had taken a three-hour break somewhere she would have caught up to me.

As we talk, more hikers congregate on the front porch as they drift in off the trail. Soon there are about fifteen hikers, all sharing stories and adventures. Tubesteak, Keystone, and Sock-in-the-Hole are a couple of the hikers who join us out front.

"Hey Sock, tell everyone how you got your name. Funniest damn story I've heard!" says Tubesteak, a chubby twenty-year-old guy from Syracuse, N.Y.

"Hell, Tubesteak, I've must have told you the story five times now. I don't want to repeat it again," Sock replies.

Tubesteak, not willing to be denied his entertainment, starts telling the story. "You see, back in Georgia, Sock shared a shelter with an ornery old prick who was out for the weekend. This hiker was loud, obnoxious, and thought he owned the whole damn place. Sock was out of toilet paper and saw that the hiker had a whole roll, so he asked if he could borrow some. The hiker told Sock to kiss off. The next morning Sock was up before the hiker, and he really had to relieve himself. Apparently the guy had hid away his toilet paper, but he did leave a pair of clean socks next to his boots. So Sock grabbed the guy's socks, went off in the woods, and after taking a huge crap, he wiped himself clean with them! Then Sock dug a hole, buried the socks, and continued on his way." Tubesteak is barely able to finish the story before he falls on the ground in a fit of laughter.

The phone rings over the laughter, and a minute later a hiker yells out asking if a Phoenix is here. Teresa goes to the phone and returns a minute later, shaking her head.

"That was Flame. He just doesn't get it. He says he's at the motel down the street and asked if I wanted to go down there and watch a couple movies with him. I think he got the hint when I told that I'm here with you and will be hiking out with you."

Teresa doesn't appear to worried about this pseudo-stalker, and she shouldn't be. She's with friends now, and if Flame still doesn't understand that Teresa isn't interested, I'd be more than happy to explain it to him.

Before I started hiking the trail I was asked numerous times, "Aren't you afraid of all the weirdos out there in the woods?" Most people's ideas of the woods are from movies and books, with backcountry men out to do evil things and serial killers looking for prey. This is the farthest thing from the truth. Ted Bundy stalked women in cities, not trails, and *Deliverance* is a Hollywood movie. The wackos and druggies are in the cities where there are soup kitchens, social services, and easy prey. There's nothing for them in the woods but in-shape hikers carrying little of value. Crime along the trail is very low. I'd much rather be in the woods than in L.A. or New York.

Kincora Hostel is the friendliest place I have ever been. Everyone is family here and there are no insults or fights. This is the perfect place to sit back and relax. I spend my zero day playing cards, telling stories, and chopping a huge pile of wood until the ax handle breaks. Never did I think that while hiking the trail I would spend a day chopping wood, but I'm learning the trail is about much more than hiking. It's about people.

After my zero day I pack up and am ready to hike when Teresa, Tubesteak and his hiking partner, Keystone, sit down to play cards. Keystone is from Boston and is thinner and quieter than Tubesteak. The two of them are good friends and are taking a break from college to hike the trail. They tell me they need a fourth player, so I join them for a game. Before I know it, afternoon has crept up on me and I am destined to stay another night.

I'm glad I stayed, because evening brings Marcus and Shiggy, as well as Isis and Jackrabbit, who are also known as the barefoot sisters. I have been hearing rumors about two women walking the whole trail barefoot, but I thought it was nothing more than trail gossip, not having seen any bare footprints anywhere to validate the claim. Now here they are and without any shoes on. They started hiking barefoot while growing up in Maine, and now their feet are masses of muscle and calluses, reminding me of an elephant's foot. They carry shoes only for the extremely rocky sections or in case it snows.

On my third morning at Kincora I am ready to hike with a refreshed Rufus, but as I make breakfast I hear a rumor that a hiker named Achilles is a handful of miles back and coming in today. Could it be the same Achilles I loaned my sleeping bag to almost a month ago? I decide to stay and find out, and by noon he walks into the hostel.

"Achilles!" I shout out as he climbs the stairs onto the porch. "I've been wondering if you were still on the trail. How's the blisters?"

"Doing good, Fruit Pie," he says, catching me by surprise. I didn't have a name when we were hiking together. "I caught your trail name in the registers," he explains, dropping his pack and plopping into a chair next to me. "There's only one person out here hiking with a Rufus, so I figured you got yourself a name. And check out my shoes." Achilles wiggles his feet, adorned with tennis shoes.

"Better than your boots?" I ask.

"Oh, so much better. I spend two more days in Hiawassee after you left, and bought these shoes. I can really move now. This looks like a cool place to stay. How long you been here?

"Um, three days," I say. "I've tried the last two days to hike out, but I just can't seem to leave."

"I know the feeling. You staying tonight, though?" he asks expectantly. "If you do, we can hike out in the morning. I'll make sure you get moving."

I stay, and in the morning Achilles helps me break the Kincora vortex that has held me hostage. Teresa still has to pack her bag and says she'll catch up. Rufus has energy again and we make great time to Watauga Lake. As we round the lake, Achilles stops dead in his tracks and points upwards.

"Look," he says, eyes sparkling like a kid's on Christmas morning, "a rope swing."

Sure enough, tied to a stout tree branch overhanging the lake is a thick, knotted rope begging to be swung on. One look is all it takes and off we go, swinging into the water like a pair of twelve-year-olds on a hot summer day. Teresa shows up, hiking with Thumper and Patch Monkey. Patch Monkey is a skinny guy my age from Tennessee wearing a bright orange Hawaiian shirt. He earned his name at the beginning of the trail when he was so weight conscious he even cut the tags off his tent. Having no sewing experience, he ended up cutting a large hole in his tent which required patching.

"Thumper! I haven't seen you since the Smokies. Where'd you go?" I ask as I climb out of the lake.

"I met Patch in Hot Springs. Turns out he lives just off the trail past Hot Springs, so we hiked to his house and spent a couple of days," Thumper says.

"Cool. Now strip off your shoes and shirt and come swing," I say, once again launching myself into the lake.

"Um, I don't think so," Thumper replies. Teresa and Patch also refuse to swing. This early heat wave creates the perfect excuse to go splashing into the

May 2, 2001. 415 miles from Springer, 1752 to Katahdin. Achilles (right) and I at Watauga Lake rope swing.

water, but try as we might, Achilles and I can't convince any of them to give it a go, so I take a couple more swings and then the five of us hike to Vandeveter Shelter.

"Who's up for getting into Virginia tomorrow?" Achilles asks while we sit around a campfire.

"What? Are you nuts? Virginia is thirty-three miles away!" Patch Monkey replies.

"No way I'm hiking thirty-three miles in a day," Teresa says.

"Me neither," adds Thumper.

"I'm feeling ambitious, I'll give it a try," I say. "No promises, but I'll see how far I get." The map shows it's fairly flat and I think I have a decent shot at it. Thirty-three miles is a long way in a day, but it'll be fun trying.

I'm up before the sun to get in some miles before it gets too hot for Rufus. As quietly as I can, I eat a quick breakfast and pack. I wake up Rufus—twice—and head down the trail. I haven't walked more than a hundred yards when Rufus' tags stop jingling. I turn around to see Rufus slowly making his way back towards the shelter. Frustrated, I grab him, put him on his leash and start walking again. He walks, but not very willingly, and I am constantly pulling to keep him moving.

May 2, 2001. Rufus taking a much needed break.

After an hour of dragging Rufus I'm tired of it. He doesn't want to walk and several times he plops onto the ground in mid-stride, curling up and refusing to move. Maybe without his pack he'll walk better, so I remove his leash and strap his pack on mine. Stupid me. As soon as I take a step forward, Rufus looks up at me with a screw-you grin, turns around and takes off running back towards the shelter. I don't care. I've already hiked two miles and I'm not going to chase him. Teresa and Achilles are at the shelter, and Rufus can catch up to me later. So much for man's best friend.

I keep walking for a couple more hours as the sun starts to come out. Rufus hasn't caught back up to me yet, and I stop next to a stream to contemplate whether I should go back for him or not. While wondering what to do, I see Rufus coming down the trail with his nose to the ground. He stops, lifts his head to sniff the air and sees me. Rufus's tail starts whipping back and forth and he runs over to me, happy to have found me. He takes a long drink of water and lies next to me, plopping his big head onto my leg. After Rufus rests a bit we are back hiking together, Rufus right beside me sniffing the plants, peeing on trees, and thoroughly enjoying his morning walk. Apparently Rufus has forgiven me for making him get up so early.

By early afternoon Achilles passes me and I try to keep up with him, but he moves way too fast. He'll make it to Virginia today, but I stop at Abingdon

Gap Shelter, twenty-two miles from where I started this morning and my longest day yet. A couple hours later Teresa walks into camp.

"What happened to you this morning? Achilles and I woke up to find Rufus curled up in the shelter asleep, but you were gone. We took Rufus with us, and half a mile from the shelter he took off running down the trail. I was worried something might have happened to you," she says, with a true look of concern in her eyes.

"Nothing happened to me, except that my dumb dog can't walk if it's still dark out. For that matter, Rufus doesn't like to hike if it's too hot, too cold, too wet or too dry either. That dog is really starting to—"

"You know what?" Teresa interrupts, her voice changing to sandpaper. "That dog loves you and you are going to have to be patient with him."

"But I—"

"No buts. Be patient with him."

"But—"

"Patience!" And with that she has the last word. Feeling bad, I walk over and pet Rufus, making sure he knows I'm not mad at him.

4

Carnivorous Death Cows

Today I will enter Virginia, 455 miles and three states from Springer Mountain. The Virginia section of the A.T. is 450 miles long, and it will be more than a month before I cross my next state boundary. Fifty percent of the hikers who started the trail with the grand expectations of reaching Maine have dropped out by now, and of the 50 percent left, half will go home before reaching the end of the state, victims of the "Virginia Blues." They will decide that walking day after day and never leaving the state isn't any fun. But for me, I love this adventure and nothing will take me from it.

Teresa and I leave the shelter while Keystone and Tubesteak are still packing up. A few miles later we reach the Virginia border and celebrate the milestone with some photos and high-fives. We keep hiking and follow the trail right into Damascus, known as the friendliest town on the A.T. The locals are friendly to hikers and the place to stay is The Place, a large house converted to a hostel in the middle of town. Damascus First Methodist Church owns the building and asks for a $3.00 donation per night. Dogs are not allowed inside the hostel but are allowed on the property, so I set up my tent outside along with half a dozen tents already here, and Teresa does the same. Tubesteak and Keystone arrive around dinner time, and they set up their tents next to Teresa and me.

The night brings rain showers and my once faithful tent springs a leak. By morning I'm able to take a sponge bath with my sleeping bag. I quickly locate the leaky culprit: several sewn seams across the roof that were not sealed properly. Easy enough to fix with the proper materials, so I head over to the local outfitter and purchase a tube of SeamSeal, a type of glue made to use on tents. The rain passes and the sun comes out as I work on my tent. By the time the glue is dry the cool morning has transformed into a very hot and humid afternoon. Tubesteak, Keystone and Teresa haven't left yet, enjoying the opportunity to stretch out on the grass and relax. I look over to Rufus, who is lying in the shade of a tree, panting like he's been chased by a cow.

"Hey guys, I don't want to hike out in this heat. It'll kill Rufus," I tell them. "I'm going to wait until it cools down a bit, then head out this evening. If you all want to leave, I'll catch up."

May 5, 2001. 454 from Springer, 1713 to Katahdin. Hanging out in Damascus, Virginia.

"Hey, Fruit Pie, we're in no rush. We'll wait for you. In the meantime, I'm going to grab some beers to help keep us cool," Tubesteak says. He isn't the type to leave a man behind.

Evening approaches and the temperature finally becomes reasonable, but now we are hungry and don't want to leave on an empty stomach, so we buy some hamburgers, hotdogs and more beer, and have a small BBQ at The Place. After dinner I slowly start packing up.

"You leaving, man? No way I can leave yet, still way too full. I have to give my stomach some time to digest," Keystone says, lying back in the evening sun.

"Me too. I can't move yet," adds Tubesteak. "Think I'll go grab a couple beers to help settle our stomachs."

Soon the sun is down and it's too dark to hike out, not to mention the fact that we can't see straight anymore, so we spend a second night at The Place. The town vortex has sunk in its claws. Towns have a tendency to do that, especially at a relaxing, hiker-friendly place like The Place. Cheap stay, good friends, abundant food at the grocery store, and nothing to do all day makes it very easy to waste away the day and never get back on the trail. Towns have broken down many ambitious hikers who decide they like the comforts of home over the drudgery of hiking and call it quits. I like towns, but not enough to leave the trail, so at 8:00 A.M. I'm packed and ready to go. Keystone and Tubesteak are also up and packed. Seems like they, too, want to escape town while it's still cool out. I don't see Teresa, though.

"Hey, Teresa! You ready to go?" I yell towards her tent.

A few mumbles and a couple of yawns later Teresa sticks her head out the door.

"No, not really. I haven't gone to the grocery store yet. I need to shop before I head out. You guys go on, I'll catch up."

Not wanting to leave her behind, as she may never make it out of town, Tubesteak, Keystone and I talk about grabbing breakfast while she goes to the grocery store. She finds out our plans, though.

"Hey, I want to go to breakfast too. Can't I go?" she whines, looking at me with pouting lips.

"Sure, but if you're with us eating, how are you going to be shopping and packing?" I ask.

"I'll go shopping after breakfast. It won't take me long."

Now I'm starting to get worried that we won't make it out today, but after breakfast Tubesteak, Keystone and I escape Damascus as Teresa goes to the grocery store. I knew that if we waited for her, we would repeat yesterday and never leave.

The three of us, with one Rufus, hike all day to Lost Mountain Shelter. Marcus and Shiggy are here, and Rufus instantly recognizes his friend, running over to greet a tail-wagging Shiggy. While the two of them are marking their boundaries, Teresa arrives. She did make it out of town.

4. Carnivorous Death Cows

May 5, 2001. 454 from Springer, 1713 to Katahdin. My place (a tent) at The Place (a hostel). Both located at Damascus, Virginia.

I get out my stove and food bag and am faced with my nightly dilemma of what to make for dinner: noodles, noodles, or noodles? I settle for a can of tuna fish mixed with a box of mac and cheese. As I finish dinner I see Keystone digging around in his pack. He finds what he is looking for and holds it out triumphantly.

"Anyone for hacky sack?" Keystone asks, holding up a worn, red hacky sack.

"I'm not good, especially with five pound boots on, but I'm in," I say, and join in a game of hacky sack in front of the shelter while Shiggy and Rufus run circles around the campsite, playing a game only they understand.

In the morning Teresa and I hike out together as we follow the trail into Grayson Highlands State Park. We slowly emerge from deciduous forests into vast meadows that could have been transplanted from Montana. Mile upon mile of rolling grasslands lie in front of us, periodically spotted with huge rock formations that we climb on for the fun of it. The best part of the park is the herds of wild ponies. Within an hour we come across one of the herds.

"Look, there they are. Ponies!" Teresa says, pointing to a spot a hundred yards off the trail. "Ooh, look. They have baby ponies. They are so cute!"

72   The Things You Find on the Appalachian Trail

May 6, 2001. Tubesteak (right) and Keystone apparently trying to hang a bear bag. How short do they think bears are?

4. Carnivorous Death Cows

May 7, 2001. Teresa in southern Virginia.

They are cute. Ten or twelve adults are grazing among half a dozen small colts, some no bigger than Rufus. Rufus looks over at them and that's the extent of his curiosity, though the ponies watch him carefully. They are much more mild-mannered than the evil cows we have previously met, and after a few minutes they lose interest in Rufus and resume eating.

I set my backpack down and slowly approach the herd, while Rufus lies down to watch. The mares with foals back up a little as I come close, but the others stand their ground and watch me with interest. I reach one of the males and he allows me to stroke his neck. This pony, one of the biggest of the herd, barely comes up to my waist and shows no fear at all. He nuzzles against my hand and I pet him for several minutes before moving through the herd, petting some and leaving alone those that make it clear they don't want to be touched.

Standing here among these quiet and peaceful animals, I have found my own Nirvana. There's no artificial noise destroying the silence, no bars or fences, no cars zipping by or mounds of garbage scarring the landscape. Just these gentle creatures grazing and living on the rolling meadows. Teresa comes down and joins me.

"See how peaceful they are. This is why I want to be a large-animal vet. To take care of creatures like this, keep them safe and let them live their lives,"

Teresa says. She manages to get close to a mare-foal pair and pets them both. She does have a touch with animals.

After almost an hour with the animals we walk back to the trail and continue through the park, camping with Tubesteak, Keystone, Marcus and Shiggy, who each share their experiences with the ponies. Shiggy was as well behaved as Rufus, ignoring the ponies while Marcus wandered among the herd.

The next day we leave the park and the ponies. Marcus, Teresa and I walk all day until we reach Virginia Road 16, a mile away from Raccoon Branch Shelter, our home for the night. Tubesteak and Keystone are taking a break next to the road. Tubesteak tells us that we crossed the 500 mile marker today, and he and Keystone are headed to a restaurant down the road to get a burger. They invite us to join them, but I have to decline. I should really eat the food in my backpack.

Teresa and Marcus also decline, so the three of us, with two dogs following, walk the mile to the shelter. As much as I want a couple of burgers, I know that tomorrow we reach Partnership Shelter. Rumor has it that there's a phone and road near Partnership, and you can have pizza delivered right to the shelter.

Tonight we share the shelter with a skinny, young hiker who goes by the name of Mouth. Mouth is considered a "go-lighter," a hiker who counts every ounce in his pack and carries only the very lightest gear available. Mouth doesn't have a tent; instead he relies on shelters and carries a lightweight tarp to use when reaching a shelter isn't feasible. He also has a very lightweight sleeping bag, titanium cookware, lightweight clothes, and other hi-tech equipment that gives him a total load of less than twenty pounds. He has forgone shoes and pants, instead hiking in sandals and a sarong, a type of skirt that is lightweight and reduces chafing by allowing plenty of airflow. He can really move with his light gear, covering the same distance I do in half the time.

Mouth is also the biggest pothead I have ever seen. His breakfast consists of a joint, his lunch is a sandwich and a joint, and dinner is, you guessed it, another joint. I understand why Mouth is a go-lighter; it's the only way he's able to carry the massive amounts of marijuana he needs to sustain himself. Unfortunately, he isn't named Mouth because he always has some type of smoking device in his mouth. He's named Mouth because he talks continuously. The guy never shuts up.

"Hey guys. How y'all doing? I'm just here having a smoke before bed, sorry about the smell. Didn't want to crawl out of my bag to smoke outside, I'm comfortable here. What type of sleeping bag is that?" he says as I lay out my bag. Before I have a chance to answer, he continues to talk.

"Hmmm, looks like a decent bag. I have a Feathered Bags Trailmaster 5000, complete with extra long zipper, Ultra-Extra Villamer 19 outer coating and 900-fill goose down picked from baby geese between the ages of 7 and 8 weeks old. I have tried a dozen different bags and didn't like any of them, so I had this one custom made and it's great. I was only going to get the Villamer 18 outer coating, but figured I'm already paying $600 for this bag, might as well spend the extra $50 to upgrade it to level 19 instead of 18...," and he continues to drone on even though it's apparent that no one is listening to him. How I long to be among the ponies again. They don't speak.

Finally his monologue is interrupted by the arrival of Keystone and Tubesteak.

"We're back, and we've brought gifts! Okay, one gift and you're going to have to share," says Tubesteak, proudly offering us a large cream pie. We share, and it is good.

I leave the shelter early the next morning with pizza on my mind, and after a quick twelve miles I'm at Partnership Shelter, which makes the Fontana Hilton look like a Motel 8. The shelter, built in 1998, stands two stories tall and easily sleeps sixteen hikers with room to spare for gear. It even has an enclosed bathroom with a hot shower. The front yard is level and grassy with several picnic tables and fire pits.

I go in search of pizza and find the rumors are true. Mt. Rogers National Recreation Area Headquarters is a mere hundred yards up the trail with a pay phone and several soda machines. Posted next to the pay phone is the number to the local pizza place, and I waste no time ordering two extra-large pies. Rufus and I make ourselves comfortable on the front lawn as Teresa, Marcus, Tubesteak and Keystone come hiking in.

The driver soon arrives with my pies. It's obvious that we are going to need more, so Tubesteak and Keystone persuade the driver to give them a ride into town. Marcus, Teresa, and I sit on the lawn and eat pizza. Even Rufus and Shiggy get a piece. An hour later the driver drops off Tubesteak and Keystone, who are holding several more pizzas and a case of beer. A 21-year-old kid named Othra hikes in with Mouth. Mouth sees us eating and has to say something.

"How are those pizzas? That was my plan as well, to order some pizza and get some beer. Hey, do you mind if I have a slice while I wait for mine to get here? I'll return the favor. Good choice, pepperoni and cheese. Can't ever go wrong ordering pepperoni on a pizza..." I hand him a slice just to fill his mouth with something other than words.

More people come in, and by the end of the day there are fifteen hikers here. We eat, drink, and play hacky sack.

"Hey Othra, what's the story behind your name? What is an Othra?" I ask as we sit around a fire. It's too dark to play hacky sack anymore.

"I know what an Othra is...," starts Mouth, but a random shoe comes flying through the air, striking him in the back of the head and ending his chance at a never-ending story. Apparently Mouth's reputation is well known.

"I'm not real sure what it is," Othra says. "In Georgia I met this Special

May 9, 2001. 522 from Springer, 1645 to Katahdin. Pizza time at Partnership Shelter, Virginia.

Forces dude hiking the trail, and one of his specialties was being able to start a fire. One night he got a fire started during a downpour. I have no idea how he did that. We hiked together for a bit and he taught me a few things before he quit the trail. So I was practicing a couple of the techniques with some other hikers one night, and one guy asks if I've ever seen the movie *Quest for Fire*. Apparently it's an old movie about a group of cavemen, with no dialogue except for the very last scene. The cavemen are all sitting around the fire, one of them mumbles the word 'Othra,' points to the fire and the movie ends. The name stuck. Man, I've got to see that movie when I get home."

The fire slowly dies down, the pizza and beer disappear, and by 10:00 P.M. every one of us is ready for bed. Rising with the sun and hiking all day doesn't leave a lot of energy for partying. Tubesteak and I lay out our sleeping bags on the lawn underneath the stars. I ask Teresa if she wants to join us, but she says she's already set up her stuff in the shelter. Considering her stuff is a sleeping bag, it's a pretty lame excuse, but I don't push it. Instead, Tubesteak and I point out constellations and look for satellites until we drift off to sleep.

Morning brings the departure of Tubesteak and Keystone. They are taking two weeks off to attend a wedding. They hitch out on the road saying they will be back in a couple of weeks, but we all know we won't see them again.

We will be several hundred miles ahead of them when they get back on the trail, and that's just too much distance to make up. Teresa, Marcus, and I hike away from Partnership Shelter, leaving two good friends behind us.

The trail drops out of the Virginia mountains and into numerous meadows and grasslands, most of which are used for grazing. Barbed wire fences criss-cross the meadows and are often built right over the A.T. Where the trail meets the barbed wire is a stile, a structure that lets hikers get over the fences.

One type of stile is a 2 × 8 wood plank that runs up one side of the fence and down the other, supported in the middle by several posts. This creates an inverted V that acts as a bridge. This idea would work if the planks had some traction on them, the fall wasn't onto barbed wire, and there was something to hold onto. Instead, the rotting planks are usually covered with a quarter-inch of slime and predisposed to dropping an unsuspecting hiker on his head.

It's tough enough for me to cross over the slippery planks, but then I have to coax Rufus over as well. The barbed wire is strung all the way to ground so Rufus can't crawl under it. Why the fence needs barbed wire six inches off the ground is beyond me. I've never even seen a cow lie down, let alone crawl. Without a way to get Rufus under the barbed wire, the only option is for him

May 11, 2001. Southern Virginia meadows.

to go over. However, Rufus wants no part of these precarious planks. Marcus and I end up often working together to get our dogs across. First we carry our backpacks over the fence. Then we take the dog's packs and carry those over. Next, I tie a long leash to Rufus and cross over, then Marcus lifts Rufus on the plank and pushes from behind as I pull on the leash, praying to God for Rufus to move. Sometimes he does, and sometimes it takes both of our efforts to make him walk. Shiggy is much better. He doesn't enjoy it, but he walks across the planks on his own.

A second stile design is just as fun to cross. For some reason, the ranchers think that these cows have an uncanny ability to jump, so the fences are tall enough to keep King Kong inside. This next design is simply a break in the barbed wire fence, replaced by a series of small logs that run horizontal to the ground and eight inches apart, forming a ladder to climb up and over. Easy enough, except no one thought to make the top of the logs flat. Instead, these round logs are covered in frictionless algae that makes crossing the log ladder an Abbott and Costello act.

I'm by myself when I come upon the first one, so my only option is to lift Rufus over. Like the barbed wire, the logs run all the way to the ground so Rufus can't scamper underneath. I can't climb these slick logs with Rufus in my arms, and I don't think he'd appreciate me picking him up and dropping him six feet onto the other side. Nevertheless, I pick Rufus up, and, using him as a counterweight, I step up onto the second log. I slowly place my knees on the highest log I can reach, then balance on my knees and lift up my feet so my stomach is even with the top of the ladder. Lifting Rufus up to my chest, I slowly begin to lean over the fence, lowering my upper body down the other side. Once I'm bent over the fence it's only a two-foot drop to the ground for Rufus, so I let him go. Good idea, bad execution. As soon as Rufus leaves my arms I slip, and before I can raise my arms to catch myself, I'm up and over the fence, crashing headfirst into the wet, manure-enriched grass on the other side. Rufus looks down at me with his big brown eyes, licks my face once, then hightails it along the trail, all the while laughing at me as I chase after him with my backpack and his. Next time I'm waiting for Marcus.

After several days of acrobatic cattle gate crossings, complete with an audience of chirping birds and laughing squirrels, I am exhausted. Haven't these people ever heard of a gate? The type with hinges on one side and a latch on the other, the type that simply swings open and then closes again? Everywhere else in the world people use gates, but not the Virginia cattle ranchers. For some unknown reason they have to invent their own instruments of terror and sow them along the trail under the guise of "cattle stiles." It's not the miles, homesickness, or fatigue that makes people quit the trail, it's these damn stiles. I'm ready to burn the next one I see.

"Hi, Kevin, whatcha doing?" asks Teresa as she comes skipping down the trail, full of smiles and happiness, while I'm working single-handedly trying to get Rufus across one of the plank stiles. I'm on one side of the fence and Rufus is on the other, refusing to take a step further along the plank no matter how hard I pull on his leash. He thwarts me by sitting his big butt down on the plank, thus sliding backwards towards the ground as I throw out string after string of profanities at him.

"What's it look like I'm doing? Metallurgy? I'm trying to get my stupid dog over this stupid gate so we can continue on our stupid hike. Isn't that right, Stupid Dog!" I yell, sweat and tears dripping off every word.

"Don't take it out on Rufus," she chastises as she helps me get Rufus across. "Remember, you're the one who took him on this hike. He didn't ask for it. You should be working on patience with him, remember? Be nice to Rufus, and be patient with him. He's doing his best."

"Doing his best? To what, piss me off? In that case he is doing a damn fine job."

"You know what will make you feel better?" she asks with a smile that melts all the anger out of my heart.

"A chainsaw?"

"Ice cream! In a couple of miles there's a road that leads to a Dairy Queen. Want to hitch in and get some ice cream? It'll make you feel better."

It would, along with several fat, juicy hamburgers. If I can't cut down the cattle fences, I'll get my revenge any way I can. Within a couple of hours we are at US 21/52, which leads into the town of Bland. It's not much of a road, just two lanes and a car every five minutes. I stick out my thumb as Teresa stashes our packs in the bushes.

After forty-five minutes only ten cars have passed by and not a single one has stopped. My vision of burgers and milkshakes is fading before me, so I tell Teresa that we might as well keep walking. She goes to get our packs as another car drives by. I stick out my thumb in desperation. They stop!

Turn out our saviors are a couple of brothers doing a road trip. They have no idea where the Dairy Queen is, but they tell us to get in. Fifteen minutes and three wrong turns later, we find the Dairy Queen next to Interstate 77. After several hamburgers and a Peanut Buster Parfait, we head out to the road to see what our chances are of getting a ride back to the trail. It doesn't look good. Our trail angels left to continue their trip, and the few vehicles on the streets are heading towards the interstate, not away from it. Fueled by ice cream, we walk the 2.5 miles back to the trail. Several hours later we stop at Dismal Falls, all my frustration at Rufus long forgotten.

Dismal Falls is a misnomer: it's not dismal at all. It is a small river cascading down a set of thirty-foot waterfalls. A huge flat rock juts out in the river, and several campsites are set back in the forest. There is a small stone fire ring on the rock, so I gather up some wood and start a fire. Teresa comes over to join me. Rufus, deathly afraid of fire the whole trip, crawls closer and closer to me until he's four feet away from the flames, just close enough to feel the warmth. I reach back and pet him as he licks my hand. We are sitting, listening to the crashing waterfalls, when Othra appears.

"Hey guys, saw in the guidebook that this is a great place to camp. Mind if I join you?" he asks.

"Come on over," says Teresa. "Pull up a rock and make yourself comfortable. So, where are you from, Othra?"

"Me? I grew up in Boone, North Carolina, not too far off the trail. I was going to college and needed a break, so took a couple quarters off and here I am. I love this, hiking every day with no worries except where to sleep, what to eat, and finding the next water source."

I couldn't agree more. I had started the hike with the idea to push myself and see if I could finish it in under five months. For the first month I did a lot of long days, but now I have a different philosophy: to go slow and enjoy my trip. I'm not real sure when the change came about; I think at Kincora. Spending three days there taught me to enjoy life and the trail. I don't want to rush it. The end will come soon enough.

Bedtime creeps up on us, so Teresa and I start towards the campsite, but Othra makes no effort to move.

"Othra, there's some great campsites over here if you want to set up your tent," I tell him.

"Thanks, but I think I'm going to set up my tent right here on this rock and fall asleep to the sound of the water."

"All right, but if it starts to rain, don't be afraid to move inland," I joke before heading to my tent. Othra has a freestanding tent. The material and poles are all that is needed to set it up, so it can be set up almost anywhere. My tent needs to be staked out or else it will fall over, so I can tent only in areas where I can put a stake in the ground. Solid rock isn't one of those places.

About four in the morning, the sound of raindrops bombarding my tent wakes me. My repair job from Damascus works as the rain is now where it should be: outside. Hoping the rain will go away, I fall back asleep for several hours, but when I wake up again it is still pouring. I peek my head outside and see that Teresa has already packed up and left, so I pack up in the rain and walk down to the river. Where we sat last night is now under a foot of water, and there's no sign of Othra anywhere. I hope he made it out before the creek rose and soaked his tent.

Rufus and I begin the morning by slogging down the waterlogged trail. By noon the storm blows over, revealing the sun, and I find Teresa in a small clearing drying her tent.

"Hey, Kevin! Come hang out in the sun with me for a little bit and dry out your stuff," Teresa says, motioning me to sit down next to her on a log. She has her guidebook in her hands and is thumbing through it. "Pearisburg is a few days away and looks like a great place to take a zero. I'm going to, how about you?"

"Yeah, I could use a day off and I know Rufus won't mind," I say, spreading my tent out and sitting down next to Teresa in sunshine. Rufus plops down between us and rolls onto his back. He is looking for a belly rub, and Teresa indulges him. Within ten minutes clouds replace the sun and a chill sets in. We pack up our stuff and keep moving.

The rain threatens all day but the sky holds until we reach Doc's Knob Shelter, where Othra, Marcus and Shiggy are already holed up. Ten minutes later the storm erupts, with lightning splitting the sky and thunder shaking the shelter. Rufus hates the thunder and hides in the corner, shaking uncontrollably. I pet him and do my best to comfort him. I set out his dinner in hopes of distracting him from the noise, but he ignores it and continues to jump every time the thunder booms. The noise doesn't faze Shiggy as he's fast asleep on Marcus's sleeping bag. Finally, I get Rufus to curl up on my sleeping bag, still scared but no longer ready to chew off his own ears to escape the noise. With Rufus taken care off, I join the others to watch the storm.

"Hey, Othra, what happened to you this morning?" I ask as we sit at the edge of the shelter, admiring the lightning as it streaks across the sky.

"I was sound asleep when I woke to the sound of rushing water. It didn't really concern me considering I was sleeping next to a waterfall. But the water kept getting louder, so I looked out my front door and saw the river was six inches from my tent! I jumped out wearing nothing but my skivvies, grabbed my whole tent with everything in it and drug it up the trail till I was clear of the river. By then I was wide awake, so I left."

"Ha, that's funny! Glad you didn't get caught in it though," says Teresa. "Kevin and I are heading into Pearisburg tomorrow to take a zero day. Either of you heading into town?"

"Yeah, I'm going in for a day. I have to pick up a mail drop," says Marcus, while Othra shakes his head no.

"I've taken too many days off already," Othra says. "I'm going to keep hiking. I've got a question for you, Fruit Pie. So, are you and Phoenix a couple now, or just hiking partners?"

Teresa looks at me and I look at her, her face illuminated by the constant flashes of lightning. She's giving me a look that says something, but I don't have the slightest idea what she is trying to convey.

"We're just hiking partners," I say. Teresa's look changes, but damn it, I have no idea what that one means either.

Deafening explosions of thunder continue to rock the shelter throughout the night. When one strikes so close we can feel the concussion blast, Teresa sits up with just a trace of fear on her face. She pulls a shaking Rufus close to her and curls up with him so they can lend each other strength. I want to take her in my arms and tell her that the lightning and thunder won't hurt her, but instead I simply lay my hand on her shoulder for support.

By morning the worst of the storm is over, but it is cloudy and misty.

Teresa and I hike the six miles into Pearisburg together, and in town Teresa goes to Holy Family Hostel, a church that has a bunk room for hikers. They don't allow dogs on the property, so Marcus and I split a hotel room for the night. Marcus decides not to take a zero day, so we check out in the morning and he hikes on. Not wanting to pay for a room on my own, I walk over to the outfitter to look at some gear, then to the hostel to tell Teresa I'm leaving. I can't find her, so I leave a note on her backpack and proceed to the best place in town to resupply: the Super Wal-Mart. After almost two months of being relegated to ma-and-pa shops with a limited supply of goods, here I am at Wal-Mart, the king of convenience. I feel like a kid in a candy store with a world of opportunity before me. Food, soap, pillows, clean socks, unlimited bottles of Gold Bond Powder; I'm in heaven. I spend an hour perusing the aisles before settling on a meager supply of food and head outside where Rufus is tied up. Several people are petting Rufus and admiring his backpack. When I sit down next to Rufus I am instantly shotgunned with questions.

"What are you doing?"

"Why does he have a pack?"

"He's hiking the whole thing too? Dogs can walk that far?"

May 19, 2001. Group shot at Pearisburg, Virginia. Left to right, front row: me, unknown hiker, Mountain Dude, Webb, Teresa. Second row: Morning Dove, Alias, Rooster, Marcus, Digg. Standing at back: Homeless (Bob) and Unemployed (MaryAnn)

"What does he eat?"

"Where does he sleep?"

"Does he get tired?"

People love Rufus and are constantly asking questions about him. I give stock answers and soon the people, realizing they are in a rush to get to work, home, school or to catch the newest TV show, take off. I'm in no hurry to be anywhere, so I take my time. I am sorting my candy bars and caressing my new socks when Teresa comes walking up.

"Hey, Kevin. What's with all your stuff? You hiking out today?" she asks, snatching a candy bar out of my hand and devouring it.

"Yeah, Marcus left already and I don't want to pay for a room by myself. Everyone is up at the hostel, and it's lonely at the motel, so I might as well hike. I'll take a zero day somewhere else. You plan on sticking around today?" I'm hoping she'll say no and come hike with me.

"I have to take a day off. My body hurts. The hostel was packed last night so I ended up sleeping on the floor. Every time someone got up to use the bathroom they stepped on me. I didn't get much rest. Say, you want to split a room with me tonight? That way you can still take a day off and I can get a real night's sleep. Besides, I bet Rufus wants a day off too. Come on, what do you say?"

"Um, ok, I can do that," I say while trying to contain the smile that wants to stretch from ear to ear.

Teresa and I have been hiking together every day for the last month, and I'm still not sure if she wants to be more than just friends. If Teresa sees me only as a hiking partner, I don't want to scare her off by coming on too strong and making her feel uncomfortable. On the other hand, if I don't make some type of move, I might never know. However, I would rather have her as a hiking partner than scare her off, so for the time being I'm content just being with her. We go back to the motel and check into a room, just the two of us.

Once in the room we each claim a bed. Teresa pulls a new hair brush out of her Wal-Mart bag and walks over to the mirror.

"I don't know if I will ever get these tangles out," she says, trying to run the brush through her knotted locks. I sit back on my bed and flip on the TV; some comedy show is on. I'm not real interested in the show, mainly using it as a distraction as I watch Teresa brush her hair. I'm smitten, bad.

"When do you think you'll reach Mt. Katahdin?" she says, looking at me in the mirror.

"I'm not sure. I'm thinking I'll finish up sometime in September. I don't have a hard and fast deadline that I need to meet."

"Me neither. Maybe we'll finish together?" she asks, giving up on her hair. She goes into the bathroom and returns wearing only a T-shirt and pair of boxer shorts.

In the morning we check out, still only friends. It's cold and foggy, but I'm excited to get moving because I have three new weight-saving devices to try out: a new stove, bleach, and lightweight hiking shoes. Up until now I've been using an old Coleman white gas stove. The stove works great and boils a cup of water in a minute, but it's very heavy. It weighs two pounds without fuel. At the outfitter I picked up an alcohol stove for $10. It's a simple device that looks like an empty tuna can. The stove has a perforated lid and sits in a slightly larger metal saucer. The theory is that I fill the stove with alcohol, put the lid on, and pour a small amount of alcohol in the saucer. When I light the alcohol in the saucer, it should burn and heat the alcohol in the stove, vaporizing it, and igniting the vapors as they come out through perforated lid.

I haven't actually tested it yet, but the whole contraption weights four ounces, an eighth of what my current stove weights. The best alcohol to use is HEET, a fuel-line additive that is almost pure ethyl alcohol. It burns hot and clean, and it's available at almost any grocery store or gas station.

I also have been using a water filter that weighs over a pound. It has worked well, but the filter is now clogged and a new one is $15, so I'm going to try bleach. Plain old chlorine bleach. Two drops per liter of water should kill everything, and I have a bandanna to filter out the larger particles before I treat it. A small bottle of bleach and the bandanna weigh two ounces and cost four bucks. Some people don't like the taste of bleached water, but I try it and don't really notice the taste at all.

My huge ground-stomping hiking boots are also going home. I should have sent my boots home weeks ago, but I spent so much money on them I've felt obligated to keep them. The boots are overkill for this trail. Instead I purchased a pair of lightweight hiking shoes. All-in-all I am sending five pounds home. I can feel the difference immediately as I throw on my pack and start down the trail.

Teresa has hiked on ahead of me, so I walk alone in the misty drizzle. Rufus and I are enjoying the morning, walking along a very flat, forested portion of the trail, when I hear a loud crashing sound coming from somewhere off to my right. The crashing gets louder, and I realize it's the sound of something very large running through the forest. Rufus immediately hides behind me as the distinct noises of bushes being plowed through and branches snapping off intensifies. Suddenly, a hundred feet in front of me, a large deer charges across the trail in a blur of speed. Three seconds later a large gray canine shape, taller and thinner than Rufus, runs across the trail in pursuit, and a second gray canine immediately follows. The animals are a light shade of gray and resemble large German Shepherds, but they're definitely not German Shepherds. The animals also aren't coyotes; I know because I saw hundreds of coyotes when I lived and hiked in California.

A piercing scream shatters the silence. It's an animalistic death cry that sends chills down my spine. As quickly as the sound began, it stops, leaving the forest eerily silent. Rufus is petrified, trying to crawl into my shoes. Some tough dog I have.

With Rufus shaking at my feet, I listen to the silence. The bushes in front of me rustle and one of the animals emerges. It walks within ten feet of me and stops, its lips peeled back in a cruel snarl that reveals huge white teeth. It stares at me for five seconds, and quietly disappears back into the woods towards its kill. My heart is racing as I realize I just came face to face with a wolf. I want to follow the animal to get a better look at it, but I believe the wolf came out to give me a warning to stay away and I'm going to respect it. I might be intimidating enough not to be dinner, but I have no doubt that Rufus would look like a piece of meringue pie.

Wolves once roamed across almost all of North America, but like many native species, they were slaughtered with the arrival of Europeans. Now wolves can be found in only a few select areas. The gray wolf roams most of Canada, Alaska, and a section of northern Minnesota, and has recently been reintroduced into Yellowstone National Park. Its smaller cousin, the red wolf, weighs between fifty and eighty pounds and isn't red but shades of gray, brown and black. It looks, in fact, like a German Shepherd. It could once be found from Florida to Pennsylvania and as far west as Texas, but hunting and expansion wiped it out. The last wild red wolf was killed in 1980, leaving only a handful in various zoos.

In 1986, several pairs of red wolves were taken from captivity and reintroduced into the Alligator River National Wildlife Refuge located in North Carolina. Finally protected from humans, the wolves were able to reproduce and build a stable community.

After the success of the Alligator River Refuge, a few red wolves were released into the Great Smoky Mountains. But while the Alligator River program was isolated and carefully managed, the Smoky Mountain program was not, and it was canceled in 1996. Lack of prey and nine million human visitors made the Smokies a poor home, and most of the wolves died. A few pair, though, not knowing they were supposed to stay in the park, left on their own, finding security and seclusion in the more isolated sections of the Appalachian Mountains.

I have no doubt the animals I saw were a pair of red wolves that have returned to the wild, though no one will believe I saw a wolf out here. Nowadays that's like saying I saw Bigfoot or Elvis.

I arrive at Pine Branch Shelter and find Teresa and Sock-in-the-Hole, and I tell them about the wolves, but neither believes me and they think I saw a couple of dogs. How often does a pair of dogs, twenty miles away from the closest town, take down a full grown deer?

After a couple of minutes of futile argument, the discussion changes and Sock states he is tired of hiking and is leaving the trail next chance he has. Two days later Sock stops at Virginia Road 42, sticks out his thumb, and hitches off the trail. Another hiker gone, victim of the Virginia Blues.

Teresa and I continue to hike together off and on. One day I am hiking alone with Rufus as the forest once again gives way to open rolling pastures. Rufus is bravely leading the way when I reach a crest of a hill and look down. At the bottom of the hill is a creek spanned by a wooden bridge, but it is blocked by our evil nemesis: hellcows. Rufus, feeling exceptionally brave, continues towards the bridge and is within a hundred feet of the herd when a giant, snorting bovine stops him in his tracks. The cow stomps the ground twice, lowers her head, and charges. Rufus knows better than to take on a charging hellcow. He turns and flees. He quickly reaches his top speed, but the cow is still accelerating and slowly gaining on my dog.

"Run, Rufus, Run!" I yell. "You can beat her, she's a cow!" Rufus reaches me and keeps going, and I realize that the cow isn't giving up. Its monstrous bulk continues to charge up the hill and I am standing directly in its path.

"Wait up, Rufus, wait for me!" I scream and start running, catching up to my dog and passing him.

When the thundering footsteps fade, I turn around to see that the huffing heifer has given up and is returning to her herd. I wait for Rufus to catch up to me, then lay out my strategy.

"Okay, Rufus, new plan. We walk together, real slow and nonchalant, and see if the cows will let us pass. No eye contact, no sniffing udders, and no jokes whatsoever about Burger King. Got it?" Rufus replies by licking my hand.

Utilizing our new plan, we creep our way back toward the cows, and this time the big one doesn't charge, but she does stare at us as we get close.

"Steady, Rufus, almost there," I say as we close to within fifty feet of the lead cow. Suddenly, the behemoth prime-rib drops her head, snorting and stomping the ground ferociously.

"Retreat!" I yell, and we quickly run away. Obviously the cow is not going to let us pass. With no other options, we walk a quarter-mile downstream from the cows and cross through the waist-deep, cow-pie-slogged creek. Rufus refuses to swim across so I have to carry him over, and we backtrack along the stream until we are on the other side of the bridge. The cow spots us, starts snorting and begins walking towards the bridge. I grab Rufus' collar and we hightail it out of there, running for a mile until we come across Teresa taking a break next to a dirt road.

"What the heck happened to you two?" she asks, as cow-pie water drips off my shorts and Rufus plops down exhausted. I tell her the story.

"Are you done laughing now?" I ask ten minutes later while Teresa is still rolling around on the ground holding her sides.

"Mad cows ... blocking the bridge ... chased you," she gasps. "You are a riot, Kevin!"

"You know, Rufus and I just had a near death experience, and all you can do is laugh. Come on Rufus, we're leaving."

"Okay, I'm sorry. I'm done laughing," she says, standing up. "I'll hike with you just in case we come across a hamburger you need protection from." With that she falls back down laughing.

Finally, she regains herself and hikes with Rufus and me. We steer clear of any more herds as we cross the farmlands. By early afternoon gigantic, black storm clouds have gathered on the horizon, and they don't look nice. Still on farmlands with nowhere to camp, we proceed through a small grove of trees to the other side, where a massive oak tree stands alone in a meadow. This mighty tree, named the Keffer Oak, is eighteen feet around and dwarfs the skinny wooden sticks that comprise the oak forest we just passed through. The canopy resembles a mushroom cloud, and the first branch is thicker than my waist. This enormous tree is over three hundred years old and was once surrounded by its brethren, all of mighty girth. Now only this one remains, the other oaks having given up their lives to be floors, desks, or book cases.

"That is a beautiful tree. I hope it never gets cuts down or dies," Teresa says, staring at the behemoth.

"I know. I was just thinking that. Something this big and solid makes us seem kind of puny. I bet this place was covered with trees like this." I know trees don't have brains or personalities, but it's easy to imagine this one does, protecting hikers as they pass below its branches.

"This would be a cool place to take a break, but I think that storm is almost here. We better get out of this meadow," Teresa says, looking up at the menacing sky.

CRACK! Teresa's warning is a second too late as a flash of light shatters the air, blinding us. The sound waves hit so hard my ears ring, and Rufus drops to the ground terrified.

"Holy shit! I think we almost got hit by lightning. Let's get out of here!" I yell as I grab Rufus by the collar and hightail it back to the small forest, well away from the open meadow and the gargantuan wooden lighting rod. Teresa and I hunker down on our packs among some of the shorter trees while the lightning and thunder continue to blast around us and the rain starts to fall. I'm getting sick and tired of rain, thunder, and lightning. Is it too much to ask for a week of blue skies, where I can walk freely in meadows and not have to worry about getting hit by twenty million volts?

Twenty minutes later the storm relents enough to give us the courage to continue, so we dash out of the woods and across the meadows towards the next forest. We make it just as the storm releases its full fury. Buckets of water pour from the sky and the wind snaps off dead limbs known as "widow makers," throwing them to the ground. Above us the trees sway and groan, any one of them a potential projectile.

A huge branch slams into the ground thirty feet away from us, sending Rufus diving under the closest shelter he can find, a five-inch-wide fern. He huddles under this imaginary protection as the rain pelts him, the lightning blinds him, and the thunder pounds his ears. I start walking, but Rufus has made his stand and refused to move. Teresa pulls on his collar, but he doesn't budge. I put on his leash and try to get Rufus walking but he digs in his feet, firmly planting himself under the fern. After five minutes of arguing with my dog in the drowning rain, I give up and walk away, leaving Rufus under his fern.

"What are you doing? You can't leave him, he's scared! Get back here!" Teresa screams when she realizes what I'm doing. She kneels over Rufus protectively, trying to comfort him. With water pouring off all of us, I walk back to Rufus and Teresa.

"Let's go. If we keep walking, he'll follow. Come on," I say.

"No! Don't you dare leave him!" she yells at me.

"What do you want to do? Sit here in the rain and mud? We have nowhere to go, so we might as well keep walking!" I yell back.

"I don't care! He's cold and scared and doesn't know what to do. We can't leave him!"

"We're all cold! The next shelter is six miles away, and if we start walking we can get inside and out of this weather. There's nothing we can do but keep going!" My patience is long gone and I'm getting angry at both of them. Our only option is to keep walking. Setting up our tents in this storm isn't feasible. The wind would rip the tents out of our hands and everything will get soaked and muddy. Sitting here doing nothing doesn't make sense either. We need to get moving and I know Rufus will follow me. He always has.

"Listen," I say, regaining my composure. "He'll follow us. If we keep walking, he'll follow. Trust me. It's better than sitting here getting soaked. Now let's go."

Teresa relents and slowly follows me. Rufus watches us until we are 200 feet away, then stands up and starts walking. He continues to stop and hide under branches, but we keep walking. He doesn't want to be left behind, so he gets up and follows.

We fight wind and rain for several hours. At last the storm passes and we make it to Niday Shelter. Rufus instantly jumps into the shelter and falls asleep in the corner. After an adrenaline-filled day of death-dealing cows and terrifying storms, he is safe.

The next few days are a mixture of sun breaks and downpours, separated by long periods of drizzly fog. McAfee Knob, supposedly one of the best viewpoints on the trail, is nothing but a large rock jutting into the great expanse of white vapor. The Tinker Cliffs, which overlook miles of Virginia, overlook nothing but fog. The trail is soggy and my gear is becoming wet no matter how hard I try to keep it dry. I've given up trying to stay dry as that is an impossible task. I walk soaked to the skin and change into dry clothes at night, hanging up my wet ones in the shelter, hoping they will dry out before morning. They never do because it's just too humid, so in the morning I change into my damp, cold clothes before stepping out into the rain. Teresa hikes with me every day, and we keep each other company in an otherwise dreary world.

While walking across a ridge, we take advantage of a break in the drizzle and sit down along a rocky stretch for some lunch.

"Look! Quick, Kevin, look!" Teresa says, pointing down the ridge. I look, expecting to see a break in the clouds giving a framed view of the valley. Instead I see two wild goats about fifty feet away. The goats, once domestic animals that have escaped (or been released), now live up here on the cliffs. One of them walks towards us, then sees Rufus, who is curled up oblivious to the world. The goat, a sleek brown creature and the bigger of the two, approaches Rufus and sniffs him. Rufus lifts his head to meet the goat, sniffs back and goes back to sleep.

Realizing Rufus is harmless, the goat comes over to us as the smaller one slowly approaches, always keeping one eye on Rufus. The little guy must have had a bad experience with a dog because every time Rufus so much as snorts, the goat jumps back, ready to run. They both let Teresa and me pet them in return for several bites of bagel and cheese.

The rain returns, forcing us to abandon lunch, and we leave the goats among the rocks. The trail has transformed into a river and we slosh our way to Lamberts Meadow Shelter. Marcus and Shiggy are inside, cooking up a hot lunch. Next to Marcus is a young grizzly hiker named Ohio and his three-year-old Husky.

"Hey guys, get out of the rain," Marcus says, and we climb into the shelter. "Can you believe this weather? Everything I have is soaked, and even though I had Shiggy's dog food double bagged, it still got wet. Now it's a brown pile of sludge. I'm heading into Troutville today to get some more food. Are you two going in?"

"Yeah. I've got a box waiting that I sent to the Econo-Lodge," I say. "Plus, I wouldn't mind a real meal."

"You getting a room? Ohio and I are thinking of splitting a room for the night to get our stuff dried out. Want to join us? Split four ways it shouldn't be too much money."

"I'm game. How 'bout you?" I ask Teresa.

"If there's a hot shower and dry bed, I'm in. Let's get moving if we are going to get a room. I'd rather be sitting in a warm room than out here in a cold shelter," she says, and I couldn't agree more. After Marcus eats we step out into the pouring rain, motivated by the thought that it's only a few hours to a warm room and a hot meal.

Troutville isn't a town but a suburban extension of Roanoke, a large city seventeen miles away. Nestled around the U.S. 220/I-81 interchange, Troutville has all the amenities needed for vehicular travels. The A.T. crosses over the highway half a mile from several motels, grocery stores and restaurants, which is why I chose this location to send a box to. We walk over to the Econo-Lodge, stopping outside the lobby. While they want business, the motel might draw the line at four grimy hikers and three wet dogs all stuffed into one room. Teresa and I decide to go in while Ohio and Marcus hide around the corner with the dogs.

Teresa and I enter the lobby, tracking mud over the rarely mopped floor, and approach the clerk, a twenty-year-old kid who quickly stashes a comic book under the counter. He looks up at us, a couple of wet, dirty hikers, and pulls the comic book back out. His attention is clearly focused on the comic, and only after a series of half-interested questions from him and exasperated answers from us does he deem us suitable clientele and grant us a room. When I tell him I've had a box delivered here, the torturous cycle begins again, with the clerk concluding — after a cursory glance at the packages of mail behind him — that my package hasn't arrived. Soaking wet, my body and my patience exhausted, I step around the counter to look for myself. On top of the pile sits my box, with my name clearly printed on it. I grab the box, and without saying another word, leave the lobby to get Marcus and Ohio.

At first I felt kind of guilty about stuffing all of us into one room, but now I wish we had a couple more dogs, a wolverine, and a flock of pigeons to leave behind. Still, with four people and three dogs, this tiny motel room is already cramped, crowded and smelly. But compared to the last six days of rain, it's also dry and warm, and right now that's all that really matters.

5

Virginia Is for Lovers

A sunny morning greets us as we check out of the motel. There's not a cloud in the sky, drastically different from the previous week. Marcus and Ohio head down the trail, and as I throw on my pack, Teresa grabs my arm.

"Don't leave yet. It's so warm and beautiful out, I want to enjoy it before going back into the wet woods. Come on, let's lie in the grass for a while and enjoy the morning," she says. Teresa grabs her pack and runs around to the rear of the motel where there's a huge lawn and small playground, and I follow. She lies down on the grass and motions for me to sit beside her. Rufus, thrilled he isn't walking or getting rained on, sprawls out on the grass to bask in the sunshine.

"Now isn't this better than walking? I don't know the last time I laid out and relaxed for a while. Probably Damascus. How long ago was that? Two weeks?" she asks, smiling at me.

"We took a day off in Pearisburg a week ago."

"That doesn't count, silly, we were at the motel most of the time, surrounded by steel and concrete. Out here we're on grass, with sunshine and nowhere to go. We can hike one mile or ten today, it really doesn't matter."

I notice she's using "we." My heart skips a beat and a smile spreads across my face.

"What are you smiling about?" she asks, jabbing me in the arm.

"Just enjoying the sunshine."

We lie next to each other, talking. Inevitably, the conversation leads to food.

"It's been a couple hours since breakfast and I'm getting hungry. How about you?" I ask.

"Mmmm, I could go for food." We find a convenience store across the street that has corn dogs, burritos, sandwiches and ice cream. While eating a corn dog and slurping a milkshake, I grab a United States atlas from a display, opening it up to New York.

"Show me where Rochester is. You said it was up by Buffalo, but point it out," I say, wanting to know everything about her.

"It's right here, an hour east of Buffalo on I-90. My parents are there, and my two brothers. That's where I went to school. My dad works at the university. In fact, I've never lived anywhere else. I've traveled up and down the East Coast, but that's been home. Now your turn," she says, flipping the map to Washington State.

"Well, when I came East to hike the trail I left from Spokane. That's where my folks live, but I had only been there for a few months. Before that, I was stationed in San Diego for two years while in the Marine Corps," I reply, flipping the atlas to California and pointing out San Diego. "I've also lived in Florida, Virginia, and Okinawa, courtesy of the Corps."

"I've never been to the West Coast before," she says, running her finger along the length of California. "I want to go to graduate school out west somewhere, I'm just not sure where yet. If I do that, would you come and visit me?"

"Absolutely. It's a date."

Afternoon has crept up on us and we need to get hiking, so we pick up our packs and leave Troutville together.

Two days later we stop for the night at Cove Mountain Shelter. Marcus and Ohio are a half-day ahead and we haven't seen anyone in the last two days, so we have the shelter to ourselves. After a good meal (mine being several slices of summer sausage mixed with a packet of Lipton Noodles) we crawl into our bags.

"I'm so glad we met, Kevin," Teresa says as she rolls towards me. "I really like hiking with you, and with Rufus." At the sound of his name Rufus looks up at Teresa, realizes she isn't holding any food, and goes back to sleep.

"I enjoy hiking with you too. It's so much better than hiking alone. Before we met I would talk to Rufus, but he'd just look at me as if I was dumb, then go about his business," I say, hoping this is leading somewhere. I don't want to do something so stupid she'd go running out of the shelter never to be seen again. I'd be quite heartbroken—and not just because she's carrying a bag of Snickers bars.

"It's not just having someone to hike with that I'm talking about. It's hiking with *you* that's made this trip so wonderful." She reaches out and finds my hand. I try to look deep into her eyes, but I can't see a damn thing since it's dark out and the shelters don't have lights. Instead, I romantically grope the air until I find her face, take her head in my hands, and kiss her. We kiss for several minutes until Rufus wakes up and decides to join in. He promptly throws his slobbery tongue at our enjoined lips, leading to a very quick, disgusted break.

"I've been waiting a long time for you to do that, Kevin. Though I could have done without the canine menage-à-trois " she says in a soft, vulnerable voice.

"I've been waiting a long time too, but was always afraid I'd scare you off."

"Not a chance," she says, curling up next to me and falling asleep.

5. Virginia Is for Lovers

I had never planned on getting involved on the trail, but I had never planned on meeting someone like Teresa either. My divorce is fading fast from my head, and being out here in the woods with Teresa really helps. I am away from everything that reminds me of my ex-wife and am starting a new life on my own. I just hope that we continue to get along and can finish the trail together.

After several incredible days of no rain, moderate temperatures, and hiking with Teresa, we stop for the night at Matts Creek Shelter.

"Okay, Teresa, how's this sound. Tomorrow we get up and hike to the road. We hitch into Glasgow, resupply, get a hot lunch, hitch back to the trail, then hike out another ten miles or so. Think that's feasible?" I ask. It sounds great, but we have a tendency to get stuck in towns.

"I think we can do that. We'll jump in, get what we need and jump out. Maybe it will break our bad town karma."

While laying out my sleeping bag, I see Teresa flick a couple of caterpillars out of the shelter. I also toss out a couple of crawling caterpillars.

"Hey, have you noticed there have been more gypsy moth caterpillars in the last couple of days?" she asks, tossing one more out into the woods.

"Now that you mention it, I have. I've seen more in the last few days than I have in the last couple of weeks."

The first time I had seen a gypsy moth nest was back at Kincora in Tennessee. Bob pointed one out to me. The nest looks like a disorganized mass of spider silk nestled among the branches of a tree or bush, a foot in diameter and full of baby caterpillars. There have been scattered nests all along the trail, and most hikers step on the caterpillars in hopes of reducing their numbers. I have killed my fair share.

In the morning we start walking, and after three quarters of a mile Teresa stops in the middle of the trail and gives a quiet shriek.

"You see them, Kevin?"

"No, what? Where is it?" I ask, thinking she sees a couple of deer, or maybe a bear.

"Look close at the trees and on the little bushes."

I look at a tree six feet away from me, and it looks like a tree; then I notice it. The bark is moving. I get closer and see it isn't the bark moving, but dozens of caterpillars. Many of the bushes and trees are covered in them, and now I notice that almost every leaf is partially eaten.

"They're everywhere. Let's keep moving," I say.

As we move, the trail itself becomes alive with caterpillars swarming over every plant and tree. A quarter mile later there isn't a leaf in sight. Every tree, bush and plant is stripped bare, not a sliver of green to be seen. Everything is crawling with the bugs and they randomly fall off the branches above us, dropping into our hair and onto our bodies. For two miles not a single tree has a leaf on it. It looks like a forest fire devastated the area, except nothing is burnt. The only sound is the constant rustling of the bugs, reminding me of a low budget horror flick. What was once a lush green forest is now an empty brown shell. Everything is gone, eaten by the gypsy moth.

The gypsy moth is a pest native to Europe and Asia, and was brought over to Medford, Massachusetts, in 1869 by Leopold Trouvelot, a French astronomer and insect buff. His plan was to combine the gypsy moth with a native moth to develop a new type of disease-resistant, silk-giving moth in hopes of creating a huge commercial silk industry. As with all great ideas, something was bound to go wrong. Several moths, not content with being breeding stock inside a strange laboratory, decided it would be a lot more fun to wreak havoc upon the eastern United States and made a daring escape. Twenty years later the first outbreak occurred, and now the moths defoliate two million acres of forest a year. The bugs have infested twenty states, from North Carolina to Canada and as far west as Wisconsin.

The caterpillars hatch around mid-spring and feed on over 300 species of trees and bushes, their favorite being oak. For several months the caterpillar devours all greenery, eating up to ten square feet of foliage in its short life. That's the size of an average coffee-table top — that many leaves eaten by a single caterpillar. Around early summer they enter the pupa stage and two weeks later emerge as moths. After mating, the female lays 100 to 1500 eggs, which incubate until spring, when they hatch and the devastation begins again. The moths are still spreading west and north, and no one knows how far they will reach.

There is good news, though. The moths sometimes regress due to a natural disease that wipes out entire populations. Mass spraying also kills large numbers. The moth outbreaks usually last for one to five years, then collapse for anywhere from four to twelve years before returning. In addition, a tree doesn't necessarily die after having all its leaves eaten. A weaker tree may die after a single attack, but most healthy trees can withstand several years of defoliation. After a tree is defoliated, it produces a second set of smaller, lighter colored leaves, which takes a lot of energy and stresses the tree. The real culprit comes from secondary bugs and diseases that attack and kill the weakened tree before it can rebuild its strength. On average 20 percent of the trees die. Here it looks like everything is dead, but with luck most of these trees will survive and by mid-summer be sprouting new leaves.

Teresa and I continue for another mile in the barren forest until we reach the James River footbridge, and once we cross the river, not another caterpillar is seen. It's like the river holds some magical shield that they can't cross. I hope they never find a way over, though I know they will. I look back and see half the mountainside is barren, a huge brown patch among the rich forest.

After picking caterpillars out of our clothes, packs, and hair — one is even crawling in my beard — and crushing them, we walk over to U.S. 501 in hopes of catching a ride into town. After ten minutes, a sedan pulls over, and a middle-aged woman rolls down her window.

"Hiking the trail and need a lift into town?" she asks as she hits the power lock switch to unlock the doors.

"Yeah, heading to the grocery store in Glasgow. We really appreciate the lift." I climb into the back seat with Rufus while Teresa jumps up front. Sitting beside me is a nine- or ten-year-old girl in a flowery sundress. As we pull away from the curb the girl leans forward and whispers, "Mommy, these people smell." She then sits back and pinches her nose with her fingers, holding it the entire ten-minute ride until we get out of the car, leaving the girl to breathe clean air once again.

I can't blame her; we do smell. Everything about hikers smells, from our feet to our backpacks. Although we shower when we can, it only takes a couple days in the woods to radiate a stench again. That's why in town we spend most of the time outside unless we have access to a shower.

The small Glasgow Grocery has everything needed to resupply. Many items, such as hot chocolate packets, granola bars and pop tarts, are sold individually. The grandmotherly clerk behind the counter is very friendly, a far cry from our EconoLodge hospitality. Teresa asks if we can sit out on her front lawn as we pack up, and she tells us to stay as long as we like.

We take her up on the offer and spread out in front of the store. Glasgow is a very small town, consisting mainly of a couple of restaurants, a motel, a tiny library, this grocery store, and very nice people. People wave to us as they drive by, and a pickup stops in front of the store. The passenger door opens and Othra jumps out, grabbing his pack from the back as the driver gives two quick honks of the horn before continuing on.

"Hey, guys. Been wondering if you two were still on the trail. Mind if I grab a piece of lawn?" he says, sitting down beside us.

As we sit on the grass, a hard-looking man in his sixties walks up to the store. He looks like he has spent his life working the land. His face is leathered from years in the sun, and he is wearing faded overalls.

"Hey, y'all. Whatcha all doin'? Don't often see people layin' here on the grass," he says in a slow drawl.

"We're hiking the Appalachian Trail and taking a break," replies Othra.

"Appalachian Trail? What the dickens is that?"

"It's a trail that starts in Georgia and stops in Maine. That's where we're headed to, Maine."

"Maine, you say? Don't think ah've ever been to Maine," he says. "Come to think of it, ah don't think ah even know where that's at. Good luck, then," and the old man enters the store to do his shopping. A little while later the old man comes back out.

"Ah thought you said you was hikin' to Maine. Ah may not know where that's at, but ah know you can't get to Maine sittin' on the grass," he says, then walks down the road with his bag of groceries.

"The man has a point. We need to be leaving if we want to do any miles," I say.

"Where you heading today?" asks Othra.

"Our plan was to get to Punchbowl Shelter, about ten more miles."

"Hmmm, that's still doable, but you guys interested in grabbing some lunch first? The restaurant across the street's advertising half-pound burgers for $3.99," Othra says, pointing towards the restaurant.

Teresa sits up at the mention of burgers. "Oooh, I like burgers," she says. "I'm in. Let's go eat." Rufus wags his tail, hoping to be included.

An hour later, with full bellies and a serious lack of motivation, we collapse back on the lawn. Time quickly slips by and suddenly its 5:00 P.M.

"Holy cow! We have got to go! So much for ten more miles, but unless we want to sleep here on the grass we need to leave," I say, looking at my watch for the first time since lunch. "There's a shelter a mile and a half away, looks like we'll have to settle for that." So much for our plan. Instead of a twelve-mile day, I'll have to settle for an embarrassing four. Can't do too many of these days or I'll never reach Maine.

We pack up our stuff and go in the store to buy some hot dogs and buns for dinner tonight. I'm inside the store for five minutes when a high-pitched female voice calls out.

"Phoenix, Fruit Pie! How are you guys?" I turn around and see a face I haven't seen since Georgia: Debbie! "You guys need a ride back to the trail? The guy who gave me a lift is waiting outside in his pickup. He said to tell any other hikers who need a ride to jump in the back."

We head outside and Teresa and Othra climb into the bed of the small red pickup as I lift Rufus in. Debbie returns a few minutes later with a bag of groceries. The driver gives us a ride back to the trail and waves goodbye. I never said a word to him, and he never said a word to me, but he was willing to give me a ride and I was willing to accept it. Where else in the world would such an occurrence take place? To jump into a complete stranger's vehicle without a single word passed. Only on the trail.

We hike to the shelter and meet a female hiker named Doodlebug, making this one of the few times on the trail that male hikers are outnumbered by female hikers. Just Othra and I to face down Teresa, Debbie, and Doodlebug.

"Debbie, how are you doing? I haven't seen you in over a month," asks Teresa.

"I'm doing all right, and guess what? I have a trail name now," Debbie says. "It's Phone Home. Every time I'm close to a phone I call home to talk to my kids, so the name stuck."

The women sit down, chatting and giggling, while Othra and I build a fire. Othra gathers kindling and starts a fire while I collect large branches and break them into burnable pieces. We cook hot dogs over the fire and enjoy a peaceful night.

The following day we climb to the top of Bluff Mountain, where the foundation of an old fire tower remains. Off to one side is a small monument in tribute to four-year-old Ottie Powell. Back in 1890, Ottie went into the woods to gather firewood for his schoolhouse and never returned. Five months later his body was found on the top of this mountain. It's amazing that over one hundred years ago people lived and thrived in these rugged mountains. Even today it is a full day's walk to the nearest road. Back then they must have been completely isolated, dependent only upon each other to survive.

Hoping to see some remnants of where Ottie lived, I climb atop one of the four-foot-high concrete pillars that used to support the fire tower, but there's no ruins to be seen, just trees and some clouds rolling in. A rather boring view, so I jump back down and lean against the pillar.

"What the heck is Rufus doing? Check him out!" Teresa says from the monument. Rufus is thirty feet from me, staring at my feet and walking towards me like he's stalking something. Rufus has never stalked anything in his life; he can't sneak up on his food dish. His eyes are fixed on my feet, so I look down. Right beside me is a coiled copperhead snake sticking out its tongue. Staying calm and keeping my wits about me, I jump six feet backwards, waving my arms wildly and shrieking like an eight-year-old girl.

"Snake! Big snake! Big mean snake!" I yell, and add another ten feet of distance between myself and this object of death. His job complete, Rufus goes back to sleep while Teresa runs over to me.

"What is it? Why are you shouting? And quit dancing around shrieking, you look like an eight-year-old girl," Teresa says, trying to calm me down. She then sees the snake and points over to it. "Wow! Hey, Kevin, check it out. There's a huge snake by the pillar over there. Quit jumping about, you're going to scare him."

Scare the snake? I'm not the one with poisonous fangs and a taste for hiker flesh. Once calm, I watch the brown reptile for a minute before tossing a couple of small rocks at it, forcing him to slither back under the pillar and away from my calves. Not wanting anyone else to be caught unprepared, I leave a note on one of the other pillars.

The next day the rain returns. June 1, my 67th day on the trail, 790 miles from Springer Mountain, and I'm walking in a downpour — again. Teresa and I have been walking all day, and we are wet and cold. Rufus is soaked and walking with his tail between his legs, but it's still eight more miles to the next shelter.

We are descending from Cold Mountain when I slip in the mud and spiral out of control down the steep trail, stopping only after I slam into a sturdy elm tree. I am covered in mud with both my body and pride bruised. Teresa helps me up and we continue down to Hog Gap Camp, where I see two giant blue tarps set up near a dirt road.

"What are those for?" Teresa asks. "Know what? I don't care what they are for. Come on, Kevin, we are getting out of the rain for a while and you can clean the mud off you."

Failing to see any flaw in her plan, I follow her to the tarps and find two people already under them. They are not hikers, though; we can tell because they are clean and sitting in lawn chairs. Surrounding them are coolers and boxes of food and a truck is parked next to one of the tarps, with what looks like more coolers and boxes in it.

"Hi, guys!" one of the men says as he stands up and walks over to us. "I'm Sherpa-dude and that's Shoe. We hiked the trail in '99. You're the first ones to arrive. Care to partake in some trail magic?"

Once again, when the day looks dark and miserable, trail magic appears and everything will be all right. Teresa and I forgo our plan of hiking eight more miles, and we sit under the tarp sipping hot chocolate until the rain lightens enough for us to set up our tents and for our to hosts to start the barbecue. Othra, Debbie and several more hikers arrive, much to the delight of our hosts. The trail angels brought enough food and drink for three days, and they want as many hikers as possible to come through and enjoy it.

Rejuvenated by the trail magic, we hike on in the constant rain, following the trail as it takes us over Spy Rock, which was used by Confederate soldiers to watch Union troop movements during the Civil War. Two wet days later we arrive at Rockfish Gap near the city of Waynesboro, 824 miles north of Springer Mountain. It's been ten days since my last shower, 19 days since our last zero day, and Teresa and I plan on taking both.

While waiting for Teresa to catch up, I hear someone shouting my name and turn around to see Mouth jogging towards me. I haven't seen him in three weeks and have no idea what he's up to.

"Hey, Fruit Pie. I've been hoping to catch you for the last week. Isn't this yours?" he says, holding a small, black nylon case.

"That's my knife! I haven't seen it in a week. I thought it was gone for good. Where did you find it?"

"Found it back at Cove Mountain Shelter. I was there the day after you signed the register, and I thought it was yours. Been hoping to catch you by Waynesboro to give it back to you."

I remember now. I was cutting up some salami at the shelter and set it down, forgetting to pick it back up.

"Why were you hoping to catch me by Waynesboro? You going somewhere?" I ask.

"Yeah, man, I've run out of money so I'm heading home to start working again. I didn't expect to hike the whole trail, but I was hoping to get farther than here. Oh well, that's the way it works. Well, Fruit Pie, I'm glad I caught up to you to give it back. Good luck, and say hi to Teresa for me. I've got to get to the bus station."

I am dumbfounded. I completely misjudged Mouth's character. I never would have expected him to do something like this, carrying my knife for a week to give it back to me. I had only met him a few times and I was never very cordial, but he carried this four-ounce tool for a week to return it to a guy he barely knew. I hope he gets back to Maine and can hike the trail again some other time. He's earned my respect.

As he walks away, I call out to him.

"Hey, Mouth. Thank you very much. I owe you one."

"No problem. We have to look out for each other out here," he says, and I watch another hiker leave the trail.

Half an hour later Teresa comes out of the woods. Rumor has it that the local YMCA in Waynesboro has free camping and free use of the facilities, including showers, so we hitchhike to the YMCA. We walk up to the front desk and find the rumors are true. They even allow dogs at their small campsite. We sign the obligatory waiver and walk a block over to the campsite, where several hikers are already set up, including Marcus. I don't see Shiggy, though.

"Hey, Marcus, where's Shiggy?"

"Shiggy is in Texas with a friend. He's done hiking."

"Oh, what happened to him?" asks Teresa.

"He started limping, so I hitched into town to find a vet. Turns out Shiggy is developing hip dysplasia, and if he kept hiking he might have suffered serious injury. I didn't want to be selfish and make him walk in pain for my hike. Really cool vet, he gave me a ride to the airport and waited while I loaded Shiggy on a flight," Marcus explains.

"Man, that's too bad. If you ever feel lonely you can always borrow Rufus for a day or two."

After setting up my tent, I go and explore a bit. Waynesboro is a great town. It has several restaurants, a huge library two blocks from the campsite with e-mail access, a large grocery store, a laundromat and even a Radio Shack where I buy a small radio to listen to while hiking. The sounds of the forest are nice, but after two months they get old. I wouldn't mind listening to music, talk radio, or news to take my mind off walking. The trail is an isolated entity unto itself. Economy, wars, and politics don't matter out here as they have nothing to do with placing one foot in front of the other five million times. I have no idea what is happening beyond the trail, and the radio will allow me to get back in touch with the world.

Homeless and Unemployed, T-Tree and Brooklyn (a couple who met on the trail), Java and Jeopardy (a married couple from New York who started out together and are still hiking together), Phone Home, and Othra arrive.

Thumper, Patch Monkey and two other hikers also come in. One is a tall, lanky mid-twenties man sporting a thick blond beard, and the other is a shorter, clean-shaven male in his mid-thirties.

"The Horsemen are here, so break out the beer!" proclaims Patch as he approaches the group.

"Horsemen?" I ask

"We are the Four Horsemen. This is Jiffy Pop," Thumper says, introducing the taller, younger hiker.

"And I'm Assface," the shorter hiker says.

"Assface? Where the heck did you get a name like that?" asks Othra.

"From an instance of my mouth speaking before my brain could stop it," Assface begins to explain. "Coming out of Georgia I was sitting around a campfire with a bunch of people when we started talking about how bad we all smelled. Well, I blurted out, 'I smell so bad my face smells worse than my ass,' and the next thing I knew everyone was calling me Assface."

With the help of the Horsemen, our quiet little campsite erupts into a huge BBQ as we grill up chicken, steaks, burgers and anything else that will fit on the grill. The sky threatens rain, but it never comes. Enjoying the first dry day in a week, we sit around and catch up on trail gossip.

"Anybody know what happened to the Outlaws?" I ask. Last time I saw them they were freezing at Groundhog Creek Shelter.

"I saw them in Damascus. They are still hiking as far as I know," says Assface.

"I met them in Georgia and they told me they were only hiking to Damascus before heading home," says another hiker.

"I think that was the original plan," replies Assface. "But Boo's pack was stolen at Watauga Lake while they were on the rope swing. Well, the three of them hiked to Damascus, but the story of Boo's stolen pack got there faster. All the hikers in Damascus took up a collection and bought Boo a new pack, and the outfitter supplied him with new clothes and other gear. Since Boo had all this new stuff, they figured they might as well use it and the three of them kept hiking."

I also find out that Tubesteak is back on the trail, but Keystone has caught giardia, a nasty little protozoan. This one-cell creature exists in animal intestines and when an animal craps near water, the little guy goes for a swim. An unsuspecting hiker drinks the contaminated water and for the next month is attacked by a myriad of symptoms, the worse being non-stop diarrhea. It usually takes several weeks of rest and a heavy dose of antibiotics to be rid of it, and many hikers who come down with giardia lose their desire for the trail and leave for good.

After the group heads out in the morning, Teresa and I take our planned day off. It's a perfect day for it, with blue skies and an expected high in the mid 80s. We spend the morning wandering through town, then go in search of a hotel. Though we've been hiking together for the last two months we haven't had any real privacy, or even gone on a formal date.

"Teresa, may I take you out to dinner tonight? Just the two of us," I ask her as we check into our room.

"Oooh, a date? I'd love that, Kevin. Where are we going?"

"I saw a great little Italian place as we walked over here. Not too formal and not too far away."

"That sounds great. Give me a minute to get ready," she says, and sixty seconds later she's dressed in her recently washed, though heavily used, hiking pants and a top that is starting to show wear from her backpack. I change into my finest nylon hiking shorts and a fresh yet permanently sweat-stained T-shirt, and off we go.

"Here we are babe, cozy and quiet. I hear they make a great pizza."

"Oh, it's just perfect, Kevin. Very good choice," Teresa says as we walk inside the air-conditioned lobby of Pizza Hut.

After a fine dinner we take our time walking back to the hotel room. The hot day has given way to a pleasant evening and the stars come out to wink at us. I take her hand in mine.

"I never thought I'd come out here and find someone as amazing as you," I say as we walk. "You have made this journey the best thing I have ever done in my life, and I want to say thank you."

"That's the nicest thing anybody's ever said to me." Teresa stops and pulls my head down towards hers, giving me the sweetest kiss I have ever experienced. We make our way back to the hotel room, lock the door, and have a perfect evening.

Checkout time is 11:00 A.M., so we lie in bed until 10:55, then in a hurricane of motion we wake Rufus, pack our bags, and are in the lobby at eleven on the dot. The hotel calls a shuttle to get us back to the trail free of charge. While waiting for the shuttle, Phone Home walks down the other side of the street. She says she is leaving the trail as she can't stand the thought of three more months away from her kids. She and Teresa exchange hugs, and she pets Rufus one last time. Our shuttle arrives and we leave Debbie standing on the corner, her trail days over.

My next adventure is just beginning, though, as I am a mere eight miles away from Shenandoah National Park. Originally the land was home to several Native American tribes, until Europeans arrived and forcefully evicted them. Along with the Europeans came destruction: the slaughter of countless animals and the clearing of miles of forest. By the early 1900s the entire Appalachian range in western Virginia was in danger of being clear-cut and settled, and the Virginia government wanted to protect what remained. Along with establishing several national and state forests, the state wanted to preserve a section of the Appalachians in the form of a national park.

June 6, 2001. Fearless Shenandoah deer.

In the 1930s the Virginia Legislature began purchasing parcels of land along the Blue Ridge Mountains. Not everyone wanted to sell, though, and 400 to 500 mountain families that had lived for generations among the mountains were forcefully evicted. Once enough land had been acquired — more than 4,000 parcels — the Virginia Legislature turned it over to the federal government for the creation of Shenandoah National Park. Since then, the forests have recovered and now the park is home to 200 species of birds, 50 species of mammals, 100 varieties of trees and over 1,100 different types of flowers.

Shenandoah National Park, or simply the Shennies, also contains 101 miles of the A.T. The park itself is 100 miles long as it follows the mountain ridge, but it's only a couple miles wide to the valley floor on either side. Running along the top of the ridge, and crossing the trail a dozen times, is the Skyline Drive — part of the Blue Ridge Parkway, which extends for hundreds of miles along the Appalachian Mountains and is designated a National Scenic Highway.

The park is less than a day's drive from Washington, D.C., and sees two million visitors a year. In such a narrow confinement the park should be teeming with people, but as in the Smokies, most people never venture far off the main road and the woods remain quiet.

Teresa and I hike a leisurely seven miles to Calf Mountain Shelter near the southern end of the park. Rufus gets to join us in this national park as the Shennies allows dogs. As the sun draws low a young, clean hiker with short hair comes walking into the shelter. He introduces himself as Dave and fires up his stove.

"My first day on the trail! Man, am I excited," Dave exclaims as he pours too much water into his cooking pot, spilling it all over the floor. Luckily, it is just the three of us, so we scoot over and Dave starts afresh with making dinner.

"First day indeed. Where are you coming from?" Teresa asks.

"It's summer break from college, and I'm going to spend it hiking. Can you believe it? Two days ago I was taking my final exam in biology and today I am out here in the woods. This is going to be fun. I plan on hiking up to Vermont, then heading back down to school for the fall. I'll see how far I get."

In the morning the three of us enter the park together, but Teresa and I quickly outpace Dave, our months of conditioning allowing us to walk harder and faster.

As in the Smokies, the camping rules here are very strict, and that determines how far we can walk each day. There are hundreds of sites to camp, but they are called campgrounds, require a fee of twenty dollars, and often are full of RV's and huge six-room family tents. The trail shelters are first-come, first-served. It is expected that hikers will stay in a shelter before setting up a tent, and there are only a couple of tent sites at each one. Camping is not permitted anywhere else, so to be legal we need to make it to a shelter each night and hope there is room.

Tonight we arrive at Blackrock Hut and join a mass of other hikers and campers. Homeless and Unemployed are here along with some new faces: Sticks, Patches, Wood Nymph and six weekenders. Sticks is a retired army colonel and is hiking with his wife, Patches. Short, stocky and barrel-chested, Sticks looks like a drill sergeant and walks with two gargantuan hiking sticks, each of which also could be called a tree. Patches is shorter, about 5'2", and can't weigh more than a hundred pounds. Wood Nymph is a young female hiker who fits her name. She seems like the quintessential nature activist: vegan, natural-material clothes, and long unkempt hair.

I start a fire, and once it is blazing away, Teresa comes over and cuddles next to me. Unemployed sees this and her eyes widen.

"Phoenix! So are you and Fruit Pie a couple now?" she asks.

Teresa and I look at each other and Teresa answers first. "More or less. Kevin took me out for a romantic dinner in Waynesboro, and we just enjoy hiking together." I nod my head in agreement.

"That's so exciting," Unemployed says, then she whispers to Teresa a little too loud, "We can hike together tomorrow and you can tell me all about it."

Tell her all about what? I thought Teresa had summed it up already, but if girls want to chat, best to just let them be.

In the morning Teresa hikes with Unemployed, leaving Rufus and me to ourselves. Hiking in the Shennies is easy, much softer and gentler than the steep, rugged Smokies. The trail has a few ups and downs, but they are short and for the most part it follows the Skyline Drive. I cross the road numerous times; its amazing viewpoints provide ample opportunity to sit and take in the beauty of the wilderness. The whole world is a lush green and the heat of the summer hasn't come on strong yet. The birds are out teaching their chicks to fly, wild flowers are ending their spring bloom, and the park is not quite full of summer tourists.

The trail itself is immaculate, thanks to the Potomac Appalachian Trail Club (PATC), which maintains over two hundred miles of the A.T., including this portion through the Shennies. The brush is cut back, there's not a single blowdown to climb over, and wherever the trail crosses the road there is a garbage can that has reduced litter to a few wrappers and the occasional bottle cap. Also, each shelter boasts a well-maintained privy, unlike the frozen tundra of toilet paper seen in the Smokies. The only blight in the Shennies are the deer.

First off, there are too many of them. I see more deer my first day in the park than I have in the last month. With two million visitors a year, the deer have become accustomed to humans as well as to dogs. Rufus and I can walk right up to one without so much as a flinch. Up close I can see they are not the soft, furry animals they should be, but instead they are diseased, sickly creatures. Each one looks malnourished, with ribs protruding through their thin skin, and many have small open sores on their faces and legs. Their ratted, patchy fur looks like a good petting would remove most of it, rendering these sickly deer bald and cold.

There are an estimated 6,000–18,000 deer within the park, two to six times what the Forest Service estimates the land can handle. Taking the average of the numbers, there are four times as many deer in the park as nature would intend. The deer's natural enemies, such as cougars and wolves, are all but eradicated from the mountains, and hunting is illegal in national parks, so there is nothing to hold the deer population in check.

Now the deer themselves are destroying the fragile balance of the ecosystem. Many animals, including various songbirds, live in the bottom five feet of the forest floor. With the deer devouring all the leaves they can reach, the populations of once common songbirds have been cut in half over the last forty years. Soon their glorious songs, now occasionally heard while hiking, will be available only as a recording in the nearest visitor center while the only noise on the trail will be the munching of thousands of deer, devouring foliage as efficiently as the gypsy moth.

While food is becoming scarce for the deer, it is in abundance for hikers. The trail passes alongside many large campgrounds, each one with a small general store and most with some type of grill or café. At least once a day we grab a burger or ice cream, and at night we carry hot dogs with mustard, ketchup, and onions to the shelter for dinner.

On our third day in the Shennies, Teresa and I take our time as we only need to cover twelve miles today to get to the shelter. Without any huge up or downs, twelve miles is a stroll in a park. Around noon we meander into the South River Picnic Grounds right off the trail. The picnic ground is a mini-park inside the park, consisting of a huge lawn studded with picnic tables and covered eating areas.

The area is almost deserted. There is a family at one of the picnic tables, and a handful of individuals scattered throughout the rest of the area. The family, a mom and dad with a young girl and boy, are laying out a huge spread of sandwiches, sodas, chips, and other goodies.

With so much food in sight I decide to give the age-old tradition of 'Yogi-ing' a try. Named after the famous Yogi Bear, Yogi-ing is not begging, but more of an art form of getting the other person to offer food. The trick is to look tired and hungry but not like a carnivorous serial killer. I, however, have a secret weapon.

"C'mon, Rufus, there's food to be had," I say as the three of us take an indirect route towards the family. Ten yards away from the family Rufus lies down on the grass. Wasn't exactly my plan, but I think he has his own plan and I'll go with it.

"No, Rufus. We can't rest yet," I say, kneeling down to pet him. "I know you're hungry, but walk a couple more miles, buddy, then we'll take a break and I'll split my last bagel with you." I know he doesn't understand a word I'm saying, but the family sure does. The mother looks over to us with big sad eyes.

"What a cute dog you have. He looks so sad and tired. Is he okay?" she asks.

"He's fine, just real tired and hungry. We've walked a long ways today," I say.

"He'll make it," Teresa adds. "He just needs to rest a few minutes." Both Teresa and I sit down next to Rufus. The girl walks over to see what is going on.

"He's sooooo cute! Oh mom, can I pet him?" yells the girl once she spots Rufus.

"Sure you can pet him. Rufus is real friendly," I say as she runs over to us and starts hugging him. Rufus loves the attention and rolls on his back for a belly rub. Behind the girl is her older brother. He's a little more apprehensive, but once he sees that Rufus is a big, brown marshmallow, he too comes forward.

"We've plenty of food here. Can your dog have a couple slices of turkey?" the mom says.

"Oh, he'll love that," I answer, and we walk over to the picnic table. I show the kids how to feed Rufus from their hands. The mom looks over to us, and her motherly instincts kick in now that we are sitting among her family.

"I bet you guys are hungry too. You sure look like it. How far are you hiking?" she asks, handing turkey sandwiches to Teresa and me.

We tell them about the trail, and they tell us about themselves. The Sampsons are from Ohio and this is their last day of a week-long trip through the park. This is what they have done almost every day: go on a short hike, then have a picnic in a different section of the park. They may not be hikers, but they have a hiker attitude. Instead of zipping through the park in one day, they are enjoying their trip and exploring the Shennies. After spending an hour with the family, we thank our hosts, give the kids one last chance to pet Rufus, and return to the lush, green Shenandoah forests.

The trail wanders through the forest, passing sickly deer, screaming squirrels, and singing birds. A couple hours later, Rufus and I are hiking a hundred feet in front of Teresa when I see movement to my left. Thinking it's another Bambi-on-crack I casually glance over into the woods, only to see a huge black bear walking parallel to me fifty feet away. The black bear doesn't seem to notice me, but I freeze, grab Rufus, and quickly place him on leash. Rufus sniffs the air a couple of times but otherwise has no idea what is going on. I watch the bear and then see a smaller shape, a single cub, right behind it. As quietly as I can, I call to Teresa about the bear. Momma bear's ears perk up, she gives one low growl, and momma and cub go romping through the woods away from us before Teresa has a chance to see them.

The whole incident lasted less than a minute, but I'll be forever grateful to the bear for allowing me this glimpse into its life — and for not tearing my arms off. I walk the last two miles to (ironically) Bearfence Mountain Shelter, thinking how lucky I am to have seen that. How many people in America have had such an experience, to see the power and grace of a bear in the wild? I'm glad I have.

Days of easy hiking pass by, each night filled with the companionship of Homeless and Unemployed, Sticks and Patches, Othra and Wood Nymph. Teresa and I reach Thornton Gap Campground late in the afternoon, and the shelter is only a mile away so we have time to kill. We buy some ice cream from the general store and spend two hours lying in the sunshine and watching the tourists until Sticks and Patches arrive. Sticks buys a six-pack of beer, Patches gets mustard and hot dogs, Teresa buys some chips, and I also throw a six-pack of beer in my pack.

"Who's got the buns?" Patches asks as we start to leave.

"Ah, man, we completely forgot buns. I'll grab 'em," I answer. I purchase the buns, and then I wonder how to carry them without mushing them. As I drop my pack to find a way to attach the package to it, Rufus walks up to me and nuzzles my arm.

"Rufus, you're a genius!" I say. Rufus, having no idea what he did but liking the praise, wags his tail. I tie the buns to the top of his pack with a little bit of rope. The buns will fall off if tossed around, but luckily Rufus doesn't toss, turn, run, play, or jump. He turns his head slightly to sniff the package, then falls in stride behind me as we hike towards the shelter, complete with bobbing buns on his burly back.

"Mommy, look at the funny dog," a child exclaims as we pass through the parking lot.

"They're not very smart," says the mom. "Why, if a bear came along and saw those hot dog buns out in the open like that, they would all be eaten alive."

Ignoring such an ignorant comment we proceed, unmolested by any wild animals, to the shelter where Homeless, Unemployed and Othra are sitting around a campfire. We get out the food and soon are roasting hot dogs over the flames.

"So, any of you guys going to aqua blaze?" asks Othra after dinner.

"Aqua blaze? What the heck are you talking about, Othra?" I say, thinking maybe he has eaten a bad hot dog.

"Aqua blazing, man! There's a place in Front Royal that rents canoes, and we can spend three days floating down the Shenandoah River to Harpers Ferry in West Virginia. I hear it's really cool, a good break from walking and we still cover the 40 miles or so. I'm thinking about it. Sounds like fun. Anyone else?"

I like the idea and so does Teresa, but she doesn't have the $75 to rent a canoe. No one else is the least bit interested in leaving the comfort of the woods for uncharted waters. Othra drops the subject and our little gang calls it a night.

Two days later Teresa and I arrive at the town of Front Royal, our week of vacation in the Shennies over. No more stopping by the grill for a burger and fries, followed by an hour-long nap on a picnic table. No more flat, easy trail punctuated with stunning views. Then again, no more strict camping restrictions. We can once again hike as much or as little in a day as we want and set up our tents wherever we want.

When I first started planning my hike, my dad asked if he could come out and hike with me for a couple of weeks. I readily agreed, and my first plan was for him to join me in the Shennies, due to its close proximity to the D.C. airports. However, he already had business commitments for June, so we went with plan B: he'll come out and hike the White Mountains in New Hampshire when I reach them in August. I am now glad he couldn't come out here because the Shennies are not representative of the trail. Anyone with $200 can hike through the park, carrying no food, taking a shower every day, and even having several opportunities to wash clothes and rent a room. That is not hiking; that's taking a series of day hikes from one developed campsite to the next. I'm glad to be back out in the wilderness — the one without cute little signs explaining what tree I'm looking at, pointing me to the next garbage can, and telling me where I can and can't sleep.

June 13, 2001. 920 from Springer, 1247 to Katahdin. Rufus packing buns in Shenandoah National Park.

5. Virginia Is for Lovers

It's a god-awful hot day today, as if Mother Nature waited for us to leave the comforts of the park before blasting the furnace. Just to make it interesting, she adds humidity too. Our plan is to re-supply, then get back on the trail, but it's difficult because Front Royal isn't a trail town. Instead, it is laid out for tourists visiting the Shenandoah National Park by car, so the services are spread out all over town.

We pick up our mail drops from the post office and start towards the closest grocery store, a mile away under the blazing sun. One bank's lighted sign puts the temperature at 98 degrees, and the concrete world we've stepped into offers no protection. Halfway to the supermarket we spy a Dairy Queen and head towards the air-conditioning. Just then, Othra walks out, holding a rapidly melting ice cream cone.

"Hey, guys! You decide to aqua blaze after all?" Othra asks.

"We weren't really planning on it. Who all is going?" I ask.

"Got a whole bunch of people, so it should only run about $50 a person. We're all splitting a motel room tonight and canoeing in the morning. You guys in?"

Teresa and I talk it over and decide that a couple days in a canoe would be a welcome break from hiking. It means skipping forty miles of trail, but neither of us is a purist who believes we need to touch every foot of the trail to

June 15, 2001. Aquablazing down the mighty Shenandoah.

accomplish it. We will still be covering the distance; we'll just be using our arms to propel us instead of our legs.

"We're in."

"Yaahooooo! This is going to be a blast!" Othra says. He leads us to the hotel room where Java and Jeopardy, T-Tree and Brooklyn, and a hiker named Duff are staying. T-Tree is a young woman who quit her job as a teacher to achieve her dream of hiking the A.T. She met Brooklyn, from Brooklyn, and formed a relationship. Duff is Brooklyn's friend from New York and is out hiking for a week. It is a good, solid group and I have no doubt this will be a lot of fun. We purchase several Styrofoam coolers, pack them full of food and beer, and in the morning the canoe rental place sends a shuttle to take us to the river.

By 9:00 A.M. the eight of us, in four canoes, are ready to shove off and give our legs a much needed break. Rufus, however, makes it quite clear that he doesn't want to ride in a canoe any more than he wants to hike in the rain, hike in the heat, or get chased by rabid killer cows. One look at the floating contraption is all it takes to send him hightailing it back to the rental shop. Luckily Rufus, being Rufus, isn't terribly hard to catch, and before he makes it off the sandy beach I grab him and place him dead center in the canoe. Once we are in the water Rufus stands up, places one foot overboard and realizes there is no ground. Defeated, he lies down to suffer the trip — that is, until we come upon a spot so shallow I have to get out of the canoe and push. Rufus sees his chance for a daring escape and jumps overboard into the ankle deep water. He looks around him and realizes he is still surrounded by water. With nowhere to go, Rufus starts whining. I call him over, hoping he'll brave the terrible wetness, but to no avail. Finally I leave the canoe stuck in the shallows, walk over to Rufus, pick him up and carry him back to the canoe. No sooner do I place him in the canoe than he jumps right back out again! Once again I lift him back in. This time Teresa holds him while I push us clear of the shallows and into deeper water.

For the next two days we paddle with the current, swim when we get too warm, and find a place along the bank to camp as dusk approaches. The eight of us, virtually strangers two days ago, share our stories and food with one another and become a tight knit, though temporary, family. When Java and Jeopardy's canoe gets stuck among some rocks we paddle back upstream to make sure they are okay. At one point the river is dammed, forcing us to portage around. We pull our canoes up to the beach, unload all the gear and, irrespective of who owns what, grab bags, coolers, and canoes and carry them the quarter mile past the dam. No one complains that one person has to carry more than the other, and no one tries to weasel out of doing his or her fair share. We all pitch in to continue our journey. Where else can eight people, who know each other only by nicknames, trust and depend on each other so completely?

On the third day we reach the rendezvous point with the canoe company's van, and they shuttle us to the KOA campground in Harpers Ferry, West Virginia. Our aqua blaze is over, and I don't regret missing forty miles of trail at all. Floating down the river, letting the current and canoe carry all of my gear and food, and watching the forest slowly drift by us is an experience I will never forget.

6

Baking with New Friends

June 17 and I have now hiked 1,003 miles to reach West Virginia. Harpers Ferry, while not the true halfway point, is definitely the psychological one. The real halfway point is another hundred miles or so in Pennsylvania. Harpers Ferry, though, is where the ATC headquarters is located and is a good place to relax for a day before leaving the south and tackling the second half of the trail.

Teresa and I walk into the lobby of the KOA, which offers a special hiker rate of $5.00. The clerk, probably an 18-year-old girl working a summer job, takes our money and gives us directions to the "thru-hiker" section. We grab our packs and follow her directions.

"What the hell is this?" I exclaim out loud when we reach our "section." Five dollars rented us a piece of rocky land either at the bottom of a 50-foot gully, or on the hill leading down to it. It is obvious the gully was formed by rainwater washing through the campground, an observation supported by the fact that several large, aluminum drainpipes jut out into the drainage. There are a couple flat spots on the hill suitable for setting up a tent, but other hikers have already claimed them.

"Well, do you feel like sleeping on the side of the gully or at the bottom?" I ask Teresa as Othra approaches and sees what $5.00 bought us.

"You've got to be kidding. I'm not sleeping at the bottom of some rain gully. That sounds stupid to me," Othra says.

"What else can we do? Unless you want to spend the $20 for a normal campsite." Teresa says.

"Look around. This place is pretty much deserted. I'm going to take one of the normal spots at the top of the gully and if they catch me, oh well. I'll just say I didn't know this wasn't one of our spots," Othra says. The idea sounds like a good one to me. We find a spot close to the gully and the three of us share a campsite. Other hikers drift in, look at the gully, and do the same thing.

There are only two places within walking distance to resupply, the campground general store or a 7–11 down the street, and neither has much of a selection. As Teresa and I discuss how to find the nearest supermarket, a small pickup truck pulls up with two hikers in the back. I recognize one of the hikers as Toast, a tall, lanky hiker that I have seen throughout Virginia.

"Hey, this guy is offering a ride to a grocery store if anybody needs to go!" shouts Toast, who jumps out of the back of the truck once it's stopped. The driver, a middle-aged balding man with the beginnings of a beer belly and a rosy-pink nose, steps out of the truck. With a low voice he turns towards Toast.

"I don't want to take everyone into town, I only offered you and the other hiker a ride. I stopped here so you can get your wallet, not invite more people," the driver says.

"What's the difference? If you're taking two, why can't you take five? Heck, we're only going to be in the back of your truck," Toast says.

"Okay, but just one trip. I don't want to be a shuttle."

Taking that for an invitation, Teresa and I, along with a few other hikers, jump into the bed of his truck. A few minutes later Toast rejoins us, and we are off to a real grocery store.

"Kind of a strange dude I found," explains Toast as we fly down the highway. "He says his name is Satellite and he claims he's a trail angel, but he seems reluctant to help. He stated he would take me and Hopper here to the store, then got upset when I asked if anyone else wanted to go."

At the store Teresa and I introduce ourselves to Satellite and thank him for the ride. He explains how he likes to help out hikers and also proudly points to the scanner in his truck.

"I'm a fire angel too. I listen to the scanner on the fire department frequency, and when there's a hot call I show up and bring the guys sandwiches and sodas. They really appreciate me," he says. He seems nice enough.

When everyone is back in the truck, Satellite mentions he's a caretaker of an old quarry and needs to stop by to check on it. Twenty minutes later we are at a huge quarry carved right out of the granite bedrock, now filled with crystal clear water and large trout. Satellite gets out of the truck and walks along the edge of the quarry with a large smile on his face.

"Here she is. Anyone want to go skinny dipping?" Satellite asks, and receives several questionable looks in return.

"Okay, anyone want to go for a normal swim?" he asks, and receives unanimous negative replies. "Never mind then."

"So, what's up with this place?" asks one of the hikers. "Why are we here?"

"This place use to be a huge mess. Kids swam, partied, and littered all over the area, but now that I have been hired I have really cleaned it up," Satellite explains. "I installed the gate and used to patrol here at night with a huge flashlight and tell the kids to leave. I bought a badge so they would think I'm a cop. They got the message not to come back. Now I come up here about three times a day to make sure no one is here without my permission. I let a few of my firefighter friends come fish once in a while, but I don't let just anyone come up here. I got to know them first."

Satellite is very proud of this place, but I think the quarry is his only shot at fame in the town and he wants to flaunt it. I have a strong feeling Satellite is a fifty-year-old groupie, looking to fit in by doing favors to hikers and firefighters. We pile back into the truck and he drops us off at the KOA. After he drives away, Toast comes over to Teresa and me.

"Hey, guys, Satellite invited me over to his house tonight for a barbecue. At first I thought he was having a bunch of hikers over so I accepted, but so far it's just me. I don't want to head over there alone, but I already said I would go. Will you guys go with me? Please?" It isn't as much a question as it is a plea, so Teresa and I agree to go with him.

A couple hours later Satellite arrives in his truck. His nose is even redder and he smells like he's had a drink or two.

"Hey, man," Toast says. "I invited a couple of friends. I hope you don't mind."

"Um, I guess it would be okay, but I don't want a whole bunch of strangers coming over," Satellite says.

As I lift Rufus into his truck, Othra comes running over.

"Fruit Pie and Phoenix, where are you headed?"

"Over to Satellite's for a barbecue. You want to come?" I ask.

"You bet I do," Othra says, joining us in the back of the truck. Satellite stomps on the gas before any more hikers can invite themselves over.

On the way to his house, Satellite's fire scanner squawks.

"Something's going on. I have to drop by the fire station and see if they need me," he says. A few minutes later we are at the station with several firefighters outside washing their rig.

"I heard the call. What's going on?" he asks them.

"Oh, it's you. Just a brush fire. We have it under control and don't need you for anything," the fireman says, barely looking at Satellite.

"Okay, but if you need anything, remember to call me if you can. I got this scanner, though, so if you don't have time to call me, I can still show up."

"Yeah, we know. We'll call you if we need you," the fireman says.

It's obvious that Satellite is a tolerated presence, not a precious commodity, at the firehouse. Though I'm sure he's appreciated when he brings them food out in the field, as much as he wants to think he is, Satellite is not and never will be a firefighter.

The emergency handled, we arrive at his house and Satellite offers us a beer while he pours himself a very stiff drink. The house is small and clean, with several pictures adorning the wall, one of a much younger Satellite holding an assault rifle in what appears to be Vietnam.

"That you?" I ask him, pointing to the picture.

"That was in Vietnam. I was in the Army and got sent over shortly before the war ended. Saw some combat over there."

I tell him about my Marine Corps days and he leans close to me and lowers his voice.

"Fruit Pie, you're a good man and have what it takes to make it. I know some old friends in Washington, D.C., that run a secret organization and they can use someone like you. They go on top-secret missions for the government, use poison bullets and stuff like that. If you're interested, come on back after you're done and I'll hook you up with those guys."

I told him I'd think about it, which meant "Hell no." I'm getting the feeling Satellite, the groupie and the alcoholic, is not all there in the head. He's a nice guy, and I appreciate all he does for the hiking community; I just wouldn't want to be alone with him.

After a day off it's time to leave the KOA. We throw on our packs and follow the trail as it meanders through Harpers Ferry. Situated on a peninsula between the Potomac and Shenandoah rivers, Harpers Ferry used to be an actual town, but now it is designated as a National Historic Park. Robert Harper founded the city in 1747 because of its ample water power and perfect location for travel and transport. He built and operated ferries to bring people across the rivers for the next twenty years. Since its foundation, Harpers Ferry has been a central point in American history. George Washington surveyed its waters and later championed the site as the location for a new federal armory and arsenal. In 1803, Meriwether Lewis, part of the famous Lewis and Clark expedition, arrived at Harpers Ferry to buy armament available only at the new federal armory.

However, the event that secured the town's historical importance occurred on October 16, 1859. Abolitionist John Brown, in hopes of freeing the slaves, formed a 21-man army with the intent of seizing the 100,000 weapons stored at the armory. He thought that with these weapons he could form a slave army and use the Blue Ridge Mountains as a base for a guerrilla war against the south. On the evening of the sixteenth, John Brown and his men overpowered the single watchman at the armory and proceeded to capture several other strategic positions in the town, none of which were guarded.

His initial success was short lived when local farmers, shopkeepers, and militiamen took up arms against Brown and his men. John Brown and his army retreated to the armory where they were surrounded by a company of U.S. Marines under the command of Lt. Col. Robert E. Lee. Thirty-six hours after the raid began, with most of his men dead or wounded, John Brown was captured. Two months later he was found guilty of murder, treason, and inciting a slave rebellion, and was hanged.

Eighteen months later, the American Civil War began. In 1862 General Robert E. Lee again returned to Harpers Ferry, this time to recapture it from Union troops. Following a barrage of artillery, General Lee and General "Stonewall" Jackson converged on the town, capturing over 12,000 Union soldiers. It was the largest surrender of the Civil War.

Harpers Ferry changed hands five times during the war as both sides sought control of this strategic location on the mouth of the two rivers. Much of the town was destroyed during the war, but the townsfolk rebuilt it. In 1963 it was declared a National Historic Site and funds were allocated to restore many of the old buildings, which are now stores and museums.

The store owners are extremely friendly to hikers, and we stop for a burger at one place, ice cream at another, and a snack at a third. Every store keeper welcomes us into his business. The town offers a self-guided tour of the major sites, and we spend half the day looking at 200-year-old buildings and reading about the town's history. Early afternoon we proceed to the ATC headquarters near the center of town. The headquarters is staffed by former thru-hikers and offers a wealth of information about the trail. They also keep an unofficial count of how many hikers pass through their doors each year. Teresa and I are numbers 343 and 344.

Finally it is time to leave town, so we cross over the Potomac River and into Maryland. Only forty miles of trail cross through Maryland, and some brave hikers attempt the "four state challenge," which involves touching four states in one day. Starting with one foot in Virginia, it is 43 miles through West Virginia and Maryland before reaching Pennsylvania. Though the challenge has a certain amount of appeal to me, I don't really feel like walking 43 miles in one day, and I know Rufus has no intention of doing so. Instead, we set out on a leisurely pace and hike seven miles before stopping for the night.

Our first full day in Maryland is hot and humid with storm clouds brewing in the distance. By early afternoon we reach Dahlgren Backpack Campground, a small state-maintained park that has several campsites, a picnic area and a shower, all free to hikers. Hot and sweaty from the miserable heat, I'm not going to pass up the opportunity to shower, so I step into the tiny concrete stall only to discover it needs a healthy dose of Napalm. The walls run green, purple and orange with mold and fungus, a three-inch mushroom grows in one corner, and the floor is slick with who-knows-what. I don't know if this place has ever seen a scrub brush. Disgusted, but only slightly scared, I enter the shower wearing my sandals and turn the knob. Surprisingly, the water coming out of the mangled pile of rust posing as a shower head is clean and clear. After a very quick shower, without touching anything other than the water knob, I carefully exit the bio-warfare lab.

"How's the shower?" asks Teresa as she takes off her shoes.

"Umm, not real pretty. But if you don't touch the walls or the floors or breathe the air, you should be okay."

"Oh, it can't be that bad, I'll risk it," she says.

Ten seconds later she's running out of the shower, still clothed.

"That's disgusting! Maybe if I hadn't showered in a week I'd have risked it, but I took one yesterday in town."

We head out, and within minutes of our leaving the park a light rain starts

6. Baking with New Friends

to fall as the wind picks up. Rufus smells the approaching storm and slows his pace. Teresa hikes on ahead, and half an hour out of the park the first lightning bolt streaks across the sky. Thunder quickly follows, freezing Rufus in his tracks. I'm on to his game, though. He wants me to stop so he can hide underneath a tree, but if I keep walking, so will he. I slow my pace for him but keep moving.

The storm intensifies as the trail turns onto a road. I follow the road into a small park and find Teresa sitting underneath a covered picnic table with water pouring off the roof. Soaked and cold, I plop down next to her.

"Where's Rufus?" Teresa shouts over a thunder clap. "You didn't leave him again, did you?"

"He's coming. He was right behind me 15 minutes ago. He'll be up here shortly." I huddle next to her and wait.

Ten minutes, fifteen minutes, thirty minutes pass and no Rufus.

"I'm worried about him," Teresa says. "What if he's lost? What if he's hurt? You left him and now he's lost. I bet he's scared and cold and thinks you don't love him anymore. You have to go find him." Tears (or well placed raindrops) are rolling down her red cheeks.

Frustrated, I head back out into the storm in search of Rufus. My first thought is that he returned to the last place we had stopped, the Dahlgren Campground three miles back. I jog to the park, but no Rufus. I turn around and start walking north, and as I cross a gravel road several hundred yards north of the campground a white sedan slowly drives by. The sedan stops and backs up until it is right next to me. The driver-side window rolls down and a middle-aged woman sticks her head out.

"You missing a dog?" she says.

"Yes, a short, stocky brown dog carrying a red backpack."

"That's the one. Twenty minutes ago I found him hiding under a chair on my back patio. Jump in, I live down the street."

A couple of minutes later we arrive at her house, and sure enough, Rufus is on the patio, but now with his nose pressed up against the sliding glass door looking hungrily inside. He sees me and runs over, wagging his tail. Little does he know we are headed back into the rain.

I thank the owner, and she gives me a ride back to the park. Teresa comes running over to hug Rufus as soon as we get out of the car.

"Are you all right, Rufus? You must have been so scared. It's okay now, he'll never leave you again — will you, Kevin?" Teresa says, glaring at me. Rufus gets loving attention while I get the evil eye. Oh well; at least he is safe and back with us again. We hang out under the pavilion until the thunder passes, then walk a silent hour in the rain to Pine Knob Shelter. Teresa doesn't talk to me for the rest of the night.

After the storm, we have beautiful weather and the trail takes us out of Maryland and into Pennsylvania. Teresa is talking to me again and Rufus has forgotten the whole incident.

Two days into Pennsylvania we arrive at Pine Grove Furnace State Park, 1,083 miles from Springer Mountain, 1,085 miles from Mt. Katahdin. Though the exact mileage of the trail changes from year to year due to relocations and maintenance, Pine Grove Furnace is the official halfway mark, and this milestone is commemorated by the "half-gallon challenge." This challenge is easier and much more fun than the four-state challenge, and I eagerly pick up the gauntlet. The test is simple: sit down and eat a half-gallon of ice cream as fast as possible. Sticking out my chest, I proudly walk into the general store and pick out a half-gallon of Hershey's Chocolate Chip Cookie Dough from the freezer. I set my prize down on the counter and pull out my money, all $1.25 of it.

"That will be $3.95, please," the clerk says.

"Um, I'm a little short on cash. That's okay, here's my credit card."

"No credit cards, sorry."

"You don't take credit cards? How about an ATM, one of those close by?" I ask.

"Closest one is eight miles up the road."

"Want to loan me $2.70, then?" I plead.

"Wish I could ... but no."

Defeated, I sit down on the front porch. I have been looking forward to this event ever since I first heard about it back in Virginia. Now, with my dream shattered, I have nothing else to do but pout.

"If I had any money, I'd give it to you, Kevin," Teresa says, coming over to comfort me in my time of need. The problem is that most hikers don't carry much money. Coins equal weight and currency is too easily lost or stolen. Credit cards are the way to go. In every mail drop I have $40 in traveler's checks, but I quickly spend that in town on food and lodging. If I need extra cash I find an ATM, otherwise every place takes credit cards — except for here.

As I sit dejected, the Four Horsemen arrive.

"You doing it, Fruit Pie?" asks Thumper, referring to the challenge.

"No man, I want to, but I'm a few dollars short."

"A couple of bucks? That's all that's standing between you and your dream?" says Assface. "Hell, you let me watch you try to eat the whole thing, and I'll give you the money."

My feet lighten and my heart fills with glee as I march into the store and purchase my container of ice cream. Thumper is the only other person to partake, and he buys plain ol' vanilla. I was thinking about vanilla, but for this I need something with a little more texture and variety, so I stick with the cookie dough. Outside, Assface starts his stopwatch as I devour my first bite, then my second, and third. I love ice cream. I have never sat down to eat a half-gallon before, but I'm a hungry hiker on a mission, and soon my half gallon is half gone.

"How you feeling, babe?" says Teresa, watching me to make sure I don't slip any to Rufus.

"Yumm, still running strong. Piece of cake. Mmmm, cake. That sounds good too," and I continue eating.

I'm down to my last few bites while Thumper sets his ice cream down in defeat. He killed three quarters of it but cannot finish, and the greedy vultures around him quickly strip the carcass as I take my last bite.

"Done! How long did that take?"

"Twenty-nine minutes and 11 seconds. You missed the record by 18 minutes. Nice job! How you feeling?" Assface says.

"Good. Real good. Give me about fifteen minutes to digest and I'll be ready to hike out." The ice cream is sitting nicely in my belly. Only one problem: I'm still hungry. I just devoured 2,880 calories and 160 grams of fat, the equivalent of five Big Macs, but I want real food. The ice cream isn't substance. I'm craving a burger from the grill, but alas, I am out of money and I am not going to ask to borrow any more.

After a couple of minutes I'm ready to leave, and we hike through the park, passing a small lake crowded with throngs of weekenders enjoying the hot day.

"Anybody up for a swim?" says Patch Monkey. Although I don't feel like swimming, my stomach is starting to gurgle, and sitting down for half an hour sounds like a good idea. We end up staying by the lake for almost an hour, Teresa lying out in the sun and me wading a bit with Rufus to cool off while the Horsemen play in the water.

No camping is allowed in the park, so we walk five miles to Tagg Run Shelter. Five miles of walking in the hot sun with a half-gallon of ice cream in my belly takes its toll, and when I arrive into camp, I drop my pack and run straight for the privy, not to be seen again for almost an hour. That much ice cream does strange things to the bowels.

The days grow hotter, and other than the brief storm in Maryland, it hasn't rained in several weeks. If this keeps up the smaller streams and springs will run dry. In North Carolina and Virginia it seemed like it rained almost every day, but the states farther north didn't receive much of it and had a very dry spring. Now it looks like it might be a very dry summer. Moving this slowly, 10–15 miles a day, it's easy to forget that I am crossing through different states and climates. It's not like driving, where in two days I can go from Georgia to Maine and instantly see a change in the climate. All that rain down south, though fresh in my memory, doesn't do me a bit of good up here.

The shade and shelter of the woods comes to an abrupt end as Teresa and I reach the southern end of Cumberland Valley, a twenty-mile expanse of exposed Pennsylvania farmland. The trail once followed roads through the valley, but with no shoulder or sidewalk to walk on, hikers became moving targets. Pressure from the Appalachian Trail Conference convinced the state to take action. Pennsylvania paid close to $6.6 million for land on 90 different farms to create a ten-foot-wide trail corridor running through the valley. The farmers, losing very little land as the trail runs along fences and through untenable areas, agreed to sell with one stipulation: no camping in the valley. This creates a twenty-mile day with no water for eleven of it.

Rufus and I, neither of us a fan of the heat, slowly walk out into the sun, taking breaks under the meager shade of scattered trees when we come upon them. After seventeen miles I run out of water and stumble through the valley until I come across a farmer who offers Rufus and me some from his canteen. We take a couple of drinks and keep walking under the blazing sun, this nightmarish crossing a day I would rather erase from my memory.

The heat hits the low 90s as Teresa, Rufus and I descend down into the town of Duncannon, an extremely friendly and popular trail town. It's been nine days since Harpers Ferry and I'm down to a couple crumbs in my food bag and some nasty red chafing between my thighs. Gold Bond is good, but it can only do so much against constant sweaty rubbing.

We walk through town and the cheapest place to stay turns out to be the Riverfront Campground, which charges $3.50 for a tent site and showers. First thing I do is take a cold shower, removing the sweat and dirt from my body so the chafing can heal.

Our plan is to resupply in the morning and be out of town by noon. We now have a deadline to make as Teresa's parents want to see their daughter and meet the man she is hiking with. We have picked a spot in the middle of Pennsylvania for them to drive down and meet us. Meeting someone at a certain place and time on the trail is quite difficult as we are never sure where we are going to end up each night. We finally had to choose a place and time, though, and central Pennsylvania seemed like a good as place as any, considering it is a straight shot south on Interstate 81 from Rochester, New York. We have three days to cover the forty miles to 501 Shelter where we will meet them; then we'll take a couple of well-deserved days off.

Java, Jeopardy and Othra arrive at the campground and set up next to us. Jeopardy's mail drop includes a pair of barber clippers he mails ahead from town to town, and both Othra and I volunteer for a Jeopardy haircut. Half an hour later, Othra, Jeopardy and I, sporting shaved heads to go along with our full beards, join Java and Teresa to walk into town to find a place to eat, ending up at the Doyle Hotel.

The Anheuser-Busch company built the Doyle in 1905. Their plan was to establish a chain of hotels across the country to promote their beer, and it worked, until Prohibition put most of them out of business. The Doyle survived Prohibition, but since then it has seen a number of owners, none of whom maintained the building, and the Doyle has slowly fallen into disarray. Fortunately, the giant four-story hotel has new owners who do care and are slowly restoring the hotel to its original beauty, from the copper-plated ceiling inside the lobby to the Victorian pillars supporting the second floor balcony.

6. Baking with New Friends

We enter the lounge and find Assface, Thumper, Jiffy Pop and Patch Monkey already crowded around a table, each with a cold draft beer in his hands. Rufus isn't allowed in the bar area, but the owner has no problem with me leaving him in the lobby where he can stay out of the sun.

"Hey, guys, pull up a chair and grab yourselves a beer. A buck buys you a glass of Yuengling and it's really quite good," says Thumper. Turns out Yuengling is a local beer available almost exclusively in Pennsylvania, and it is good. The food matches the beer in both price and quality. For less than ten dollars I have a huge sandwich, several orders of fries and a couple of beers. The long hot day catches up to us all, and by 10:00 P.M. Teresa and I are back in our tents asleep.

"Come on, babe. We have a lot to do if we want to be on the trail by noon," I call over to Teresa the next morning.

It's 9:00 A.M. and already the temperature is in the mid–80s. We grab our dirty clothes and walk a quarter mile into town to the laundromat, only to find a note posted on the door: "Washing machine temporarily broken. Will be closed until repairs are made." My guide shows there is another laundromat located in a truck stop, but that is three quarters of a mile on the other side of the campground. We walk to the truck stop to wash our clothes and once done, it's almost two miles back through town to the grocery store. Once we have what we need, we head towards the campground while the temperature reaches the mid–90s.

"Let's sit down for a minute and cool off in the shade," Teresa says as we walk by a bench tucked under a store awning, directly across from the Doyle. I take advantage of the shade and sit down.

So far we have walked five miles today in the blazing sun, yet according to "trail math" we haven't hiked a single mile, as we are no closer to Maine than we were this morning. Trail math conveniently leaves out hiking to find water, hiking to the shelters, and walking around town, all of which can add several hundred miles to the trip. I hate trail math. We rest on the bench for an hour as the sun moves across the sky and into our shade. Once again we are exposed to its burning rays with Rufus trying to hide under the bench to escape.

"Teresa, it's noon already," I say, looking at my watch. "We've got to get going. Let's go grab some lunch and get out of this town."

"Sounds good to me. Where do you want to eat?"

"Let's do the Doyle. It's right across the street and we know they have good food." A few minutes later we are sitting in the air-conditioned bar, Rufus lapping up a bowl of water in the lobby and Teresa and I each holding a cold Yuengling.

As our food arrives, so does Othra, who joins us for a meal and a beer. Soon the Horsemen walk in. Assface breaks out a deck of cards and starts dealing "Presidents," a drinking game.

"Just a couple hands, guys, we've got to head out soon. We're meeting

June 26, 2001. 1124 from Springer, 1043 to Katahdin. Taking advantage of the shade in Duncannon, Pennsylvania. Doyle Hotel across the street.

Teresa's folks in a couple of days and have some mileage to cover," I say as I pick up my cards.

Four hours later and blissfully drunk, I have no intention of leaving. Teresa, however, has other ideas.

"Come on, Kevin, we have to get going," she says as she moves my beer away from me and takes my cards.

I look to Othra for help, but he's lying face down on the table, drool leaking from his mouth. Jiffy Pop is staring at the window making little pictures in the dust with his fingers, and Assface is trying to arrange his cards for the third time.

"One more game. Why don't you head down to camp and pack up? I'll meet you there in half an hour," I tell her, taking back my beer and cradling it to my chest.

"Not a chance in hell. Get up, we're going now. We've got to meet my parents in a few days."

"Can't they meet us here?"

"No!"

6. Baking with New Friends

Defeated, I stagger back to the campground with her. After guzzling a gallon of water we head out of town, with Teresa behind me every step of the way to ensure I don't go back to the Doyle. The sun sets as we begin the uphill climb out of town, leaving us to stumble over rocks and roots guided by the light from our small headlamps. A long and sobering four miles later we find the shelter, and three minutes after I crawl in my sleeping bag I am fast asleep curled up with Rufus.

I wake to a pounding hangover and 85 degree heat. Walking in the heat is no fun, but walking in the heat dehydrated and hungover is as much fun as covering yourself in honey and playing tag with a grizzly bear. Just to keep things interesting, we've come upon the "Pennsylvania rocks." For weeks I have heard about Pennsylvania's rocky trail, waiting to snap an ankle if you blink too long. Hikers say the boulders roll underneath your feet like marbles. Up until now, however, we have only come across very small sections of rocks and I thought the rumors were fireside stories. We have now found the rocks, and while they are not dangerous in the conventional sense, what makes the rocks so bad is that they are sharp, uneven and very hard. The arches in my shoes are breaking down, and my feet and knees are beginning to hurt every time I step on these jagged stones. Another problem with the rocks is that they slow down our pace. Rufus has a really tough time because where I can step up 18 inches onto the next rock, he has to jump. He is expending a lot of energy, so we take longer breaks, and I constantly check his feet to make sure they're not cut or raw.

Due to the rocks, the heat, and the fact I spent a full day drinking in a bar, the only way we can make it to the 501 Shelter in time to meet Teresa's parents is to hike two twenty-mile days, something neither of us wants to do. This trip is supposed to be enjoyable, and walking to exhaustion for two days doesn't fit my idea of fun. While sitting in an ice cold creek we come up with plan B: yellow blaze. Yellow blazing is skipping a section of trail by car, either a taxi cab (hence the name yellow), a ride from friends, or hitch hiking. I didn't come out here to ride the trail, but we have a deadline. We spend the next two days covering a leisurely 27 miles, then stick out our thumbs at a major road and accept a ride to the 501 Shelter, skipping 13 miles of trail.

The 501 Shelter sits at the crest of Pennsylvania Highway 501 as the road crosses the Blue Ridge Mountains. The shelter is fully enclosed and has numerous bunks, several tables and chairs, and lots of old magazines to read. Though it is right next to a major road, it doesn't see the hoodlums or partiers that other shelters near roads attract because there is an on-site caretaker. The Blue Mountain Eagle Climbing Club bought the land and renovated this shelter. The caretaker lives next door in a house also owned by the Climbing Club. The club does an outstanding job of maintaining the place and the shelter has water, a porta-potty, and a solar-heated outdoor shower.

I lead Rufus inside and find an older couple peering over maps, and I introduce myself. The couple's names are Rocky and Bedouin, an older couple slack-packing the trail. Rocky, the wife, explains that because she has had reconstructive surgery on both knees and her husband, Bedouin, blew his knee out several years ago, the only way they can hike the trail is to slack-pack it.

Slack-packing is simply a fancy name for hiking without a pack. It can be as complex as having a full-time support vehicle that picks you up at the end of every day, spending every night in a motel or hostel, and never having to carry more than a light day-pack. Or it just be finding someone to take your pack and drop it off at the next road crossing, so you can enjoy half a day of hiking without a heavy burden. Rocky and Bedouin are living the hiker life, but are finding hostels, shuttles and trail angels who will help them slack-pack. There are many ways to hike the trail and slack-packing is just one of them.

Some hikers are purists, believing they must pass every white blaze. Many shelters are on blue-blazed side trails that loop around a section of the trail, and a purist will backtrack to ensure he doesn't miss an inch of the A.T. Then there is the blue-blazer. A blue-blazer hikes the A.T. how he wants, taking side trails or scenic routes and not intent on passing every white blaze. While there is no right or wrong way to hike the trail, it is wrong to criticize how someone else does. The philosophy of "Hike Your Own Hike" is an important one, and if you walk, crawl or run from Georgia to Maine, you are a thru-hiker.

While we are waiting for Teresa's parents, Toast arrives and we learn that Othra is off the trail. Apparently, the day after our drinkfest at the Doyle, Othra was very sick, but he attributed it to too much alcohol. The day after that, he was still just as sick and visited the local doctor, where he was diagnosed with Giardia. He will have to take several weeks off before he can hike again.

While we are talking to Toast a car pulls up.

"It's them. They're here!" Teresa screams. "My mom and dad are here, come on!" Teresa runs outside and instantly embraces her mom and dad with big hugs. After several minutes of acting as giddy as a 16-year-old girl, she calls me over and introduces me to her parents, Paul and Joyce.

Paul is a tall, bearded Italian man with a deep voice and a strong handshake, while Joyce is an older version of Teresa, right down to the curly hair. I reach over to shake Joyce's hand, but Teresa wraps her back up in a hug.

"Enough hugging already. Joyce, let go of your daughter. You can hug her some more back at the hotel, but right now I bet these two hikers are hungry. Any takers for dinner?" Paul says.

Now, that's a silly question. We pile into the car and drive towards Allentown, a city of 100,000 people about forty miles away. On the way to town, Teresa and her mom talk non-stop, leaving Rufus and me to sit back in silence. We find a small diner and head in.

"Well, tell me about yourself," Paul says to me while we look at our menus. He's eyeing my bushy beard and shaved head, probably hoping that his daughter isn't hiking with a hippie or a lunatic.

"Okay, Mr. Bufano—"

"Come now. None of that Mr. stuff. Call me Paul."

"Okay, Paul," I say, and I tell him about my degree in pre-law and my tour in the Marine Corps to prove I'm not a bum.

"Any plans for after the trail?" he asks.

"To find a job. I'll probably head back to Spokane and stay with my parents for a couple of months until I land something, most likely in law enforcement."

Paul digests that for a second then reaches over the table, extending his hand, which I shake. "Good to have you along, Kevin," he says. "Lunch is on me. Order whatever you want." I must have passed the interview.

After a gargantuan meal we head to the hotel — a real hotel with a pool, towels and clean sheets. A few people turn to stare at us as we walk through the lobby. Along the trail most people don't give us a second look when we walk into a restaurant or hotel, carrying a huge backpack and wearing ratty clothes with a week's worth of stench and grime attached. Away from the trail it's different.

"Mommy, look at those people. They're dirty and stinky," a child says as we pass by.

"Don't point, it's not polite. Homeless people don't always have a chance to shower and wash their clothes," the mom says. An elderly couple isn't so kind, though.

"Look at those bums and that poor, starving dog," says an old man, purposely loud enough for us to hear. "They should be ashamed of themselves, probably taking advantage of those nice older folk."

"Shhhh, Joe," says the elderly wife. "Don't make them mad. I've heard that the vagrant kids now-a-days are dangerous."

Teresa and I chuckle at the comments as we pass. Soon we will be clean and "respectable." Joyce and Paul treat us spectacularly, paying for our room and meals and refusing to take any money from me, for which I'm relieved because I don't have a whole lot to spare. We spend the days swimming in the heated hotel pool and eating. Lots of eating. Rufus spends two whole days sleeping. Our days off quickly come to an end, though, as Joyce and Paul have to drive back to New York and return to the mundane working world. They take us back to the shelter, where Joyce and Teresa engage in multiple rounds of hugging and crying. Paul eventually breaks up the two, ushering Joyce to the car while I lead Teresa back to the shelter. We watch them drive away, two streams of tears rolling down Teresa's face.

"I really miss my mom. It was so good to see her again," she says, burying her head into my shoulder. I enjoyed meeting her parents, and it gave Teresa the emotional support she needed to continue. For the longest time Teresa has been telling me how close she and her mom are. At almost every town Teresa calls home, and her mom sends cards and other spiritual uplifts to keep Teresa motivated. After these last few days I am beginning to understand their relationship. They are both mother and daughter and very close friends.

As we spend the night at the shelter (it's too late to hike out), a thunderstorm hits. It has been weeks since the last rain and this storm will help refill the streams and springs. Refreshed from two days off, and rejuvenated by the cool air, we continue north on the Pennsylvania rocks to Eagle's Nest Shelter, where we meet Preacher and Squirrel.

Preacher is a Southern Methodist preacher whom I have seen on and off since Georgia but never really had the chance to talk to. Though he leaves inspirational Bible quotes in the shelter registers, he doesn't preach on the trail or try to convert anyone. Squirrel is a short, skinny man in his mid–50s with a long red beard and scraggly hair. He has the look of a hardened alcoholic fighter, and the profile that all mothers warn their kids about. His looks don't match his personality, though, as Squirrel is simply a man nearing retirement and taking a break from ordinary life.

Traveling with them is Bear Bait, a bouncy, jovial eighteen-year-old girl from Texas, with a cute face framed by large round glasses and long, straight hair. Bear Bait looks like she should be at a senior prom, not out here in the woods. Turns out she did just graduate from high school. Wanting some adventure before starting college, she decided to hike the trail.

Naïve about the trail and having never camped before, she was under the impression she could make it to Maine in three months. She started hiking in Georgia well after the hiker season had passed and found herself alone most of the time. Two lonely weeks after starting out she hitchhiked to Harpers Ferry, and within a couple of days she met up with Squirrel and Preacher, who took her under their wings and taught her about trail life. Squirrel and Preacher tease her about being so young and out here on her own, but she knows how to deal with them.

"Hey, Bear Bait, why don't you go run that pretty face into town and get us a couple of beers?" Squirrel says as he climbs into his sleeping bag.

"Hey, Squirrel, why don't you go to sleep before I shove my hiking stick where you don't want it?" she responds. Yup, she manages just fine.

It's easy to figure out how Preacher and Squirrel received their names. Bear Bait is a bit unique, though, so I prod her for her story.

"It's kind of embarrassing and I didn't know any better when I chased that bear out of camp...," she starts to explain.

"Wait a minute, you chased a bear out of camp? Start from the beginning," I interrupt.

"Quit putting on a show and tell your story," Preacher chides, so Bear Bait starts over.

"Well, it was my first night on the trail and I was sharing Springer Mountain Shelter with a couple of weekend hikers. I put my pack outside and went to sleep. A few hours later a bunch of noise woke us all up, and I saw this big, brown animal running off with my pack in its mouth. I'd never seen a bear before, heck, I'm from Houston. I thought they're like big dogs so I grabbed my pocket knife and took off running after it, yelling for it to drop my pack. The bear stopped and looked at me. Man, it was huge, but so are my Rottweilers in Texas and I'm not afraid of them, so I yelled at the bear to drop it and waved my knife at it. The bear dropped my pack, pulled out my food bag and walked away with it. I picked up my pack and walked back to the shelter. It didn't do too much damage to my pack except he took most of my food."

Dumbfounded, I stare at Bear Bait with a gaping mouth.

"You chased a bear and brandished a pocket knife at it because you thought it was like a big dog?"

"He had my backpack. I didn't have a choice because if he took my pack, I would have had to go home. I carried my pack back to the shelter and the two guys there were like, 'Ooh, that was so cool.' They gave me some of their food so it was okay. Bear wasn't so tough. In fact, it looked a lot like Rufus, only much bigger."

"That's our Bear Bait!" Squirrel says. "Naïve as the day God made her."

The next day, July 4 and three months on the trail, we all walk in silence. The Fourth of July is a time for family barbecues, and every one of us is thinking about home. Squirrel should be home with his wife, Bear Bait with her brothers and parents, and Teresa with her mom. While I have a loving family as well, I have spent the last four years away from them and have spent the last two July Fourths standing duty in the Corps. Before the Marine Corps, though, I spent the holiday with my family. We would barbecue all day long, then drive to Riverfront

July 5, 2001. Rufus taking a break halfway through Pennsylvania.

Park in downtown Spokane to watch the fireworks. There won't be any fireworks tonight and our families are hundreds, if not thousands, of miles away. We are each other's family now.

Together, we stop at Eckville Shelter to take a break. Like the 501 Shelter, this one is next to a road and is owned and maintained by the Blue Mountain Eagle Climbing Club. The shelter itself is a remodeled garage, and next to it is the caretaker's house. The caretaker is currently out in the front yard, attaching a propane tank to a barbecue. He sees us approach and calls out.

"All right! I was hoping to get some hikers today. Happy Fourth of July! Come on over and eat!"

He has hot dogs, burgers, chips, watermelon, beer, soda, and tons of ice cream. The fridge containing the food has a price guide on the door and a metal pay box inside, but the caretaker tells us everything is free today and to eat what we want. I am forever grateful for people like this who, for nothing more than love of the trail, open their houses and hearts to complete strangers. He invites us to stay the night at the shelter, but as we just took two days off, Teresa and I hike another handful of miles, accompanied by Preacher and gang.

The morning brings a cold rain, and the general consensus is to push 18 miles to the "jail" in Palmerton, Pennsylvania. The "jail" is the basement of city hall, which is open to hikers. Teresa and I get a late start out of camp and we tell Preacher, Squirrel and Bear Bait to head out without us. Teresa and I hike together in the foggy drizzle for hours, but by early afternoon the clouds lift and reveal miles of Pennsylvania farm land stretching out below our ridge. For the last several weeks the humidity has created a dense haze that reduced visibility to a few miles, but now we can see as far as our eyes will take us. Though we are not on a high ridge, our location — maybe 1000 feet above the surrounding lands—gives us a majestic throne to survey the countryside, dotted with houses and farm buildings.

"Kevin! Snake!" Teresa cries out in front of me as we walk along the ridge. I immediately stop and look at my feet. I see two big brown shoes and a pair of dirty hiker legs.

"Not by you! In front of me on the trail. I think it's a copperhead," she says, watching me stare in wonder at my own feet.

I walk up to her, and sure enough, a fat copperhead snake is coiled in the middle of the trail, either fast asleep or just pretending to be sleeping in an attempt to lure us into its trap. Luckily, I'm too smart to fall for that old trick. We do seem to be in a dilemma, though, as the trail is surrounded by waist-high thorn bushes and the snake doesn't appear to have any plans of moving.

"Hey, snake. Yeah, you, I'm talking to you. Move!" I yell.

No luck, but the snake does lift its head and stick its tongue out at me. I knew it wasn't really sleeping. In an effort to get the snake to move, I pick up several small rocks and toss them at the snake. Two pebbles bounce in front of him and one smacks him right in the head. The snake isn't even fazed; he just continues to look at me with his beady little eyes. It must be a Rufus snake. I pick up a ten-pound boulder and take aim.

"What are you doing? You can't hurt it, it's not hurting anything," Teresa says, grabbing my arm. "I won't let you hurt the snake."

The snake won't move after being hit with small rocks, and I can't crush it with a big rock, so now I have no choice. Walking very slowly, I approach the snake, holding both my hiking poles out in front of me. I poke the snake several times, but he fails to get the hint and keeps staring at me. Using both sticks like giant salad tongs, I try to pick up the snake like I have seen on the Discovery Channel. And like I've seen on the Idiots Messing with Poisonous Snakes Channel, the snake slips out of my chopstick grasp, lunging at me in midair with his mouth agape and steaming venom dripping off his fangs. Okay, I may have imagined the venom, and it might even be possible that the snake simply fell, but anyway the snake hits the ground, slithers several feet closer to me and recoils its body, still in the middle of the trail. Admitting defeat, we resort to taking the detour through the thorn bushes.

I go first through the bushes to stomp them down so Rufus can get through, and the sharp thorns extract a fair amount of blood from my legs. It would have been easier to stone the snake, but oh well. We cut back to the trail after twenty yards of walking through the thorn bushes, and five minutes later we come to a small, level clearing overlooking the valley. The clouds have passed and the sun is just beginning to set, bouncing hues of pink, red and orange across the sky. I can make out the headlights of cars as the unknown drivers head home after a day of work.

"Oh, let's stay here, Kevin. This is beautiful, and so much better than sleeping in some basement tonight," Teresa says.

"What about the snake?"

"What about it? It's two hundred yards behind us, and you're the one who wanted to kill it, not the other way around. Let's stay here, what do you say?"

"Sound good to me. I really didn't want to sleep in a basement either."

It's nights like this that make the all the rain, heat, and misery worth the trip. Most nights we are in the forest, unable to see anything except endless trees, but tonight we lay Rufus' blanket out on the ground and sit silently, watching the brilliant color display as the setting sun shares its magic.

7

Tribulations of New York–New Jersey

Teresa and I wake to a brilliant sun that washes the dew-covered grass in sparkling light. After taking in the morning warmth, we cover a quick 2.6 miles to the road that leads to the town of Palmerton in one direction and the town of Slatington in the other. Teresa shipped a mail drop to a hotel called Fine Lodging in Slatington, so that's where we are headed.

"This should be quick. I'll pick up my box, we'll grab some breakfast, and we'll be back out on the trail by noon," she says as we watch car after car drive by on the highway.

Half an hour later we are still watching cars drive by, so we give up the idea of hitching and walk the two miles into town and find the Fine Lodging hotel. Once a fancy place, built in the 1850s during Pennsylvania's coal boom, the hotel now appears to be more of a run-down boarding house than any type of public lodging. Paint is peeling off the exterior, half the windows have blankets or sheets hung instead of blinds, and the cracked concrete front porch does nothing to enhance the structure.

Posted on the front door is a handwritten sign in black marker: "Appointments by reservation only. No walk-ins allowed." Right under that is another sign reading, "Hikers always welcome." Under that is another sign stating, "I won't be in until noon today," and signed by Mr. Fine, the owner. So much for getting in and out.

With nothing else to do we look for a place to eat and stumble upon the Slatington Diner, which has the lowest prices for a home-cooked breakfast anywhere on the trail. A stack of pancakes costs $2.00 and a three-egg omelet with hash browns runs a whopping $3.00. We eat our breakfast and sip our coffee until noon, then return to the hotel, but Mr. Fine isn't here yet. We do meet one of the tenants coming out of the building, a gaunt, sunken-eyed man with a deep tan and a slight case of paranoia.

"You guys waiting for Mr. Fine?" he asks, shifting from foot to foot and speaking incredibly fast. "I hope you have your application ready. He doesn't take just anyone you know, good man is Mr. Fine."

"We're hiking the trail and have a package to pick up. You know when he's supposed to be back?" Teresa asks.

"Hikers, huh? Yup, some of you guys have been through already, he likes you guys I guess. Don't know when he'll be back, he's usually here, unless he has something else to do. Should be back soon, I guess," he says, his eyes darting around as if someone were sneaking up on him. "I can't be seen talking to you for this long. I have to get to work."

The man walks down the street, looking behind every corner and garbage can before passing it. Soon he is out of sight.

"Well, Kevin. Now what?" Teresa asks.

"We wait some more, unless you want to skip your package and keep walking. Do you have anything in it you need?"

"Yes, I have a book I want and some fresh socks and a new shirt. The book and socks I could do without, but the shirt cost me forty dollars, and I don't want to leave it."

"Then we wait. He can't take too long, come have a seat with me," I say, motioning over to where Rufus is lying in the sun. Most women I have dated would be upset by now, blaming Mr. Fine, Rufus or me for having to sit here and wait. Teresa takes it all in stride and isn't upset at all. I like how flexible Teresa is, how she is able to cope with something when it doesn't go according to plan. She doesn't get upset or mad; she simply accepts it.

We end up exploring the town, drinking a few Yuenglings at a local bar, and checking back every thirty minutes until 4:00 P.M., when Mr. Ira Fine finally shows up. We have shot the whole day waiting.

We tell Mr. Fine about needing to pick up a package, and he quickly apologizes about running so late. He explains that most hikers don't show up until early evening so he didn't think anyone would be waiting. We follow him into a lobby that is painted mental institution beige. Half a dozen handwritten signs cover the walls, listing rules and explaining basic manners such as not urinating in the corners or spitting on your neighbor.

Mr. Fine hands us the box and again apologizes. To make up for his tardiness, Mr. Fine offers us a cheap room and will take us to a grocery store tonight and drop us off at the trail head in the morning. It is too late to get more than a couple of miles in tonight, and a warm bed and shower is hard to pass up. We agree to his offer, and Mr. Fine leads us to our room.

The room is old but very clean. Each floor shares a common bathroom, but the door locks so Teresa is able to shower in peace. Signs cover the bathroom, instructing residents not to throw garbage out the window or use electric appliances while showering. One note even explains how to flush the toilet: "Pull silver handle."

After our showers Mr. Fine runs us to the grocery store. I buy a paper and check the weather report. Yesterday's rain looks like the last rain we'll see for a while, as the temperatures are supposed to soar again.

July 6, 2001. 1233 from Springer, 934 to Katahdin. Teresa and Rufus on a Pennsylvania ridge, a day out from Slatington, Pennsylvania.

Wanting an early start before it gets too hot, Teresa and I are up with the sun, and Mr. Fine drops us off at the trail head at the base of Blue Mountain. The trail ascends a barren, rocky ridge 1000 feet to the top of the mountain, and if we don't get to the top before the sun comes out strong, it will be a very hot climb as there isn't a single tree or bush to provide shade. A hundred years ago Blue Mountain was like any other Pennsylvania mountain, covered in forest and home to numerous animals. Then in 1889 the New Jersey Zinc Company arrived and built a zinc smelting factory at its base. Over the next 82 years the factory pumped 300,000 tons of zinc, lead, copper, and arsenic into the air, killing the mountain.

Two thousand acres of forest were annihilated; the trees died where they stood, plants withered away, and the animals fled. The lack of vegetation allowed the rain to wash away the topsoil, leaving nothing but dead trees and exposed rock. The trees couldn't even rot because the toxins killed everything down to the bacteria, leaving the dead and weathered trees standing upright like petrified guardians.

In 1980 the EPA got involved, shut down the plant, and in 1986 declared Blue Mountain a Superfund Site, pumping in millions of dollars to restore the

7. Tribulations of New Year–New Jersey 133

forests. The topsoil is slowly being replaced with a mixture of municipal sludge and fly ash. (No, fly ash is not the remains of thousands of burnt flies. It is an ashy by-product from burning coal in coal power plants.) Thousands of seeds are combined with the mixture and spread out across the mountain, and it is working. Small pockets of saplings are fighting for survival and the undergrowth is slowly returning. Eighty percent of the mountain is still dead trees and rock, but someday it will be a forest again.

The heat comes on full force as we climb the bare, rocky summit. We pass dead tree after dead tree and come upon a spring seeping a rust-colored sludge. We continue walking across the lifeless mountain, and slowly the forest reasserts itself. Within three miles we are again surrounded by trees and under the canopy of shade. Teresa and I follow the forested ridge for several days until we run into Bear Bait hiking alone. Squirrel and Preacher are nowhere to be seen.

"What happened to your guardians?" I ask.

"I left them. I only have a month left and I want to reach New Hampshire. They're good guys, just slow and poky, and they stop at every place that offers a beer," Bear Bait says, and the three of us hike together to Kirk Ridge Shelter.

Two people have already set up residence in the shelter, and they are definitely not thru-hikers. I drop my pack and take stock of our bedfellows. One man, who introduces himself as Dan, is wearing blue jeans and cutting up a block of cheese with a gigantic hunting knife usually used to hunt elephants. His brother, with the trail name of White Indian, is forty pounds overweight and has half the shelter floor covered in clothes, food, cooking gear, and other junk. Both men have greasy black shoulder length hair and look like they haven't had a shower in two weeks or a job in a year.

"Hey, guys, think you can make a little room for three more?" I ask. The shelter sleeps nine, but the two of them are taking up the entire floor.

"Oh yeah, man, we can do that. Hey, White, grab your stuff and scoot over to this side. Plenty of room to stay," Dan says, patting the floor next to him while looking at Bear Bait.

"Um, Fruit Pie, I don't think I'm going to stay here with these guys," Bear Bait whispers to me. "I don't like them, they give me the creeps. I'm going to continue on to Delaware Water Gap."

I don't blame her. I don't like them either and have a feeling that something is not quite right here, but I don't know what it is. However, I still have Marine blood flowing through me and I'm not going to be scared off by two bums, so I lay out my sleeping bag. Teresa sets up hers between the wall and me, as far away from Dan and White Indian as she can get.

"So, where are you two heading?" I ask.

"Nowhere in particular. We're Native Americans and we received a huge tax credit so we came out to hike for a while. Just spent the last ten days hiking south through New York and New Jersey. We have a month left so we're going to keep hiking south and see where we get to," Dan answers very quickly.

Teresa nudges me a couple of times, and I know what she is thinking. These two are about as Native American as Rufus is cat.

"Then you guys just came from Jersey and Delaware Water Gap?" I ask.

"Left there this morning. It's one long-ass hike. Man, it was tough. You'll be going downhill, though, so it shouldn't be too tough for you," says White Indian.

Something doesn't add up here. One hundred and sixty miles of trail run through New York and New Jersey, and these guys say they hiked it in ten days. Sixteen miles a day for ten days, but today, according to White Indian, it took them all day to cover a mere 6.6 miles up a 1,200-foot climb.

"It wasn't so tough today, man. We took our time to take some pictures and stuff," Dan quickly says, as if to cover his brother's mistake. "So, you guys know about the Jersey rules?"

I have heard rumors that New Jersey has strict rules on camping, much like the national parks. I have also heard that rangers patrol the trail looking for violators and having a dog off leash is an automatic ticket. I don't know how much is truth, so maybe I can learn something from hiking guru Dan.

"No, I haven't heard. What's up with Jersey?"

"It's a rough place to hike, man. Rangers are all over the place enforcing the rules. We must have seen four or five rangers. I saw one ranger approach a dude who had a dog off leash. The ranger yelled at the dude, then took his dog. Just took the guy's dog. For no other reason than it being off leash. I heard they take 'em to the pound and the owner has a day to collect the dog, or else it's shot dead."

I express my disbelief, but Dan is adamant.

"No, I was right there and I swear that's what happened. I'm telling you to watch your dog, else they'll take it. Those rangers are mean. I saw a ranger write a hiker a $500 ticket for camping in the wrong spot, and another guy was arrested for having a campfire. Snatched right up out of the dark by two rangers. It was like watching a movie. Bet ya didn't know that. No campfires are allowed in New York or New Jersey."

"Real communist manifesto they have going up there, then," I reply. Dan cocks his head sideways and looks at me the same way Rufus does when I talk to him.

"Umm, okay." Dan then lowers his voice almost to a whisper. "Speaking of rangers, have you heard of any asking about us? Some of them are looking for us for no reason. They think we did something we didn't do," he says, glancing around and looking very nervous.

"Rangers asking about you? No, I haven't heard anything. Why, what do they think you did?" I ask, wondering if staying here tonight was such a good idea.

"They think we are thieves, man," White Indian says, his voice rising. "A few weeks ago at Eckville Shelter the owner accused us of stealing his money jar. We didn't steal crap. He's an asshole and blames us because we're Native American. Now we got the rangers looking for us."

"Yeah, we didn't steal anything! Do we look like thieves?" Dan shouts. He glances outside again and lowers his voice. "We may not be rich, but we don't steal. It was some other people that took it. I saw 'em take it but the dude wouldn't believe me, told us to get off his property and said he was calling the cops. What an asshole."

I have no doubt they stole the money. I don't believe a word they say as their story is full of holes. It doesn't make sense that two weeks ago they were at Eckville shelter fifty miles south of us, jumped up to New York, and are again hiking south towards Eckville. Why would they do that if the rangers are looking for them down there?

Dan continues to ramble about how bad they are treated because they are Native American. (Even though they are the whitest Native Americans I have ever seen.) After talking to himself for several hours he finally falls asleep. I'm glad they are heading south (or so they say). They are hiding from something, and when the time comes that whatever they are running from finally catches up to them, I'd rather not be around. Teresa and I rise early, quietly pack up, and are out of the shelter while Dan and White Indian snooze away. I'll be happy to get a few miles between them and us.

Six quick miles later we are at the Presbyterian Church of the Mountain hostel in Delaware Water Gap National Recreation Area. Delaware Water Gap, a small canyon carved by the Delaware River, is the Pennsylvania–New Jersey border. Our plan is to take a shower, hit the grocery store and get back out hiking, but once again the town vortex sucks us in. The hostel is like Kincora and The Place, offering all the amenities of home. It feels so good to take a hot shower, kick off my musty hiking shoes, and sink back onto a large comfy chair out of the heat. It'd be easy to give in and stay the night at every hostel along the way, but we'd never make it to Maine.

This time it's my turn to drag Teresa out of town after she lies down with Rufus on one of the beds. A mile from the hostel we cross the Delaware River and leave Pennsylvania behind. One more state done, and one state closer to Mt. Katahdin. Since we spent most of the day at the hostel, nightfall creeps upon us before we make it too far into Jersey. However, unlike the last time we hiked in the dark, this trail is void of any rocks or obstacles. It's a simple five-mile climb up and out of the gap until we find a place to camp.

The following day we follow the summit ridge, and contrary to the words of Dan and White Indian, New Jersey is one of the best sections of the trail. We don't see a single ranger, and camping spots are plentiful as long as we stay away from the roads. The rangers are mainly concerned about partygoers coming in on the weekend, starting fires, leaving mountains of beer bottles, and turning a small meadow into three acres of scorched earth. They patrol near the roads and rarely venture a mile into the woods, knowing that no self-respecting group of kids is going to lug a keg more than a couple hundred yards from their cars.

What makes Jersey incredible is the condition of the trail and the views. The trail is dirt and grass, unlike the rocks of Pennsylvania. It ascends from the gaps and follows the path of least resistance along the ridge line, hitting high points only if there is a view and going around puds and rocks instead of over them. And the views! I come from the West Coast, and my preconceived notion of New Jersey was millions of people swimming among syringes and puffing pollution. I thought I would be walking on miles of roads through the outskirts of towns, not on ridges overlooking miles of forested valleys and hills sparsely populated with houses and farms.

On our second day in Jersey we descend into Culver's Gap to Worthington's Bakery, the smell of fresh baked rolls, donuts, and bagels wafting through the air. In operation for the last 45 years, Worthington's Bakery has become a traditional stop for hikers to grab a sticky bun or bagel sandwich, and we indulge in both before heading up the other side of the gap.

The trail gently leads up to the summit of Culver Mountain topped with a giant fire tower that beckons us to climb it. The fire tower is no longer used to spot fires (satellites and aircraft do that now), but it is still maintained for the benefit of anyone who wishes to hike up from the gap. Teresa and I scramble up the ten flights of stairs to the top, but Rufus decides he likes solid ground better and waits at the bottom. Today, with blue skies and almost no humidity, we are able to see halfway across Jersey, and I don't see a city anywhere, only farms and forests.

After taking in the scenery, we walk a leisurely three miles to 1,600-foot Sunrise Mountain and are surprised to find the summit crowned with a huge pavilion, half a dozen picnic tables, and a paved road that leads to the top. Unlike the other mountains with roads to the top, this one is quiet on the summit; there isn't another soul up here. And once again we have a 360-degree view of New Jersey's forested ridges and valley. I never would have suspected a park like this would exist in Jersey. I expected that every square inch would be developed, but I am pleasantly wrong.

"Looks like a good place to stay to me," I say to Teresa.

"We can't camp here. Says no camping allowed. Look," Teresa says, pointing above my head to a white sign with bold red letters stating, "No Overnight Camping Allowed."

"So? Rufus isn't supposed to be off leash either," I reply. Rufus is sauntering around the pavilion, sniffing for the perfect place to relieve himself.

"What if someone comes up here?"

"Then we say 'sorry,' pack up, and walk down the trail a quarter mile and camp. Heck, it's a Wednesday. Who's going to come up after dark on a Wednes-

7. Tribulations of New Year–New Jersey

July 11, 2001. 1299 from Springer, 868 to Katahdin. Self-portrait with Teresa at the top of Culver Mountain fire tower, New Jersey.

day? Besides, we have a flat, covered spot to sleep and views of the sunset. You like sunsets, don't you?"

"Yes, I like sunsets," Teresa says, slowly giving in. "Okay, I'll stay, but if someone wakes us up in the middle of the night and tells us to leave, it's your fault."

I could live with that, so we sit down to cook. We don't lay out our sleeping pads or bags yet. We'll do that just before we crawl into them. That way if anyone comes up, it looks like we are just taking a dinner break.

After dinner I break out my Data Book to figure out how to meet my dad in New Hampshire. He needs to buy his plane ticket soon. So far, we have been averaging 12 miles a day, and it is 488 more miles to North Woodstock, New Hampshire. If we average 13 miles a day, we can get there on August 20. Teresa and I think it is doable, so I plan on calling dad in the next town, Vernon, 29 miles away. We can no longer afford getting stuck in towns, so we decide to hike 23 miles tomorrow. This will leave us an easy six-mile hike into Vernon the day after, which will leave us plenty of time to resupply and hike out.

After a night's sleep undisturbed by rangers or rowdies, we start out hiking strong, and by afternoon twelve miles lie behind us. Now, though, we are walking in the hottest part of the day and the miles catch up to us. The last four miles are on a road, our first road walking in New Jersey, and the hard pavement adds to the pain in my knees and feet. We are also out of water. The last couple streams have been dry and now the trail approaches a huge, mosquito-infested wetland with green and brown sludge floating across the top, daring any to drink it. I'm starting to worry as the guidebook says the well right before the shelter has been removed due to contamination. It looks like we might spend a very thirsty night. With no water to drink I lick my lips to keep them moist and walk along to the sludgy pond.

That's when the first mosquitoes find us. They tell their buddies dinner has arrived, and we are quickly swarmed by a black cloud of the buggers. A quick application of Jungle Juice, a military bug repellent made almost entirely of DEET, gives marginal relief, but the majority of bugs think it's salad dressing and move in for the feast. I kill four mosquitoes with a single slap to my leg, but the hundreds of others don't even notice. They fly into our mouths, eyes and ears, and I can feel their little needle noses stabbing into my skin.

I run and Teresa and Rufus follow, no longer caring about our painful knees or parched mouths. Our only desire is to get away from the little winged demons. Finally we reach the intersection where the trail leaves the road and heads back into the serenity of the forests, away from the mosquito breeding ground.

Even better than the forest is the sight of a huge white "water bull" sitting at the intersection. A water bull is a 400-gallon water tank on wheels with numerous spigots on it, and it is used by the military to supply troops with fresh water. This one has "New Jersey Forest Fire Service" painted on the side. It is here to replace the contaminated well. I love New Jersey!

We stop and fill our water bottles. Unfortunately, the mosquitoes take full advantage of our inactivity and attack with a vengeance, carrying away our blood in jars, canteens, and paper cups. As soon as our water bottles are full we tear up the trail, and within half a mile the mosquitoes have dwindled down to just a manageable handful that we slap to death. A mile into the woods we reach the shelter, devoid of the bloodsuckers, and I'm asleep in minutes after hiking 23 miles today.

It's a sore, slow walk to New Jersey Road 94, but we are thankful that at the road is Heaven Hill Farm, a huge bakery and fruit stand that caters to thousands of people who drive out from the New York suburbs for fresh fruit. After a week of noodles and bagels I'm ready for any type of fruit. I purchase a huge container of orange juice, several fresh donuts, an apple and a banana. Teresa and I sit down at one of the many picnic tables and begin eating. As usual, Rufus attracts attention.

"Mommy, look at that dog! He's so cute! And he has his own backpack!" yells a girl followed closely by her mom. The mom, in her late thirties, looks out of place out at the fruit stand, with her new leather purse, designer shoes, and fresh makeup. Her daughter, who looks to be about twelve, is also immaculately dressed. They should be at a power lunch in Manhattan, not out here in the country.

"Don't touch it, honey, you don't know where it's been or what germs it might be carrying," the mom says, grabbing her daughter's arm. Rufus stoically ignores the insult.

"Oh, you can pet him," I say. "He's clean and real friendly. We gave him a bath yesterday. Come on over and pet Rufus, he'd love it." She doesn't need to know that Rufus is afraid of water and hasn't had a bath in months.

The mom says no, but the girl throws a tantrum until her mom shrugs and gives in, a scene that has probably been played hundreds of times. They both walk over, and the girl gives Rufus a big hug.

"What are you guys doing that your dog needs a backpack? Taking a walk?" the woman asks, her manicured nails sparkling in the sun.

"You can say that. We're hiking the trail." This of course brings the standard question of "what trail," so we explain the Appalachian Trail. The mom's eyes open wider.

"You're hiking the whole thing? All at once? Where do you sleep?" she asks.

"We sleep in the woods in our tents. It's just like camping night after night."

"Oh, I'm familiar with camping, we go quite a bit," the mom says.

"Whatever, mom! We go camping like once every four years!" the girl snorts.

"No, I'm sure we go more than that," the mom says, giving her daughter a hard look as if to say, "Don't make me look like a fool in front of complete strangers I will never see again."

"So, do you have a TV?" the girl asks, avoiding her mother's stare.

"No TV. There's too much to see and do as it is, and there's nowhere to plug one in."

"Six months without a TV? I'd die!" the girl says.

"Six months of camping and no TV? What do you eat, a bunch of nuts?" the mom asks. This woman needs to get out more.

"Just nuts. I have stock in Planters, and I keep a couple almond bushes in my backpack—" I start to explain, but Teresa interrupts my fun.

"No, we eat normal food just like you. We cook it on a stove and even use silverware," Teresa says.

"Normal food? Where do you get that?" the mom says, watching me eat an apple.

"Same place you do, grocery stores. In fact, we're trying to get into Vernon right now. It's a couple miles down the road and we'll have to hitch in," I say, hoping she'll get the hint and offer us a ride.

"You hitch hike too? Isn't that dangerous? What if you get picked up by a crazy person?"

"Well, most people are like you. Good, honest people willing to give us a lift into town," Teresa answers meaningfully.

"I don't think I could ever hitch hike. Too dangerous," she says.

"It's not dangerous at all. We come into places like this and find a nice person who might want to help a couple of hikers get into town. In fact, we're ready to start hitching now," I say.

"Good luck with your trip, and finding a ride," she says. She takes her daughter's hand and they climb into a Mercedes SUV, driving off in the direction we need to go. I'm not sure if she is dense, ignorant, or afraid, but I feel sorry for her daughter, who is going to grow up with the idea that stopping at a country fruit stand is "roughing it." Luckily, ten minutes later an older gentleman in a pickup offers us a ride and we head off to Vernon. Vernon is a great hiker town because the major services are all located within blocks of each other. There is also a church hostel in town, but the plan is to avoid it.

"Remember the plan, Teresa. We get our stuff, eat, and head back out on the trail," I remind her, knowing our tendency to get stuck in towns.

I find a pay phone and call my dad to tell him the August 20 date; then we hit the grocery store. We buy a couple of sandwiches, a half gallon of ice

July 13, 2001. 1333 from Springer, 834 to Katahdin. Rufus getting a ride into Vernon, New Jersey.

cream and a two-liter bottle of root beer, and settle down in a park for our lunch and dessert. After finishing our second root beer float we relax in the sun. The heat is quite pleasant when I'm not walking uphill with a forty-pound pack strapped to me.

"Hey, Kevin, as long as we're just hanging around for a bit I want to go over to the hostel," Teresa says.

"I don't know. At hostels we end up staying the night, sometimes two. I think we should stay here for another hour, then hike out," I reply, not wanting to be sucked into another town.

"Please?" She looks at me with her huge brown eyes, and I cave.

The hostel is actually the basement of the St. Thomas Episcopal Church and has a fully furnished kitchen, washer and dryer, showers, Internet connection, and TV. There aren't any bunks, but instead hikers sleep on the carpeted floor, all for a five-dollar donation. No pets are allowed inside, so I tie Rufus out on the patio where he can see me through the sliding glass door. Homeless and Unemployed are here and packing up to head out. Homeless is looking great, as he has lost over fifty pounds since the Smokies. After chatting for a few minutes, Teresa and I let them finish packing and we check our e-mail.

"You ready to get going?" I ask after Teresa e-mails her mom.

"Just about. I want to take a shower first. Might as well take advantage of it while we're here. Won't be but a few minutes," Teresa says, heading towards the shower.

Forty-five minutes later she returns. I'm not happy.

"You ready to go now? It's starting to get late and I would really like to set up camp before it gets dark."

"I can't go yet, I haven't showered. It'll just take me a few minutes," she says.

I'm beside myself, not understanding how she could have left to take a shower forty-five minutes ago and somehow not managed it.

"What do you mean, you haven't showered? What have you been doing for the last hour?" I can feel my patience quickly slipping away.

"I was talking to Unemployed. She's so fun to talk to. Has it really been an hour? I'll go hurry up and we can leave."

"You know, babe, if you want to stay here just say so. I would like to hike out tonight but if you don't want to, just say so."

"No, I want to hike out tonight, really. I'll go hop in the shower and we'll be out of here before you know it." She walks away, this time (I hope) to actually step in the shower and get wet.

Thirty minutes later Teresa walks back into the room, towel wrapped around her wet hair. Now it is 6:30 and will be dark in two hours. I have a strong feeling we're not leaving Vernon tonight.

"Feel better? Now are you ready to leave?" I say.

"I'm clean!" she shouts in triumph. "It feels so good to be clean. You should go take one."

"No, we'll never get out of here if I do. I'm packed up, Rufus has eaten, and we're waiting on you. Throw the rest of your stuff in your pack and let's get going."

"You might as well go shower. I want to wash my clothes before we go. I can't stand having dirty clothes against a clean body." Teresa bends over her pack and pulls out the rest of her dirty clothes. My patience is gone.

"Why the hell didn't you wash your clothes when you first got here? They could have been washed and dried by the time you finished your stupid girl conversation with Unemployed and we could be out by now! The whole point of doing twenty-three miles was to be able to hike in and out of here the same day! If you wanted to stay, just say so and quit playing these stupid games!"

I walk outside to sit with Rufus. He doesn't play games, he just rolls over for a belly rub. By the time Teresa's clothes are clean it is too late to hike out, and we spend a hostile night at the hostel.

In the morning I apologize for yelling at her, and she apologizes for delaying until we had to stay. Happy again, we make breakfast as the beautiful day turns hot and humid, and before we realize it we waste away the afternoon watching movies and playing cards in the air-conditioned basement.

Thumper, Jiffy Pop and his sister, who is hiking a section of the trail with him, arrive around noon. Teresa and I decide, together, to take a zero day. The twenty-three mile hike of pain was accomplished for nothing. I don't mind it now because this is a great place to take a day off. Thumper, Jiffy Pop, his sister, Teresa and I all pool our money and make a fantastic spaghetti dinner accompanied with several bottles of wine. I'm glad we stayed. My joints welcome the day off, and I get to spend the evening with some great friends, enjoy life and have fun — the whole reason I'm hiking the trail.

The following day we finally escape Vernon and say goodbye to New Jersey and hello to New York, the border marked by a line painted on a rock. The trail in New York, while only a stone's throw from New Jersey, is noticeably different the minute we cross the line. While the trail in New Jersey followed ridges, avoided rock piles, and climbed hills only if there was a view, the trail builders in New York were evil. If there is a hill, the trail climbs it. If there is a rocky section, the trail finds it. If there is a view, the trail avoids it.

Several times the trail comes to a length of rocks requiring hand-over-hand scrambling to get up, then follows the hundred-foot-wide pile of ankle-twisting boulders before dropping back down to the forest, when it would have been just as feasible to walk around the rocks. At the third pile of stones Teresa and I do walk around, using a faint but clear trail that is very easy to follow. Why the trail has to go up every single hill and over every boulder in New York I will never understand.

Adding to the miserable trail is the miserable heat, constantly reaching the low nineties in the day and seventies at night. Even some of the springs have turned warm, making breakfast a barely palatable bowl of cereal mixed with warm powdered milk (I gave up oatmeal a long time ago). Shelters have become impossible to sleep in because of the swarms of bugs that have emerged. We eat and sleep in our tents, where the temperature is ten degrees warmer than the outside air. The mesh walls provide adequate protection, but the mosquitoes can still poke through if I sit too close to the walls. The mosquitoes are bad enough by themselves, but there are black flies to deal with as well. A black fly is a gnat on steroids and it packs a wallop of a bite, removing tiny chunks of flesh and sending the strongest hiker into a skin-slapping frenzy.

As much as I hate the trail in New York, it does have one good view. Standing on top of Mombasha High Point I am barely able to discern the Twin Towers of New York City among the thick haze. I look at the towers for several minutes and comment to Teresa how someday I would like to visit New York City. We descend Mombasha and walk within 34 miles of that city, the closest I have ever been to it. Teresa, coming from upstate New York, has been to the city many times and promises me that someday we will spend a week there.

Past Mombasha, after a long and hot 18-mile day, Rufus and I arrive first at Tiorati Circle, a huge developed picnic area and campground on Lake Tiorati. I find a picnic table in the shade and wait for Teresa, but an hour later she still hasn't arrived. She couldn't have been more than a mile or two behind me and should be here by now. Another hour passes and still no Teresa. My imagination goes wild with possibilities. What if she broke a leg somewhere? What if she was bitten by a rattlesnake and dying on the trail? What if, God forbid, some perverted scum found her, an attractive woman hiking alone, and did things I'm afraid to imagine?

After thirty more minutes of waiting I decide to go look for her, but before I can saddle up Rufus she comes half-walking, half-limping into the park. Her face is red, her hair drenched with sweat, and she moves with the speed and grace of an arthritic turtle. As soon as she reaches me she collapses on the ground in a pile of tears.

"I hate this! I just hate this! Every muscle hurts, I don't want to walk anymore, I want to go home."

I take her in my arms to comfort her the best I can, my own heart breaking to see my love in such a condition. After a ten-minute cry Teresa starts to recover.

"I can't believe how hard it was today, so hot and thirsty and tired. All I wanted to do was go home and if I would have come across a pay phone I would have called my folks to come get me. My head hurts, my feet hurt, my legs hurt. I hate this damn trail!" Teresa rants while I make dinner.

Teresa eats, but now we have to hike out because camping in the park is only allowed at the established campground, which charges twenty dollars just to sleep in a tent. That money would be much better spent on food. After I convince an exhausted Teresa that we should hike another half-mile, she gath-

July 20, 2001. The only flat section of trail in New York!

7. Tribulations of New Year–New Jersey

July 20, 2001. Time to head to Maine in Style.

ers the strength to put her pack back on and we walk twenty minutes until we are out of the park, where we set up our tents on the trail, too tired to look for a campsite.

After sleeping in and taking our time packing up, Teresa begins to feel better and no longer wants to get off the trail. Bad days happen to everyone, but they are much easier to get through when you have someone by your side. If she was alone she probably would have gotten off, but with Rufus and me for support she realizes that she wants to complete the trail and we keep walking north.

On our sixth hot and muggy day in New York, Teresa and I plan to head into the small town of Pawling to get groceries and a good meal. Around noon, several miles from the road leading to Pawling, we catch up to a hiker walking the same direction as us. She's a day hiker, which is obvious from her clean clothes, small day pack, and most noticeably, her smell. After months in the woods my senses are enhanced, and I can smell the perfume or cologne of people before I see them. Just as my body stench must be overpowering to her, her use of perfume is overpowering to me. We tell her we are headed to town, and she offers to give us a ride. We walk to her car, which is parked underneath an enormous oak tree. Our trail angel explains that this is the Dover Oak, over three hundred years old and the largest oak tree on the Appalachian Trail.

It is an enormous tree, very close to the Keffer Oak down in Virginia but not quite as tall or as big around, but I don't mention this. I don't want to harm our chances of a ride. I have no idea how the Dover Oak has survived for so long next to the road. The Keffer Oak is off the road and hidden from view, but this one is less than ten feet from traffic. Drunk drivers, bored kids, or an idiotic road maintenance crew should have destroyed it years ago, but I am glad they haven't. Something is protecting this tree.

Our trail angel takes a couple of pictures of Teresa and me in front of the tree; then we get into her car and head to town. She drops us off at the library, which is only a couple of blocks away from the grocery store and a good restaurant.

I call my dad from a pay phone in front of the library, and he says he has bought his plane ticket and found a bus that runs from Boston to North Woodstock. He is ready to go; now Teresa and I need to get to North Woodstock in time. I ask my mom to ship out the boots I sent home in Virginia, as the arches in my shoes have completely broken down and every step is painful. She tells me they will be in the mail tomorrow and soon I will have good arch support again. Until then, I settle for a ten-dollar arch support from the grocery store and hope it does the trick.

We waste the rest of the day reading in the library. Unlike Vernon, this town has no hostel to stay at, so we catch a ride back to the trail and walk three miles until it starts to get dark. Not finding anywhere to camp, we pitch our tents in a farmer's field, staying hidden as much as possible to avoid eviction. Early morning, even before farmers get moving, we leave the fields and the possibility of being run over by a tractor, and cross into Connecticut. After 117 days and 1,400 miles of hiking, I am in New England!

8

Hot and Hotter Still

When my older brother and I were in grade school our parents took us on a two-week vacation every summer. We saw the Redwood Forests, Glacier National Park, Yellowstone, the barren deserts of the Southwest, the green forests of the Northwest, and every state west of the Rockies. The Marine Corps took me to the East Coast, from Maryland down to Florida, and when I was transferred to California I drove cross-country across the northern and Great Plains states. The only part of the country I have never seen is New England. Now I am here, able to see for myself the northern Appalachians and, when fall comes, the breathtaking wash of colors as the leaves change from green to gold, red, yellow and orange. New England also means the end of cheap lodging and meals as tourism now dictates the costs, and because it is mid-July, we are in the middle of tourist season. However, lots of tourists also means lots of cafes and ice cream parlors, and we come across something every couple of days.

None of the stores in Pawling stocked Heet, the methanol fuel we use for our alcohol stove, and I don't want to use isopropyl alcohol because it is very sooty and doesn't burn as hot. Also, my bleach container, a Visine bottle I've used since Harpers Ferry, is starting to leak, and the bleach has already eaten through the bandanna wrapped around it. The town of Kent, Connecticut, is a few miles away, so I plan to go into town for fuel and a new bleach bottle. Teresa will keep hiking with Rufus and I'll meet up with them tonight at Silver Hill Campsite.

As soon as I reach the road leading to Kent I meet a young couple who are finishing up a morning run, and they ask me if I need a ride into town. Not wanting to walk a mile along the road under a sun hot enough to melt the pavement, I take them up on the offer. They drop me off at a drug store and within thirty minutes I have fuel and a new bleach container.

Kent is a very trendy and expensive place, and it is by no means a hiker town. Running through the middle of it is the Housatonic river, and the town is a popular tourist destination. The eateries are fancy; the "lunch special" at one restaurant is a lemon-glazed chicken breast sprinkled with rosemary, laid on long-grain wild rice, for the low price of $15.99. Sixteen bucks for lunch! I can buy a whole lot of peanut butter for sixteen dollars. One hotel offers a special "hiker's rate" at a discounted $95.00. I have a feeling they don't see many thru-hikers.

One good thing about Kent is that it has a great outfitter, Backcountry Outfitters, which quickly proves to be the best outfitter since Damascus. The store is well stocked with quality gear and only slightly inflated prices. A very knowledgeable salesman introduces himself and tells me to browse as long as I want in the air-conditioned store. Since my boots are in the mail I'm not going to buy new shoes, but I do decide to try out a new alcohol stove made by Trangea. It is a couple ounces heavier than my current stove but has a very solid base, unlike my current stove, which has a small wire potholder apparatus that tends to randomly fail, dumping boiling water towards whoever's closest to it. As I pay for my new stove, Teresa and Rufus walk into the store. Rufus wags his stubby tail when he sees me, and Teresa comes bouncing over.

"I thought I'd find you here! Get what we need?" she asks.

"What the heck are you doing here? " I ask, flabbergasted. "I thought I was meeting you this evening."

"I wasn't planning on coming in, but when I reached the road a guy with a cooler was handing out sodas to hikers and asking if anyone needed a ride into town. So here I am!" Getting a ride with a strange man who happens to be passing out free Cokes anywhere else in the country would be considered insane, but on the trail it's called luck. I'm glad to see her. We grab a quick lunch at an overpriced, but still affordable, fast food grill and start walking out of town.

"Hey, Teresa, want to take a shortcut?" I ask. "The map shows a road that follows the Housatonic River for five miles before connecting with the trail. The road along the river is completely flat, and we'll avoid climbing and descending the St. John Ledges, which the book says 'puts a hurting on the knees.' You up for it?"

"It sounds like fun, but are you sure we'll meet back up with the trail?" she asks, doubting my route-finding skills.

"Of course I am, trust me." The best skill I learned in the Marine Corps was how to use a map and compass. I have full confidence in my abilities, and soon Teresa will too.

As we walk along the river we pass the Kent School, a very expensive prep school, with its crew team practicing on the river.

"Look, Kevin! Crew! I forgot about this place. I used to row in college and came here every year to race. We would set up on the riverbank where those boats are and lie in the sun until it was our turn. I miss crew. That was a lot of fun. Hard work, but fun."

Crew is not a big sport on the West Coast and I know very little about it. "You used to row?" I ask, prompting her.

"Yes. We used to get up before the sun almost every day to practice. That was the best time because the water was so still. Anyway, we raced all over New England."

We walk along the river as Teresa tells me about her rowing days. The road proves to be flat just like the map showed, and we walk underneath a canopy of oak and elm trees blocking out the hot sun. Twice we stop for a swim in the clear and surprisingly warm river. The road passes beautiful houses, and the farther from town we get the smaller the houses become until they are just a scattering of forest cabins, all immaculately cared for. Teresa and I are able to walk side-by-side on the road, something we rarely are able to do on the trail, and it makes talking easier. While Teresa tells me about crew I also find out she used to be a gymnast, and in college she taught kid's gymnastics.

There is so much about her that I want to know, but the end of the trail is coming up soon. I don't know what we will do then, but for now we spend the day with an easy walk along the river like a couple of lovers out for an afternoon stroll.

After the last house the road passes through a rusty old gate. The pavement changes to hard-packed dirt and eventually we come across the A.T. We leave the road and follow the trail up a gentle climb to Silver Hill Campsite, which has a covered cooking area, privy, swing, and small deck overlooking the beautiful valley we ascended from. To top it all off, there is a hand-operated water pump that spouts ice cold, delicious water. I take a quick, body-numbing shower in the freezing water to wash away the day's sweat and grime. This nightly rinse, along with plenty of Gold Bond, is a very effective ritual to prevent chafing. Teresa doesn't do any more than wash her hands and face in the water, as she would rather have the skin rot off her body than take a cold shower.

Half an hour later Homeless, Unemployed, and a male hiker named Dig arrive.

"Fruit Pie, Phoenix!" yells Unemployed, hobbling over to give Teresa a hug. "It's good to see you again. How did you like those ledges?"

"We skipped the ledges. We went into Kent, then walked along the river to get here. Completely flat, and we swam twice!" Teresa says.

"Oh, god, that must have been nice. The ledges were so steep and slippery I fell twice, banging my knee real bad. It was miserable. I wish I could have walked along the river, but Dig would never go for it," she says, dropping her voice.

Dig is a forty-year-old guy taking a break from his construction business. He started out alone but now Homeless, Unemployed, and Dig have become a hiking team; Dig has someone to hike with and Homeless and Unemployed have someone new to talk to. Dig is a purist, with the goal of touching every foot of the trail, and he won't skip a section.

We spend the rest of the evening sitting on the porch and swinging on the two-person swing until the sun sets over the valley and bugs drive us into our tents, ending one of my best days on the trail.

Little did I know I would awake to my worst day on the trail. Rufus and I begin a long ascent to the top of a nameless peak as the temperature climbs and the bugs realize breakfast is coming to them. By noon it is in the low 90s and almost 100 percent humidity, making every step miserable. I don't do well in the heat, and Rufus does even worse. My only saving grace is my little radio. I like talk radio the best. Music tends to be background noise, but with talk radio I have to pay attention, taking my mind off the mundane task of walking, the burning heat, and the biting bugs. Today the trail follows a roller coaster path up and down ten steep hills, and that is wreaking havoc with the reception. The radio is clear near the summits, but as I drop down into the valleys the reception fades except for one lone country music station. I hate country! I can either listen to Hill Billy Bob singing about his 1975 truck and blind dog, or turn off the radio and listen to the threatening buzz of the mosquitoes, gnats, and blackflies.

The bugs are the worst they've been so far and are relentless in their attacks. I use liberal doses of Jungle Juice but it seems to lose its potency as I sweat buckets. I have received ten new bites since this morning and am constantly swatting bugs off Rufus' lips and eyes. The bugs work together: the gnats buzz my ears and eyes, distracting me, while the mosquitoes attack all exposed skin. As I climb the next pointless hill, listening to Coverall Boy singing about his ex-wife taking his prized hubcaps, the bugs coordinate an all-out assault. This time they change tactics. A swarm of mosquitoes attacks first, sending me into a well-rehearsed slap-dance. Once the mosquitoes are done with my veins, the gnats come in to cover their retreat, and a young kamikaze flies into my eye, temporary blinding me.

"God damn gnat! Get out of my eye. I said get hmmphf galgg hawwwth!" Another gnat, trying to save his brother, flies into my open mouth and lodges in my throat. Blind and choking, I try to cough up one insect and remove the other from my retina as I keep walking. To stop not only means surrender but would bring on hundreds more bugs. As much as they enjoy a moving target, they go into an absolute frenzy over a stationary one.

"Rufuth, leath the way," I try to say while attempting to cough up the bug. "Aaahhhhhhhhh!" My foot catches a root, sending me sprawling across the trail onto a handful of sharp rocks. Defeated, I sit down and throw Rufus' blanket over me to keep the bugs off while I regain my composure. Sitting underneath a fleece blanket in 90 degree heat doesn't provide much relief, and as soon as I dig the bug out of my eye and cough up the one in my throat I stand up and keep moving.

The heat, hills, and bugs wear Rufus and me down, and by early afternoon Rufus lies down in the shade of every tree we pass, waiting until I am out of sight before standing up and walking. He's panting very hard, his heart's pounding faster than mine, and his eyes are begging me not to continue. I want to cool him down but the streams have dried up, leaving me with one liter of water to share between the two of us until we can find a flowing creek or spring. At the dry creek beds Rufus stops and digs, knowing there is supposed to be water and confused because there isn't. As the day progresses, Rufus and I get into a rhythm of walking for forty-five minutes, then resting for thirty.

Finally, after taking nine hours to cover twelve miles, we reach Belter Campsite nestled among a grove of red pines where Teresa, Homeless, Unemployed, and Dig have already set up camp. The spring here, though small, is very cold. I dump bottle after bottle of water over my head, then do the same to Rufus. The bugs intensify as dusk sets, but Rufus and I are safe inside my tent.

The heat isn't going anywhere for a while. For two days we walk in the heat and at the Mountain Café, a small eatery along one of the many roads we cross each day, the paper says the highs are supposed to be in the mid–90s all week. Teresa and I take our time walking, stopping for a three-hour break in a hiker-friendly cemetery just outside Salisbury. (The tenants don't mind, they're dead.) We spread out Rufus' blanket, make Gatorade and pass the hottest part of the day reading the gravestones, many of which date back to the 1700s. After the heat of the day has passed, we walk to the shelter for the night.

I awake to my second worst day on the trail. It begins with a long, rocky climb to the 2000-foot summit of Bear Mountain, which is devoid of any shade-producing trees. A giant, one-hundred-year-old stone tower marks the summit, but I don't feel like climbing a pile of hot rocks so we descend off the mountain and into Sages Ravine, crossing the Massachusetts state line, our 51 miles of Connecticut behind us. Sages Ravine is an icicle delight compared to the heat of Bear Mountain, as the ravine is shaded by massive trees and cooled by an icy stream. The ravine is short, though, and soon the trees give way to burning rocks and blazing sun as we climb over the next mountain. The previous days' heat has beat me down and today I have no energy, stumbling over my own feet. I know Rufus feels the same way.

"Kevin, you look terrible!" Teresa says as I fall down again.

"I'm okay, just a little hot. The sun will set soon. Let's sit here until it does. That sounds good, doesn't it?" I say, my cognitive ability slowly ebbing away.

"It's only eleven in the morning. The sun's not going to set anytime soon. We'll just take a little break here, okay?" she says, forcing me to take a drink of water.

We sit, but without any shade the sun bores into me, and Rufus is clawing the rocks trying to escape its rays. I struggle to my feet within a few minutes of sitting down.

"I've got to keep moving, Teresa, I'm burning up sitting here. It's too hot to sit and too hot to move, and it's too damn hot to hike this stupid-ass trail." There's not a wisp of wind today, and at least when I am walking a little bit of air moves across my skin.

152   The Things You Find on the Appalachian Trail

July 25, 2001. 1482 from Springer, 685 to Katahdin. Bye bye Connecticut, hello Massachusetts.

"Okay, let's hike. We'll go slow, and once over this mountain a side trail leads half a mile down to a creek and some waterfalls. Come on, we'll head down there and take a long break. How's that sound?"

"Sure, I don't care. I just need to cool down," I state, putting my pack on upside down and walking a hundred feet before realizing my mistake.

After an hour of walking in the sun I have retreated into myself, trying to ignore the heat, my parched tongue, and my half-dead dog. It takes everything I have to keep placing one foot in front of the other, and that's all I am concentrating on.

"Come on, Kevin. Here it is, let's go down to the stream," Teresa says when we reach the turn-off.

"No, I'm walking and I don't want to stop. It's too hard to stop. Let's keep walking."

"Kevin, you are not making sense. You and Rufus are cooking. Come on, we're going down to the stream," she says, and takes my hand, making sure I follow her down the trail.

The trail quickly drops off the mountain and into a lush, cool forest with a stream flowing into several pools. Once I am out of the sun I am able to think a little more clearly. I strip down, grab Rufus, and plunge into one of the icy pools of water until my feet grow numb and lips turn blue.

After several hours of lounging by the stream and drinking the cold water, Rufus and I are refreshed and feeling good. I follow Teresa back up the mountain and towards the summit of 2,600-foot Mt. Everett. Hiking towards us is a group of very hot kids led by an overweight adult. The kids, who look to be about ten to twelve years old, are carrying small overnight packs and don't appear to be enjoying their trip. The adult sees us and comes over to me with an expectant look.

"Wow, sure is hot out here, isn't it? You know how long this heat is supposed to last?" he asks, sweat pouring off his brow.

"I don't know. I haven't been in town for several days. How long have you been out?" I ask.

"Just came from Jug End this morning," he says, referring to a road four miles to the north.

"What? You left town this morning, and you're asking me for the weather report? You didn't check before you left?"

"Um, no, I didn't look. We've had this trip planned for a long time, it's just harder and hotter than I thought it would be. Do you know where the next water source is? We're almost out. We're drinking more than I thought we would."

"Pull out your map and I'll show you," I say, already knowing his answer.

"Um, I didn't bring a map. I mean, why should I?" he says, his tone turning defensive. "We start at Jug End, follow the Appalachian Trail for two days, and get picked up in Salisbury. I don't need a map for that."

I drop my pack to pull out my map. If it were only him, I would leave him to his own stupidity, but I don't want to see eight kids suffering heat stroke because their guide is an idiot. I point out the next water source, the creek we just came from, and explain that it is also a great place to camp for the night.

"The creek is half a mile off the trail? That would add an extra mile to our trip today. I don't know if we can do that. There's got to be water somewhere else," he says, grabbing my map. "What about this stream right here? It crosses the trail!"

"Sir, that stream is ten miles east of here and that line isn't the A.T., it's a highway. We just came from the south and the only water is the creek I told you about," I say, taking back the map so he doesn't decide to follow another "trail" elsewhere.

"We can't go down there, we're on an agenda. We have to make it to Sages Ravine tonight to stay on schedule."

"Um, sir, that might not be possible. Look, it's 3:00 already and Sages is still six miles away. What time did you start out this morning?"

"Ten this morning. Why does that matter? We started a little late, but we can still make it." He starts to walk away, hollering at the kids to get up and start hiking. I reach out and grab his arm. So far he has shown an extreme lack of judgment, bringing these kids out here on a hike that is too much for them. Trying to push these kids six more miles in this heat is bordering on criminal. The kids are all sitting down with their packs off, drinking the last of their water, all of them wishing they were elsewhere.

"I know it's your trip," I say, "but face it. It took you five hours to walk four miles, you are almost out of water, and none of you are having any fun. If you try to push six more miles today, someone is going to get hurt. It's your job to take care of these kids. If I were you, I'd hike down to the falls; it's all down hill and should only take an hour. Spend the night, let the kids play in the water, then hike back this way and head home."

He says he'll think about it, takes one last look at my map, and herds his group down the trail. I don't know if he'll heed my advice, but I hope he does. Some people don't have the common sense it takes to walk in the woods. That's all it really takes.

Teresa and I continue on slowly to Jug End, where a break in the haze gives us incredible views of the Massachusetts valley 1,000 feet below us. We can barely make out the bulk of Mt. Greylock rising from the valley floor far out in front of us. Mt. Greylock is the highest point in Massachusetts, and of course the A.T. has to go over it. We drop down to the road and set up camp on the trail. I turn on my little radio and hear that the thermometer reached 98 degrees today, breaking the old record. No wonder it felt so hot.

As we head towards Great Barrington to resupply, the humidity finally builds up into a thunderstorm, drenching us with warm rain as we approach Massachusetts Highway 23. Wet and muddy, I stick out my thumb in an attempt at a mercy ride. Within 15 minutes a new tan Lexus pulls over and a white-haired lady rolls down the window, displaying the car's immaculate leather interior.

"Where are you heading in a storm like this?" she yells over the raindrops pummeling her car.

"We're hiking the Appalachian Trail and are trying to get to Great Barrington," I say.

"Really? Then jump on in. I'll give you a ride."

"You sure, ma'am? I have a dog and don't want to mess up your car."

"Your dog is the reason I stopped. That poor thing's getting soaked in the rain and it's breaking my heart, so jump on in and don't worry about the mess. It's only a car and I can clean it out later. Anything to get that cute dog out of the rain." I knew there was a reason why I brought Rufus.

She drops us off at a shopping center about half a mile from downtown in what we discover to be the rudest town on the trail. As soon as we enter the grocery store we receive a dozen stares from shoppers and employees alike. Several people turn up their noses and others give us the evil eye before walking away. I don't know if they think we are bums passing through, or if they just don't like hikers.

We get our groceries and proceed to the checkout line where we place our food on the counter. The clerk, who looks to be about thirty and wears her hair in a tight bun, stares at us for several minutes before very slowly scanning our items. She stares at us the whole time, as if expecting us to try to rob her. She doesn't even bag our groceries; instead they just stack up at the end of the conveyor belt.

After bagging our own groceries, we head back into the rain that has slowed to a steady drizzle. Our next stop is the laundromat across the parking lot. It has a large awning that extends out over the sidewalk, and I tie Rufus up under the awning so he can stay dry. Teresa and I walk into the empty establishment, but before I can pick out the type of soap I want to use, the laundry clerk comes over to us and says that I have to move Rufus as he is intimidating the customers. I look over at Rufus, who is curled up in a ball asleep. Just then, an elderly lady walks into the laundromat, passing within inches of Rufus, who doesn't even move.

"What a beautiful, friendly dog out there," the old lady says as she walks over to a washing machine. The laundry Nazi is not so easily defeated, though, and insists that I move Rufus.

Not wanting to make a scene, I untie Rufus and move him in front of the video store next door, which has a two-foot-wide awning running the length of the storefront. With nothing to tie Rufus to, I sit with him on the concrete sidewalk while Teresa starts the laundry. She joins me after our laundry is in a machine. As long as we stay huddled up against the store we can keep out of the rain and still watch our laundry. This lasts for twenty minutes before the video store Gestapo comes out.

"Hey, you can't be sitting in front of my store. Nobody wants to come in if they have to walk around you and all your stuff," she yells. I look across the barren parking lot and shake my head.

"Ma'am, all we're doing is waiting for our laundry to finish. We're not even close to your front door and are just trying to stay out of the rain," Teresa says, hoping to play on her feminine sympathies.

"I don't care. All I know is that you are keeping away customers," the mustached Gestapo lady says.

"But there's no one even here."

"That's because you've scared them all away!"

It's tough to argue with that logic. Not wanting to force the issue, we pick up our stuff and move over to the far side of the grocery store, where there are a couple of small tables, covered by battered umbrellas that let in as much rain as they keep out. As soon as our laundry is done we leave this miserable little town and return to the sanctuary of the woods.

This rainstorm breaks the unbearable heat and in the morning the temperature is in the mid–60s. It isn't even supposed to reach 80 today. Hiking is once again fun now that every step isn't a re-creation of Dante's Inferno. The bugs are still out in force, but it's also blueberry season. Blueberry bushes so tall I can't see over them are scattered through the forest, and every hour Teresa and I stop and stuff handful after handful of sweet blueberries into our mouths. Even Rufus enjoys a few. Wild strawberries also start to show themselves, but the dry summer has left them small and tasteless.

Other than the heat, Massachusetts really is a great place to hike, with easy trail, lots of blueberries, and an amazing amount of history. This whole area was once bustling farmlands in the 1700s, but the forests have long since reclaimed the land. We walk past forgotten two-hundred-year-old buildings that are slowly decaying in the woods. Low stone walls built when George Washington was president cut through the forests; once they mark personal boundaries, but now they mark only the passing of the years. The trail even passes right through an old Shaker community, home to several hundred Shakers in the mid–1800s. Now the only thing left is a meadow and the broken remains of old foundations.

The trail also passes many ponds, and when we come upon the fourth pond today Teresa stops and stares at the water.

"Check out all the frogs, Kevin! There must be thirty of them," she says, pointing towards the bank. None of the other ponds had any frogs, but here dozens of hand-sized amphibians are sunning themselves on the shore, and I suddenly have a great idea.

"Want to watch me catch a frog?" I say.

"Ha! That'd be funny, especially if you trip and fall in the pond," Teresa answers. Not quite the support I was looking for, but I give it a go anyways.

I try to sneak up on the frogs, but just when I think I have one, the slippery creature escapes into the security of the pond and then pops up a few feet away, croaking at my dismal failure. Bringing the fight to their turf, I take off my shoes and socks and wade after the frogs, but they simply swim around me.

After watching for several minutes, Teresa takes off her shoes and socks and wades into the muck right beside me.

I have never known a woman as easygoing and fun as Teresa. Most women I know would think that spending an hour chasing frogs is either childish or beneath them. Teresa thinks it's fun. She sees it as something different, an excuse to go splashing around in the pond instead of hiking. I am falling for this girl, and concerned about what the end of the trail will do to our relationship.

Finally tired of being outsmarted by frogs, we hop back on the trail and walk until we come to Pittsfield Road. We leave the trail and follow the road a mile to the famous "Cookie Lady's" house. The Cookie Lady's real name is Marilyn Wiley, and she lives on a large parcel of land next to a blueberry farm that is run by her husband, Roy.

There are other hikers here already, so Teresa and I sit down at the picnic table in her front lawn, and a few minutes later Marilyn comes out with a plate of fresh baked cookies. She tells us we can get water from her hose, and if we feel so inclined, we can set up our tents on her front yard and spend the night. She gives Rufus a quick pet and walks inside, leaving us to make ourselves at home in her expansive yard. Bear Bait, whom we haven't seen since Pennsyl-

July 28, 2001. 1535 from Springer, 632 to Katahdin. Snuggle time at the Cookie Lady's house.

vania, is here with Tabasco and Hemlock, two twenty-something hikers with matching bushy black beards. They look like brothers but two months ago didn't know each other. Like many hiking teams, they became good friends and are now inseparable.

A young, clean couple smelling of perfume and soap are also here, unloading coolers and chairs out of an old station wagon. The couple, Tom and Christy, hiked the trail last year. They met on the A.T. and are now engaged, another successful trail romance. This year they decided to return some of the trail magic they received and have spent the last two days looking for a spot to set up. The spots they drove to no longer have reliable water sources because of the heat, so they finally came to the Cookie Lady's house, bringing with them hot dogs, burgers, chips, more cookies, soda, fruit, salad, and anything else a starving hiker might want.

Originally planning to take a quick break here and keep hiking, Teresa and I decide to spend the night with our new friends. We eat until we are unable move, but barely make a dent in the food our two trail angels brought. They understand how much hikers eat and planned accordingly. They bought several hundred dollars worth of food to feed complete strangers, the only bond being they walked the same trail a year ago. In the morning Tom and Christy have dozens of doughnuts spread out on a table with gallons of orange juice, and are brewing coffee on their stove.

Roy, who talked with Teresa for about an hour last night, comes walking over to us from his barn with a couple of fresh eggs in his hands and gives them to Teresa. Teresa takes the still warm eggs and fries them up on our little stove. I don't know if it's my appetite or that the eggs are fresh, but they are the best tasting eggs I have ever had. When I finish the trail I may have to get myself a chicken or two. But for now, it's time to hike. Not wanting to overstay our welcome, we say goodbye.

The last twenty-mile stretch of the Massachusetts A.T. passes through three small towns and we come to Dalton, the first one. While walking down High Street we see a sign posted in front of a house: "Hikers welcome to get water from back." The extreme heat has returned and I'm low on water, so we walk around to the back of the house into a small fenced yard with a picnic table. After filling our water bottles we take a break at the table. The homeowner comes out, carrying several dishes.

"Thought you guys might like a little snack before heading out. Enjoy," he says, setting down an ice cream sundae, a brownie, and a large slice of honeydew melon in front of Teresa and me. It is delicious, and again I owe thanks to a complete stranger.

After finishing our food and saying thanks, Teresa, Rufus, and I continue our hike through town with the heat radiating off the pavement. We pass air-conditioned shops and cool swimming pools, but our only reprieve is to get back into the shade of the woods, and we reach Crystal Mountain Campsite right before sunset. A twenty-year-old male hiker named Shambala has set up camp along with Tabasco and Hemlock, and an hour later Bear Bait arrives, her huge pack replaced with a small day pack.

"Bear Bait, what's with the tiny pack? You got school tomorrow?" Hemlock asks.

"Ha, you're so funny," she says with a mocking laugh. "Actually, I do start school soon and I only have a week left on the trail. I want to get to New Hampshire before I go home, so I went to Wal-Mart and bought this little cute pack. All I have is the clothes I'm wearing, a blanket to sleep under, a little stove, and a week's worth of food. I hope I make it!"

New Hampshire is 160 miles away, so Bear Bait has to average twenty-three miles a day for a week to get there. It will be tough, but with such a light pack and the knowledge that she only has to hike hard for one week, it can be done. I hope she makes it and someday can return to hike the whole trail.

In the morning Shambala and I are the first ones out of camp, Teresa deciding to sleep in a bit.

"Shambala, where did your name come from?" I ask as we hike down the trail together.

"It really doesn't mean anything as far as I know. I just like the sound of it when yelled off a mountaintop. A couple of hikers heard me yelling it and the name stuck."

"SHAMBALA ALA ALA LA A," we yell for the rest of the day, feeling like Swiss yodelers.

We hike into the town of Cheshire and stop at the post office. My boots have arrived and I put them on, tossing my worn down, broken shoes into the garbage. The arch support I bought in New York helped, but it wasn't made for hundreds of miles and now is paper thin. I finally have some decent support again and hopefully my arches will stop aching.

Envious of Bear Bait's light load, I send home my multi-tool and compass. I have carried the four-ounce multi-tool this whole time and the only thing I have used is the knife. Teresa had two small folding knives that weigh less than an ounce each and she gave me one, so I don't need this heavy thing anymore. I have now sent home everything that I don't use on a daily basis, except for my tent. My pack before food weighs about twenty-five pounds, a far cry from the forty I started out with.

Shambala continues on while I wait for Teresa, and when she arrives we begin our way towards 3,491-foot Mt. Greylock. First though, we have a warmup climb over Saddle Ball Mountain, our first 3,000-foot mountain since Shenandoah Park. The mountains once again are tall and steep, and surprisingly, we are out of shape for them. We have been hiking almost every day for the last four months, but the relatively flat hiking from Harpers Ferry to here hasn't pushed our muscles the same way as these 3,000-foot climbs do.

We top out over Saddle Ball, drop down, then begin the long ascent up Mt. Greylock. Like Clingmans Dome in North Carolina, the summit of Massachusetts' highest peak is accessible to anyone with a vehicle. After several hours we reach the summit, a huge clear-cut meadow dotted with various service buildings and roads all surrounding a huge stone tower, built in tribute to the state's fallen war heroes. A large glass globe that lights up at night crowns the tower, and the light can be seen from miles away. Also on the summit is a large, rustic lodge for those brave souls who survived the elements in their car and wish to spend the night on the mountain.

According to the guidebook, the lodge is very hiker-friendly, employing past thru-hikers to work the summer months and offering showers for $1.50, including a towel. It has been thirteen days since our last shower and Teresa is ready.

"I get to take a shower. I get to take a shower," Teresa chants as we approach the lodge.

"Come on, babe, we can go a couple of more days without showering. Let's break our record of fourteen days," I say, instantly receiving a dirty look.

"No way! I want to be clean!"

"Two more days and we break our filth record! You don't want to be a quitter, do you?"

"If you want to remain nasty and smelly you go right ahead, but stay away from me. No more hugs or kisses or anything!"

Hmmm — I like hugs and kisses, so I follow Teresa to the lodge.

Next to the huge oak front door is a chalkboard with the weather forecast: very hot and humid for the next week. Written in chalk below the forecast is "A.T. hikers may get water from the park maintenance building." Sounds harmless, except for the fact that the maintenance building is a quarter mile back down the trail where we just came from. No way am I hiking backwards when I know there are perfectly good faucets inside the lodge. This place might not be as friendly as the book states.

I tie Rufus outside and we walk up to the check-in counter, staffed by a young woman in pigtails. We tell her we want a couple of showers, and with an awkward look, she tells us it will be five dollars each. She informs us the lodge is under new management and has raised the price for showers. Five bucks for a shower? That can buy me a burger and fries, something I could really use. I'm only going to get dirty again.

"You take one, Teresa, I'm not going to spend five bucks for fifty cents' worth of hot water. I'll meet you in the lobby — that is, if it doesn't cost anything to sit in a chair."

The clerk assures me that sitting in a chair is still free for hikers, but may not be by next summer. The new management doesn't like hikers and told the staff they would be fired for bending any rules for us. How nice.

I sit in the lobby with Smokey, another hiker who I have seen on and off and the only hiker I know who smokes cigarettes while hiking uphill. Half an hour later Teresa returns to the lobby, clean and smelling once again like a girl.

"It feels so good to be clean!" Teresa says, flinging her wet hair in my face. She sits beside me and whispers, "The showers are right up the stairs as part of the communal bathrooms. No special key or tokens or anyone watching them."

I suddenly have an urge to do a little exploring of this old, historic lodge and walk upstairs to look around. Passing the open rooms I notice that every bed has a towel laid out on it. Out of curiosity, I pick up a towel to see how it feels. Before I can lay it down, nature calls, so I carry the towel into the bathroom, where somehow I stumble naked into the shower and find warm water spraying all over me. I fight to get out but the shower door closes and my wet, soapy hands are too slick to open it. I resign to rinsing the soap off my body before I can even contemplate attempting an escape. Once downstairs, I tell Smokey and Teresa about my terrifying ordeal and Smokey decides to go upstairs to investigate. Fifteen minutes later he too returns with a story about the possessed shower that pulls a person in against their will.

Now that we are clean, Teresa and I walk over to the observation tower, only to find that it closed at 5:00 P.M. No 360-degree views for us, so we settle for walking around the summit perimeter. For almost an hour we watch paragliders jump off a launching point on the eastern edge of the summit. They set up their gear, and when the right draft hits, they run off the side of the mountain and soar into the air, sailing like an eagle. I can just imagine the adrenaline rush they must feel, the intense sense of absolute freedom from everything, including gravity, and I envy them. However, their trip lasts just a few hours while mine has lasted months, and I'm not done yet. Teresa, Rufus, and I leave the paragliders floating above the farmlands, and we set up camp off in the woods just below the summit.

In the morning Teresa and I leave the flanks of Mt. Greylock and walk into North Adams, our last town in Massachusetts. Between the heat and the increasingly steep and long climbs I need to start carrying more food. The trail has passed by dozens of towns, cafés, and bakeries through Connecticut and Massachusetts, so for the last month I haven't had to carry more than four days' food. That is about to end because the trail is going to be a bit more remote the rest of the way, and I am going to have to start carrying a week's worth of food again. With my metabolism, a week's worth of food weighs over twenty pounds.

We hit the grocery store to stock up before our last climb in Massachusetts. Then, loaded down with a heavy pack but lifted by Teresa's encouragement, I attack the mountain and climb out of Massachusetts and into Vermont. We take a break at the Massachusetts-Vermont border, marked by a small sign simply reading: "Southern Terminus, Long Trail." We have now hiked 1,577 miles through eleven states, and the trail wanders another 530 miles through three more states before ending on Mt. Katahdin.

9

The Greens and the Whites

For the next 105 miles the Long Trail and the A.T. follow the same path. The Long Trail is the country's first long distance trail, extending 270 miles through Vermont's Green Mountains from the southern border of Vermont all the way to Canada. The A.T. is once again steep and rugged, reminiscent of Georgia and North Carolina. It marches up the side of a forested mountain with no view, and drops down the other side before it immediately begins climbing the next one.

Though hard, the mountains are beautiful. The lower slopes are covered in oak, elm, alder, and other hardwoods. The hardwoods slowly give way to pine trees as I climb the mountains, and by 3,000 feet, the summits are almost exclusively conifer forests. The mountains, small in stature compared to the Rockies or the Sierra Nevadas, are still a challenge and are pocketed by microclimates that can change the temperature by twenty degrees over a mere 2,000-foot change of elevation. The trail has also become quite crowded with north bounders, south bounders, and Long Trail hikers. The south bounders started from Mt. Katahdin after black fly season ended in early June, and now our paths are crossing. They are a great source of information about what springs and streams are still running and the best places to eat, and we share the same information about the sections we have just come through.

On my second day in Vermont, Teresa and I startle a momma moose and her two babies, all gangly-legged and awkward. Rufus gives as much attention to the moose as he does to bears, deer, and ponies. The mom looks at us, though. She gives a snort to her two children, and all three of them go charging off the trail into the undergrowth, the young ones tripping over their own legs trying to get away.

The moose behind us and mountains in front of us, we keep hiking, crossing mountain after mountain to the summit of Stratton Mountain, the purported birthplace of the A.T. We have hit one of the microclimates and the summit is shrouded in a cold fog. For the first time in two months I put on my fleece jacket. Up until now it had been demoted to a pillow, but today I'm

August 2, 2001. Taking a break at Caughnawaga shelter, Vermont. Built in 1931.

glad I have it. As we drop down the other side to Stratton Pond Shelter the temperature returns to a comfortable 80 degrees and sunshine filters through the trees.

Stratton Pond is a simple campground with a brand new two-story shelter near the north end of the pond. A paved road ends at a parking lot a half-mile away, making the pond a very popular camping and picnicking destination. There are several dozen people here and it's not even noon yet. A new camping fee of $5.00 has been instituted at some of the more popular areas along the trail in Vermont, this being one of them, with the idea of controlling crowding. The fee is collected by a full-time caretaker during the peak summer months. As soon as we drop our packs at the shelter the caretaker approaches us.

"Hey, guys, you planning on spending the night? Five bucks a person, and if you want to stay the night I should collect your money now so you can claim your space," the caretaker says. He introduces himself as Eric and makes it clear he has hiked the Long Trail. He doesn't mention hiking the A.T., though.

"We're just taking a break before moving on," I say.

"Okay, but be aware that any camping within half a mile of the shelter requires the fee as well."

This was news to me. Someone had to build the shelters, so while I don't like the fee, I can sort of understand it. But no one built the woods. They should still be free, and I tell Eric that. He has a quick answer.

"It's because too many people come out here, and the fee's a way of keeping this place clean. In fact, this year a day-use fee of $2.00 has been instituted, and by the book, it applies to everyone, but I don't charge thru-hikers the day-use fee."

"Two dollars to take a ten-minute break next to a pond in the middle of the woods? And even if I didn't stop, it would cost me two bucks to hike through the woods? I have an idea. It may sound crazy, but how about closing the road farther back so people actually have to walk to get here?" As I am talking, an overweight woman eating an ice cream bar walks down from the parking lot, followed by her two kids each carrying a six-pack of soda.

"We can't do that, it wouldn't be fair. Not everyone can walk several miles and they wouldn't have a chance to come here," he says, surprised that I would even suggest such a thing.

"Gee, and wouldn't that solve the problem of overuse? For crying out loud, it's a pond out in the woods, not a city swimming pool. Let people hike two miles to get to it. Look around! Half of these people wouldn't be here if they had to walk two miles to get here."

Eric rolls his eyes and starts rambling on about discriminating against overweight and out-of-shape people, and I can see that no amount of arguing is going to change his mind. I don't understand the line of thinking used to create the fees. If a place in the middle of the woods is overcrowded, make it harder to get to. Problem solved. Instead the government has to use the only solution it knows: fees and taxes.

Homeless and Unemployed arrive while I'm discussing the fee with Eric. Unemployed is walking with an obvious limp.

Teresa goes over to her, and Unemployed, with a grimace of pain, walks up the stairs into the shelter and sits down. She explains how she stubbed her toe this morning, and again just before reaching the shelter. She pulls off her shoe and sock, revealing a very red and swollen toe with a hint of bruising forming around the nail. Homeless says that they can stay here tonight, and that brings Eric over.

"Camping here tonight? That'll be ten dollars for the two of you," he says to them.

"What? You're going to charge an injured hiker to spend the night here, even though she can't hike on today? How is this supposed to reduce impact on this area again?" I say.

"Sorry, everyone who stays has to pay. That's what my boss tells me, and I'm not about to give hikers special exceptions on the overnight fee. Heck, I'm already giving you guys a break on the day-use fee," he says with a smug look.

Frustrated at the absurdity of this, I pick up my pack and lead Rufus down the trail, leaving Teresa chit-chatting away with Unemployed. She'll catch up with me at the next shelter (a free one) tonight.

Two days and several pay sites later it's August 4. It's also Teresa's twenty-fourth birthday. It's tough to throw a proper party on the trail because there's no way to bake a cake, and presents would consist of a half-eaten candy bar and old packets of oatmeal scrounged from the bottom of a food bag. So instead of attempting a party, Teresa, Rufus and I reach Vermont State Road 11 and hitch into Manchester Center to spend the day.

Manchester Center is a tourist town with trendy eateries, an upscale outlet mall and several overpriced hotels, but it also has a post office, a laundromat, and a grocery store all within a few blocks of each other. The people are nice too, not as friendly as the small towns in the south but much more hospitable than Great Barrington. A nest full of pissed-off copperheads is more hospitable than Great Barrington.

I treat Teresa to breakfast, and we stop at the post office to pick up a package her mom sent her. We sit down on a bench in front of the post office and Teresa rips into her box.

"Look, my mom loves me!" Teresa says, pulling out a small teddy bear and birthday card.

"I have a present for you too. Happy birthday, Teresa." I give her a handmade card I have been carrying in my pack, watching her eyes light up as she opens it.

"Kevin, this is amazing! You drew — well, tried to draw — a picture of us hiking. Little stick figures with stick backpacks, and your rendition of a hiking stick is perfect. I love it. You had people sign it too! How did you get the Horsemen to sign it, and Preacher and Squirrel? We haven't seen them in weeks."

"I've been carrying it for a month. I've had people sign it in anticipation of your birthday. I hope you like it."

"I do, I love it! This is the most thoughtful gift I've ever received. Thank you!" Teresa wraps me up in her arms and gives me a huge hug. Her happiness is all the thanks I need.

We end up spending most of the day in the town. We wander over to Eastern Mountain Supply, a large chain outfitter and a favorite stopping point of many hikers. I want to replace my sandals, which have fallen apart. Sandals are one of the few luxury items most hikers carry. The ability to get out of hiking boots at the end of the day is a glorious feeling, not to mention good for the feet. The sandals will also come in handy in Maine where the trail fords through a dozen streams. As I weigh different models in my hands, looking for the lightest pair, Homeless and Unemployed walk into the store.

"I thought you guys might spend the day in town, and was hoping to find you here. Happy Birthday, Teresa!" Unemployed says, giving Teresa the mandatory girl hug. She's still limping.

"Thanks, MaryAnn. How's your toe?"

"Still hurts, but it's not as bad as it was. We're going to take a few days off here. I think it's just jammed and a couple of days off should be all I need, but I'm going to see a doctor tomorrow to make sure. I hope we'll catch up to you, so don't walk too fast."

We can only talk for a few minutes because it's late afternoon and we need to get going. I purchase my sandals and say goodbye to Homeless and Unemployed, and we walk to the edge of town to start hitching. A nasty looking thunderstorm is moving in and I think we've waited too long to get out of town. We stand for thirty minutes on the side of the road with our thumbs in the air. Hundreds of cars pass us by, but no one stops. It was so easy to get into town, but now we can't get out. Talk about a tourist trap.

The clouds take over the sky and lightning is visible in the distance. It's five miles to the trail, mostly uphill, and no one is stopping. As the storm positions itself overhead and the clouds threaten to drown us, a trail angel arrives, disguised as a middle-aged woman driving a rusted Honda.

The car pulls over and the woman rolls down her window. "You guys need a ride somewhere?" she asks.

"Yes ma'am, trying to get to the Appalachian Trail before the storm hits. The trailhead is five miles down the road," I say, looking up at the menacing clouds.

"The Appalachian Trail? I know where that's at, I drive by it almost every day. Jump on in and we'll be there in a jiffy."

Three minutes later the storm hits, sending down torrents of rain that make Niagara Falls look like a leaky faucet. As the car starts to pull away from the shoulder it dies. Unperturbed, our driver smacks the steering wheel several times and turns over the ignition. The car finally starts, only to die again at the next red light. She tells us she has a reliable car at home, and if we don't mind, she can drive us to her place to get her good car. It is still pouring outside, so we don't mind.

Half an hour later we reach the trailhead just as the rain lets up. We thank our angel several times and take advantage of the lull in the storm to get moving.

Ten minutes later the storm returns from its break, this time bringing gale-force winds with it. The trail has turned into a stream, but at least the thunder and lightning are over with, else Rufus would again be attempting to hide under fern leaves. The wind continues to increase as we hike up the mountain, and soon walls of stinging rain are attacking us. The wind is bending full-grown trees and we hear widow makers crashing to the ground.

An hour from the road we stumble upon Bromely Tenting Area, a primitive campsite that offers no protection from the storm. The only other person in the campsite is a poor soaked soul sitting on one of the elevated wooden tent platforms, huddling under a light tarp with his gear all around him. The tarp is flapping around in the wind and I can only imagine that he and everything he owns must be drenched.

Blinded by the horizontal rain and chilled by the cold wind, Teresa, Rufus and I take temporary refuge in the tiny privy at the tenting area. It's so small we are not able to close the door. The stench is nauseating from this over-used toilet but it is minimal shelter from the wind and rain. I am hoping the storm will pass, but after five minutes of gut-wrenching sewer smell in these cramped quarters I have had enough.

"Babe, we've got to do something. We can't hide in here all night."

"Yes we can. It's dry and warm in here, and I don't mind sleeping standing up," Teresa says, but I know she is as uncomfortable as I am.

"The smell is choking me," I reply. "Look, we have two choices. Either we set up our tents here, or keep hiking to the summit of Bromley Mountain. The book says there's a ski-patrol hut on top that's usually open to hikers."

"What if it's not open, or full? What then? I don't want to hike up there in the rain for nothing," she says, shivering now that we are not moving.

"Then we set up our tents up there. Either the hut's open and we get out of the rain, or it's not and we set up camp in the rain, same thing we'd have to do here. We have nothing to lose, so let's give it a try."

Teresa agrees, and I drag Rufus out of the privy. He doesn't mind the smell and has no desire to go back into the storm. It's a cold, wet hike, and several times branches the size of small trees come crashing down near us. Rufus jumps at every cracking sound, and I don't blame him. After an hour, though, the wind dies down, and three quarters of the way up the mountain the rain stops. By the time we reach the summit the storm is over. Breaks in the huge, billowy clouds grant access to the sun's setting rays, throwing a multitude of colors across the sky. I love the aftermath of a storm when the world looks fresh and new after a good cleaning, and the air resonates with a sense of tranquility.

The hut is open with plenty of room. It is occupied only by a couple of south bounders, a Long Trailer, and two older gentlemen out for a three-day hiking trip. They welcome us and make room so we can spread out our wet clothes to dry. We spend a very enjoyable night with the group while Teresa and I split a bottle of wine I carried up. Teresa's twenty-fourth birthday, one I'm sure she will never forget, comes to an end.

The heat returns, and the morning sun draws the moisture out of the ground, turning the trail into a sauna. My boots, though comfortable with great arch support, are not designed for this type of heat. Whenever the trail crosses a stream I take off my boots and socks to soak my feet. A painful heat rash is developing around my ankles and shins, and I want to keep it from becoming open and raw.

When we reach a small river at Clarendon Gorge I dip my feet into it, finding it surprisingly warm. The river, with deep swimming pools and small waterfalls, is a hundred yards from a highway and is a popular swimming hole. Grandmas wading up to their knees, families out for the day, and rambunctious teenagers starting the weekend all gather along the river. Even with the diverse mix of people it is a very friendly atmosphere.

After an hour of playing in the water my fingers and toes have pruned up, a sure sign it's time to go. I force an unwilling Rufus into the water to cool off before we hike across the highway and ditch our packs in the tall grass by the trail. I throw on my sandals and we walk half a mile down the road to the Whistle Stop Café, reportedly one of the best places to eat on the entire trail. The reports prove correct. For less than eight dollars I devour half a cow's worth of meatloaf, an acre of mashed potatoes, and a field of vegetables. Rufus also gets a slice of meatloaf, which he thoroughly enjoys.

Stuffed from the meal, Teresa and I begin the leisurely walk back to the trailhead, but halfway there it hits me: my bloated stomach pushing on my bowels.

"Um, Teresa, I've got to walk faster. I really need to take a crap." I say. After hiking 1,600 miles with someone, talking about bodily functions is as natural as talking about the weather.

"We're almost to the trail. Can you hold it until then?" she says. I really don't have a choice because we are walking along the shoulder of the busy road and my toilet paper is in my pack. Returning to the restaurant isn't an option; it is a farther walk back to it than to the trail.

"I can make it, we just need to walk faster." I pick up the pace but the pressure builds.

"Um, I don't think I'm going to make it," I say and break into a run, the bouncing not helping one bit, forcing me to run faster.

Teresa and Rufus run behind me as I make a mad dash to the trail, clenching my butt cheeks as tight as possible. Without a second to spare I grab my pack and turn it upside down, shaking out everything inside in an attempt to find the toilet paper as fast as possible. Once I find it, I look around for a place to go, but we are in a huge meadow without anything to hide behind. Unable to hold it any longer, I have no choice but to go where I stand. I hope the tall grass and weeds will shield my lower half from the road a hundred feet away. Armed with my toilet paper, I rip down my shorts and squat when a searing pain tears through my foot. I have interrupted a sunbathing yellow jacket, and he promptly flies between the arch of my foot and sandal, attacking vigorously.

"Ow! Get it out! Ouch, holy crap, that hurts! Get out, get out!" I shriek, dancing around on one foot with my shorts around my ankles, trying desperately to rip the sandal off my other foot. Teresa, unaware of what is going on, watches me dumbstruck.

"What the heck are you doing, Kevin? Everyone driving by can see you. Just relax and it will come out, no need to force it. We're in no hurry," she says, trying to coach me through taking a crap.

"I got stung by a bee, dammit! Oh shit, that hurts, and I still have to go! A bee stung me and I have to shit! This sucks!" I scream with my shorts around my ankles and my bare ass flashing whoever happens to be driving by. I finally get the sandal off, releasing the bee, who quickly flies out of reach. I look over to Teresa for comfort but she is rolling on the ground in an uncontrollable fit of laughter. Even Rufus is chuckling at me.

"Hahahaa! You got stung trying to go! That's so funny! You should have seen yourself jumping around naked! Hahahahaha! And I just thought you were constipated. This is so much funnier!" she screams, holding her sides.

"It's not funny! My foot hurts and I still have to go!" I yell back, now inspecting the ground for any more surprises.

Still laughing, Teresa walks over to me holding her sports bra.

"Here, wrap your foot in this. It's still wet and cold from swimming. It'll make your foot feel better. Haha, you got stung by a bee trying to take a dump! Wait till I tell everyone about this. Too funny!"

I wrap my foot in the bra and it does ease the pain a little. I squat down again, wet bra wrapped around my foot, and relieve myself.

The next day, with my foot and bowels back to normal, we follow the trail towards Sherburne Pass and the Inn at the Long Trail on Vermont Route 4. The inn is a huge bed and breakfast built in 1939 and was Vermont's first ski resort. It still caters to skiers in the winter and tourists in the summer, but it is fairly expensive so not a lot of hikers stay here. However, it's been over a month since we have slept in a bed, so I decide to splurge and get a room for the night. We stop for lunch under the shade of some oak trees, and I pull out my map to see how far away we are from the inn.

"Hmmm. Teresa, you mind blue-blazing a bit to get to the inn?" I ask her after studying my map for a few minutes.

"It depends. Is it faster?"

"Oh yeah, a lot faster. The trail used to pass right by the inn, but now a relocation has moved the trail almost half a mile west of it. I say we take the old A.T. and get there."

"If it's faster and shorter, I'm all for it."

At the beginning of the hike I was opposed to blue blazing, yellow blazing, or any sort of hiking other than passing every single white blaze. I quickly gave up that idea when I realized many of the blue blaze trails were once the A.T. This new relocation adds an extra mile to the trail, then half a mile on the road to get to the inn, while the old trail will take us directly to the inn. As long as I am hiking north towards Maine I see no difference how I get there, be it completely on the A.T. or by other trails that are more convenient or efficient.

By 6:00 P.M., following the very gentle old trail, we arrive at the inn and ask the clerk for a room. He tells me the room will cost $88, twice what it says in the guide book. I am shocked and ask why, and the clerk explains that because

August 7, 2001. Looking down towards Sherburne Pass from Killington Peak, Vermont.

of Rufus, I have to get one of the rooms with a private entrance. Dogs aren't allowed in the main portion of the inn, and the rooms with the private entrances are actually suites with fireplaces so they cost more. It's twice as much as I had budgeted, but one look at Teresa's disappointed face convinces me to splurge, and her smile returns.

The rooms are very nice and are part of an addition built onto the main lodge. I don't need the fireplace as it is blazing hot outside already. Better than the fireplace, though, is the fact that the room has air conditioning. It is well worth the $88 to get clean and spend a comfortable night out of the heat and humidity.

The inn also has a great Irish pub that offers incredible food and beer at very reasonable prices. I take Teresa to dinner in the pub, have a couple of pints, and sleep in a cool room on a very comfortable bed with Teresa in my arms and Rufus on the floor. I can't ask for a better life.

We check out at noon, then catch a bus into the town of Rutland to resupply, leaving Rufus tied up under a tree in front of the inn. I give him a big bowl of water and leave my backpack next to him so he knows I'll be coming back. Wearing my sandals to give my heat rash a chance to heal, I walk around with Teresa in town, where one sign puts the temperature at 95 and another says

9. The Greens and the Whites

August 8, 2001. 1676 from Springer, 491 to Katahdin. Sherburne Pass, Vermont. Home to a great Irish pub.

101. I grab a newspaper and the weather forecast calls for seven more days of upper 90 degree weather, not something I enjoy hiking in.

After visiting the library and a supermarket, we catch the last bus back out to the inn and find Tabasco, Hemlock and a female hiker sitting in the shade with Rufus.

"Phoenix and Fruit Pie! I saw Rufus and was wondering where you guys went. This is my girlfriend, Moss. She's out to hike with me for a while," Hemlock says.

"We went into town for the day. You two staying here?" I ask.

"Nah, it's too expensive. I did talk to the manager, though, and he said it was cool to set up our tents in the field across the street. That's where we are. No shower privileges, but oh well. Hey, we're heading into the pub for dinner and a couple of beers. Want to join us?" Hemlock asks.

Teresa and I hadn't planned on taking a zero day today and if we don't leave now we won't leave at all, but I have no problem not leaving. I don't feel like walking this late in the afternoon in 95-degree heat, and we have hiked an average of 15 miles a day for the last three weeks without a break. I'm all for taking a day off.

"So, Teresa, how bad do you want to hike out today?" I ask her.

"Me? I don't want to hike out at all today if we can stay in an air-conditioned pub and eat real food. I was worried that you would want to leave," she says.

"Well, Hemlock, count us in. We'll set up our tents, then meet you in the bar," I say.

Preacher comes hiking up the road as we set up our tents. I tell him about being able to sleep in the meadow for free, so he claims a spot and joins us in the pub for dinner. There are a couple of Long Trailers in the bar that weren't here last night, and one of them is the hiker we saw huddled under a tarp in the storm coming out of Manchester Center. He doesn't look healthy; his face and eyes are sunken and he looks anorexic. There is a weariness to his eyes that I have never seen before.

"You all right, man? You don't look too good," I say to the hiker.

"I'm done. I'm not in shape for these hills. I haven't eaten enough food, and I need to sleep for a week," he tells me as he slowly sips his beer.

"Sorry to hear that. How are you getting home?"

"I'm staying here tonight and my dad is picking me up tomorrow." Even his voice sounds tired.

"Want to join us for a couple beers?"

"No. Thanks for the offer, but I'm just too tired. I'm going to bed after this beer and not waking up until my dad is here."

He must be exhausted. To get here at the same time as us, he has to have been moving about 15 miles a day. It wasn't smart for him to start out doing 15-mile days in this heat over the steep Green Mountains. Quite a few Long Trailers exhaust themselves in the first couple of weeks. The problem is that they see northbound A.T. hikers covering 15 miles a day without much trouble and think they can do the same. We have 1700 miles of conditioning behind us. They never saw us during the first weeks on the A.T., sore, tired and moving slow. I hope he tries it again some other time, at a slower pace.

Preacher says that Othra is back on the trail after his bout with Giardia. He took almost a month off to recover, jumped ahead, and now is only a couple days behind us. I hope he catches up; it'll be good to see Othra again. We party it up, drinking Guinness and shooting darts. Even the bartender buys us a round. However, by 11:00 P.M. it is time for bed. Our bodies have adjusted to sleeping when it gets dark and waking when it is light, and not even hanging out in a bar with friends can overcome the weariness.

Just as the newspaper predicted, the scorching heat continues as we leave the inn, bringing Rufus and me to a crawl. Rufus is so hot he can't walk more than a hundred yards before needing a break, even when I carry his pack. My boots have become ghoulish footwear, making every step painful. The heat rash has progressed and is now oozing bloody pus. I need to get out of these boots. I walk in my sandals but the ground is too steep and my pack too heavy. After I twist my ankle for the third time I collapse on the ground defeated.

9. The Greens and the Whites

"Kevin, let's just hitchhike the rest of the miles we had planned to hike today. There's no reason to kill ourselves in the heat and Rufus can't walk another step," Teresa says. I don't have the energy or the heart to disagree. I don't want to skip portions of the trail, but right now I am in pain and Rufus is in danger of heat stroke if we keep moving. We need to meet my dad in ten days and have to cover the ground, but skipping ten miles or so today isn't going to hurt my feelings.

We walk another mile to a road and stick out our thumbs. Within twenty minutes a car pulls over with a man in his mid–50s driving.

"You thru-hikers? Where do you need to go?" he asks us.

"Actually, we're trying to get as close as we can to a certain shelter. We're skipping a portion of the trail because of the heat. I guess if you can give us a ride to Vermont Highway 12 we can walk the eight miles to the shelter," I answer, looking at my maps.

The man, lean for his age, gets out of his truck and walks over to us. On the map I point out Thistle Hill Shelter, which has a forest road passing within a couple miles of it.

"I'm Steve," he states, holding out his hand. "I hiked the trail 37 years ago and know about bad hiking days. Tell you what: I run a summer camp up the road and need to drop off some supplies to the kids there. If you want to wait here until I'm done, I'll come back and I'll get you as close as I can to that shelter. In the meantime, would you like a couple of apples?"

Once again, when we need it most, a trail angel arrives. It just seems to work that way on the trail, like someone is looking out for hikers. It may be coincidence, but it has happened enough times to us and other hikers to make me think there might be something more to it. I'm not a religious man, but after meeting this many trail angels, I may have to think about it again.

We wait, and Steve returns half an hour later. He breaks out his road maps, and after an hour of driving on dirt forest roads he drops us off two miles from the shelter, as close as we can get. He could have easily dropped us off on Vermont 12 and been done with it, but he spent several hours of his time helping two complete strangers. That is a trail angel.

In the morning we blue-blaze our way into the small town of Norwich, following roads instead of the trail. I enjoy blue-blazing, taking different trails and roads and seeing sights other than mile after mile of forest. People wave at us as we pass by, some getting their mail and others out mowing their lawn. I feel like I'm taking a walk around the neighborhood, except that I have a 35-pound pack on. One person yells out to ask if we need some water and lets us fill up from his hose. Rufus drinks for a long time. Then we are back walking along the flat road that takes us right over the Connecticut River and into Hanover, New Hampshire.

Hanover is unlike any other trail town as it is a college town, home to the very affluent Dartmouth College. While other New England towns are upscale, this one is downright rich. The town's main hotel, the Hanover Hotel, charges $240 a night for a room. The less expensive hotels run $100 for a room. There is a silver lining, though, in the form of two fraternities, Tabard and Panarchy.

For years these two fraternities have allowed hikers to spend a night at their place for free. More fraternities once opened their homes, but too many hikers didn't realize they were guests and took advantage of this hospitality. The trail has seen an increase of party hikers, no longer out here for the spiritual or physical journey but instead seeing a hike as a six-month party.

We walk over to Panarchy because it is closest. After ringing the bell and knocking on the open door for several minutes with no answer, we let ourselves into the dirtiest, most disgusting place I have ever seen. Beer bottles are everywhere. The floor is sticky from stale beer, and several pools of congealing vomit only add to the decor. A second-hand store would burn the furniture, and Mr. Clean would burst into tears. The kitchen makes the living room look inviting. Vast mounds of dirty dishes cover every countertop, most host to a wide variety of colored mold, and a rotting stench emanates from the room.

"There's no way I'm staying here. If I have to I'll tent out back, but let's go check out the other place first," Teresa says. I heartily agree.

We walk over to Tabard Fraternity and find a couple of fraternity members chatting with Marcus, Wood Nymph, and Shambala on the front porch. Marcus is on a schedule now because he has to pick up his dog before the end of September. He's only here for the day and is on his way out. Shambala tells us Othra has quit the trail. He was trying too hard catch up to our small hiking community and burned himself out. I wish he had hitched a few days ahead and caught up with us. We also find out Bear Bait did make it here, and left for Texas a couple days ago. Wood Nymph and Shambala seem to be traveling together more or less, much like Teresa and I were for the first couple of months. It'll be interesting to see how things develop between them.

"Hi. I heard that you guys allow hikers to stay here." I say to the two members.

"Thru-hiking? Yeah, you can stay here. The sign-up sheet and rules are right inside on the corkboard. You can tent on the lawn or find a comfortable piece of floor to sleep on," he says.

"So you don't mind if my dog stays here?"

"Does he bite?"

Rufus looks up at the member, offended. Rufus doesn't even like to bite his own food. I tell him this and he says it's no problem then. "Oh, one more thing. Our shower plumbing is broken so you need to use the shower at Panarchy or sneak into the gym."

Tabard, unlike Panarchy, is clean and livable. The rules are simple: respect the members' privacy, clean up after ourselves, and remember that we are guests. The house has a large common room with several comfy couches, a big screen TV, and a DVD player with lots of movies. This town will be hard to leave.

9. The Greens and the Whites

Teresa and I do head over to Panarchy for a shower and somehow it is even dirtier than the rest of the place. I shower first, making sure nothing burrows into my legs or turns my skin orange. After Teresa showers we waste no time getting out of the place. Teresa then takes me to the art museum on campus, where I see authentic Picasso and Monet paintings for the first time. I have never been a real art fan, but it's fun with Teresa as she explains the different artists and styles of paintings. She's a bit more cultured than I am.

With nothing else to do we hit the Dartmouth Co-op, a trendy pseudo-outfitter, to get some hiking shoes to replace my hot, heavy boots. While we are looking at overpriced shoes a young woman, immaculate in a designer shirt and carrying a matching Gucci handbag, comes in with her mom. They walk over to the shoe rack and stand right in front of me.

"Mom," the girl says, loud enough for the whole store to hear, "I need new hiking boots. Mine are no good anymore."

I'm assuming that to her "no good" means that they are last year's style, not devoid of tread with holes in the toes and the soles falling off like most hikers' shoes are.

"Honey, do you really need new ones right now? None of these are on sale," the mom says.

"But mom, I need new ones!" she whines. She grabs a $200 shoe off the rack and sticks it in her mom's face. "Look, these are on sale! These will work just fine."

"Those aren't boots, honey. I thought you wanted boots. Those look more like shoes," the mom replies.

The girl glares at the shoes as if it is their fault they are not boots. She isn't ready to be defeated so easily, though.

"M-o-m," she says, drawing out the simple word into a three-second whine. "I need shoes too. They're Gore-Tex and I need Gore-Tex so my feet will stay dry." Keep her feet dry? I bet she hikes in the rain about as often as I get a pap smear. She continues to whine and beg for another five minutes until her mom finally gives in and buys her the shoes.

Teresa and I stand in awe at this childish, materialistic display and the mother's lack of backbone. A grown adult whining to her mother like a five-year-old to get her way — and it works! It never would have crossed my mind in college, or even in high school, to act that way towards my parents. If I did that, my mom would have said no and my dad would have knocked some sense into me. That young woman certainly looked old enough to buy her own shoes if she needed a new pair. I'm ashamed at how our culture has produced rich, snobby whiners who can't separate what they really need from what TV and magazines say they need.

We finally escape Hanover after two zero days and new shoes on my feet. I hadn't planned on spending two days at Tabard, but it was so dang comfortable it was tough to leave. I still have plenty of time to meet my dad. The air is cooler than it has been in a while, and the first night out of Hanover we camp in a field at the base of Dartmouth College Ski Resort, a fairly large hill with two chair lifts. I've never known a college to have its own ski slope. Dartmouth engineering projects are also along the trail. A suspension bridge and a couple of shelters, one shaped like a hexagon with a matching privy, are courtesy of the engineering students working on their craft.

The engineering projects disappear as we increase our distance from Hanover, and I know why. These mountains are steep, making Vermont's Green Mountains look like Kansas. Still, with the cooler temperature, Teresa and I make up the distance we lost by spending the extra day at Hanover. We trudge up the near-vertical Smarts Mountain, and are able to see the White Mountains that lie before us, including the imposing Mt. Washington 100 miles away.

The hot, dry summer has taken its toll on the streams and springs. In the fifty miles since Hanover there have been only five water sources. Teresa can get by on a couple of liters a day — I think she's half camel — but Rufus and I require a lot more. At each spring I fill anything that will hold water, which adds up to almost a gallon, and hike with the extra eight pounds of water until

August 15, 2001. 1751 from Springer, 416 to Katahdin. Heading over Cube Mountain, New Hampshire. The White Mountains are on the other side.

Rufus and I drink it all, hoping the next source is not too far away. We reach Glencliff as it starts to rain, the first rain since Manchester Center two weeks ago. Where the trail crosses a road is the much appreciated Hiker's Welcome Hostel situated near the base of Mt. Moosilauke. I haven't been eating enough for these climbs and I am severely calorie-depleted; every step is exhausting. I am going to stuff my face here.

The Hiker's Welcome Hostel is a good place, run by Packrat, a 1994 thru-hiker. He has a small stock of supplies: frozen pizzas, ice cream bars, candy bars, granola and more, all on an honor system and at the same prices as in town. I hope no one like White Indian and his brother take advantage of this and ruin it for honest hikers. The hostel is packed with people, half of them south bounders. While we are complaining and bragging to the south bounders about miles we've covered, the mountains we've climbed, and the pain we've endured, all of which they still have to look forward to, a short, bearded hiker named Gnome sits down.

"Are you done bragging? While you were standing on Springer Mountain I had already hiked almost the equivalent of the A.T. to get there, so don't whine too much about your pain," he says, munching on an apple.

"Huh? What the hell are you talking about?" I ask, perplexed.

"I'm hiking the Eastern Continental Trail. It runs 4,400 miles from Key West to Cape Gaspe, Canada. By the time I was standing on Springer Mountain I had walked 1,600 miles. In 400 miles when we're standing on Katahdin, you'll be done with your trip, but I'll still have another 680 miles to go."

I shut up about my pain. Forty-four hundred miles! That's walking from New York to Los Angeles and halfway back again. I can't fathom walking that far. Gnome is a braggart, but he has a right to be.

"Forty-four hundred miles! What was the hardest part, Gnome?" I ask. I hope he'll say the part he's on now, because it has been kicking my ass. If these steep mountains are still hard for him after 3,200 miles, I won't feel like such a wimp for resting every hour.

"The Florida Keys Trail. That was hard. Heck, it's not even a trail. It's 175 miles of road-walking on the Keys Highway, no shade from the sun and very little water. Easy by car but it's a real ass-kicker by foot."

"Ha, I'd just yellow blaze all of that! Then I wouldn't have to walk it! I yellow blazed through most of the Whites. A lot easier than walking," shouts another hiker that I haven't met. He's a young, skinny guy with a patchy beard and one large bucktooth next to a hole where the other one should have been.

"Hey, dumb-ass. The point of hiking the Keys Trail is to hike it. If you're going to skip it, why even go down there?" Gnome says. The other hiker walks away, dejected.

"Hey, man, wasn't that a little mean? You may have walked 3,200 miles, but you're not special," I say, a little put off by his attitude.

"Fruit Pie, wait until you talk to J-the-A. Then you'll understand why I told him off. He's an idiot."

That night a group of us head into town for dinner. I tie Rufus to a tree in the front yard and jump into the back of Packrat's pickup. At the restaurant I find myself sitting across from J-the-A. He interjects himself into everyone's conversation, saying he has hiked harder stuff, climbed steeper mountains, and survived harsher weather. He overhears me telling another hiker that I was in the Marines and decides this is a good time for him to jump into our conversation.

"You were in the Marines? Wow, I've heard most Marines are crazy. I was going to join, but I have tennis elbow and they wouldn't take me. Too bad for them. I'm J-the-A, hiking southbound," he says to me, emphasizing his name. I know he's dying for me to ask what it stands for, but I don't take the bait.

"It stands for Jason the Argonaut," he says after several seconds of silence. I have a feeling J-the-A named himself and is trying to be clever. I'm too tired and hungry to play his game right now. I just want to eat.

"I named myself that because I'm chasing my golden fleece," he continues. Again he looks at me and waits, and when I don't ask him to explain, he does so on his own.

"My golden fleece is Springer Mountain. You know what a fleece is?" he asks with a superior air. I wonder if he really believes Marines are crazy, and I decide to find out.

"A fleece is my favorite type of blanket used to suffocate people who annoy me," I reply in a cold voice. J-the-A doesn't say another word, allowing me to eat in peace.

When we get back to the hostel Rufus is ecstatic at my arrival, but he is whining and barking with a hoarse voice. Gnome, who did not go eat with us, walks up to me.

"Hey, man, your dog went nuts when you left, barking and trying to get free. I tried to comfort him, but he kept barking so I didn't want to get too close," he says, now kneeling down to pet a calm Rufus. Augh, I'm the idiot. I was in such a hurry to eat that I didn't even think about where I was tying him. I tied Rufus in the front yard away from all the hikers and without any of his or my stuff within sight. He saw Teresa and me get in the truck and leave. He must have thought we were deserting him. If I had left my pack next to him or tied him in back with the other hikers he would have been fine, but now he has barked himself almost voiceless. I feel terrible and spend some time consoling Rufus. I cook him a microwave pizza as an apology, which he accepts.

After an hour of socializing, Teresa and I retire to the upstairs loft in an attempt to get some sleep. Most of the other hikers have also called it a night, but a small group is still awake in the downstairs common area. One of them is J-the-A, talking loud enough to keep hikers in Vermont awake.

"I've killed 124 mice so far!" he shouts to the other hikers downstairs, none of whom are farther than ten feet away from him. "My record is 15 in one night. Let's see someone try to top that!"

"They're mice," a quiet female voice answers. "Are you afraid of mice? Let them be. They don't harm anyone and they actually help keep the shelters clean."

"I don't care. I'm not going to have one of those nasty creatures running across me while I sleep. I'll kill them all," J-the-A yells, trying to sound tough but coming across as a complete jackass.

I yell down the stairs for him to quiet down so we can sleep. He does, but five minutes later his voice rises again.

"I've been doing twenty-mile days through these mountains. They're not so hard. My first day on the trail I did twenty-five miles," he yells.

I reach over and grab Rufus' small green fleece blanket. Taking one end in each hand and wrapping it around my knuckles, I walk downstairs and look J-the-A in the eye.

"Jason. I've already asked you once. This is your last chance. Shut up so I can get some sleep. Understand?" I say, making a loop with the blanket just big enough for a neck to fit in before snapping it tight. The color drains from his face and he nods his head yes.

I crawl back into bed, and for the rest of the night J-the-A is quiet. I'm relieved that he didn't call my bluff. I have never killed anyone with a blanket, but he doesn't need to know that.

Teresa and I awake early for our first slack-pack. For a small fee Packrat is going to take our packs to a ranger station on the other side of Mt. Moosilauke. I haven't hiked a foot of the trail without my pack, and I'm looking forward to the change. It's drizzling, so we borrow a couple of day packs from Packrat to carry some food and rain gear. We place our big packs in Packrat's truck and sit down for a quick breakfast. J-the-A wakes up and walks over to us.

"Sorry for being so loud last night. Sometimes I don't know how loud I can get," he tells me. I'm taken aback by his apology.

"No problem. You heading out today?" I ask.

"It's raining. I don't hike in the rain."

"Not at all? How many days have you taken off so far?" I ask, curious.

"Fifteen. Some for rain but sometimes I just don't feel like hiking. I hike when I want, yellow blaze when I want, and spend a lot of time in towns. Anyway, no hard feelings?" We shake hands and he crawls back into his sleeping bag.

He has traveled 400 miles, yellow-blazing half of that, and has already taken fifteen days off. Teresa and I have walked over 1,700 miles and have only taken eighteen days off. At his rate he will never make it to Springer before winter and I really don't think he intends to. J-the-A is the type of hiker that gives us a bad name, the type that finds a comfortable, cheap place to stay and doesn't leave until his welcome is long over. Then he packs up and finds the next place, either hiking or hitchhiking to it. J-the-A isn't a hiker, he's a hobo. Leaving J-the-A behind us, Teresa and I start towards Mt. Moosilauke.

Mt. Moosilauke is our introduction to the White Mountains and is our first peak on the trail that rises above tree line. Most of the mountains in the Whites are a part of longer ridges, but this one stands alone at 4,800 feet high. The trail is steep and rutty, but with light day packs we easily cover the 3,700-foot vertical climb. Rufus runs up the trail and I jog after him. After a hundred yards we both stop to catch our breath, then run again. I now know why people slack-pack the trail: there's very little work involved.

The drizzle continues as we reach the cloud-enshrouded summit, and we are in a cold, wet whiteout that reduces our visibility to less than twenty feet. The summit is a mass of trails all converging into one junction. Several signposts stand at the junction, each supposedly pointing in the direction of its respective trail, but none of the signs actually line up with a trail.

To make matters worse, the Whites use local trail names instead of the commonly used A.T. symbol. Also, in an attempt to keep the wilderness 'pristine,' blazes are few and far between. In short, I have no idea which trail to take. In an effort to save a few ounces, I sent my compass home a month ago. Now, without a compass, my map is worthless because I can't see any terrain features. In this fog and drizzle I can walk right past a blaze painted low on a rock and never see it.

Teresa and I take an educated guess and choose a well-used trail marked by huge cairns. After walking downhill for an hour we drop out of the clouds. I stop and pull out my map.

"This isn't right, babe. We should be walking down a ridge, but we're in a ravine following a stream. Have you seen a blaze lately?"

"No, I haven't. I wasn't really looking for one, but I can't remember seeing a single blaze since the top. You think we went the wrong way? I don't want to hike three miles back up the mountain," she says, and Rufus lies down in protest of hiking back up.

"Yeah, I'm pretty sure we're on the wrong trail. There are a dozen trails coming off this mountain but I think we're on this one," I say, pointing to a trail on the map. "It looks like it runs into a road. I say we keep hiking, find the road, and hitch to where we need to go."

"What if no one picks us up?"

"Then we walk halfway around the base of the mountain and hook back up with the trail. At least it would be flat, unlike hiking back up this mountain and hoping to find the right trail down."

Teresa agrees, and we follow the trail for another hour. The trail descends down the mountain to a huge lodge constructed of massive spruce trees. The parking lot behind the lodge is filled with several dozen cars, so our chance of finding a ride looks good. We enter the lodge, appropriately named Ravine Lodge, and find the manager. He is a 22-year-old Dartmouth student working a summer job. We learn that the lodge and the surrounding 4,500 acres are owned by Dartmouth College.

9. The Greens and the Whites

After we explain our situation to the manager, he takes pity on us and drives us an hour to where we should be. I thank the manager and try to pay him for his gas and time, but he refuses. Our little detour ate up the afternoon, and by the time we retrieve our packs from the ranger station it's too late to keep hiking, so we wander off into the bushes and find a place to camp, ready to take on Kinsman Ridge in the morning.

Sixteen-mile-long Kinsman Ridge separates us from the town of North Woodstock, where I will meet my dad in two days. The ridge is steep, rocky and very hard and will probably take two full days to traverse. The problem is that I am completely out of food. I've eaten my week's worth of food in five days. Teresa isn't much better off. Rufus has plenty of food, but I would have to be pretty hungry to dip into his chow.

"Well, what do you want to do, Kevin? We can push forward and go hungry for a day, or head into town and come back out," Teresa says.

"I've got to get food. I'm burning way too many calories to try to go a day without eating. I don't have any fat left to burn," I tell her.

"Then let's hitch into town, grab two days' worth of food and come back out."

By road it is six miles into North Woodstock, so we try to hitch in. Two hours later we are still standing by the side of the road. Hundreds of cars have passed by, but they are all city-folk who probably have never heard of the Appalachian Trail and only see us as a couple of vagrants. With no other choice, we begin walking into town and after three miles a car does stop, a local who has picked up hundreds of hikers around the Whites. By the time we hit a grocery store it's too late to get back to the trail as we would probably have to hike the six miles back.

According to my book, the only affordable place that takes dogs in this expensive tourist town is a small place called Cascade Lodge Bed and Breakfast. We find the lodge, a ramshackle three-story building, and I walk through the front door that opens up into the owner's residence, currently occupied by a man in his seventies.

"What?" he asks in a low, growling voice when he sees me.

"We're hiking and I'm hoping we can get a room for the night. You take dogs, right?" He looks me up and down for several minutes before answering.

"Cost $18 per person. Dog got to sleep on the porch, not in the room. You want a room?"

"Yes sir, I do."

"Okay, $36 dollars. Cash. I don't take no credit cards and I don't take no checks. You got cash?" he asks challengingly. I think he's hoping I don't have the cash so he won't have to do anything. Unfortunately for him I just picked up my mail drop with my traveler's checks, which he takes.

Our accommodations are basic to say the least. Our room has a full size bed covered by a single yellowed sheet, a thin blanket, and a comforter that should have crumbled into dust by now. An old chair sits in one corner and a cheap dresser fills out the room. The room doesn't have a TV and the only window opens a mere six inches before jamming. The room also doesn't have a bathroom; instead it shares a filthy communal bathroom that doesn't even have toilet paper.

With nothing to do in the room we head down to the porch to keep Rufus company. As we sit reading our books, Hemlock, Tabasco and Moss come rolling in, Hemlock carrying a large jug of rum. They are staying the night as well, and invite us to join their little party. With nothing better to do, Teresa and I partake of rum and Cokes until it gets dark and the cranky old proprietor yells at us for making too much noise. Not finished for the night, we head over to a bar across the street, but my many rum and Cokes catch up to me. I head off to bed, but not before I sneak Rufus up to the room. There's no way I'm going to leave him tied up on the front porch overnight after all we've been through together.

The plan is to get up early and slack-pack the 16 miles of Kinsman Ridge we missed. Teresa heads downstairs for the breakfast, and I start to get up but my hangover says no. I listen to my headache and crawl back under the covers. Teresa comes back a few minutes later.

"Guess what? This bed and breakfast is now just a bed. They no longer make breakfast. We'll have to grab something on the way out. Why are you still in bed?" she asks.

"Not hiking. Head hurts," I tell her, shielding my eyes from the light.

"I told you not to drink so much. Maybe next time you'll listen to me. I talked to the owner downstairs and he said he'd shuttle us to the trailhead. I'm still going. I'll see you tonight," and she's gone.

Around noon my headache releases its grip on my skull and Rufus and I wander around town. Not much here but antique shops, souvenir shops, and T-shirt shops. I meet a few other hikers in town, including Rocky and Bedouin. Most seem to be taking a day off before venturing into the White Mountains. An hour after nightfall Teresa comes back to the room.

"My god, that was hard! Steep, rocky and slow! It would have taken us two full days with our packs on. I'm glad I slack-packed it. But you should have seen the views, it was gorgeous," she says, collapsing on the bed, and she's asleep before she can tell me about the views.

The next day it rains, so we kill the day playing cards and reading, waiting for my dad to arrive. Hemlock, Tabasco and Moss left yesterday. We'll catch them in Maine. While we're sitting on the porch, Homeless, Unemployed and Dig arrive. Unemployed is in obvious pain and almost in tears.

"MaryAnn, your toe still bothering you?" Teresa says, rushing out to her. I grab her pack and the three of them sit down on the porch.

9. The Greens and the Whites

"My toe has healed, but my knees are killing me. I hurt everywhere and I feel sick," she tells us. I can see why. She is very thin; she's lost too much weight out here and her body is starving.

"We're going to take a couple days off here to recover, but I'm worried about the Whites. I don't know if her knees, or mine, can take the mountains," Homeless says. An idea comes to me.

"Hey, I was talking to Rocky and Bedouin yesterday. They found a guy who is going to slack-pack them through the Whites. They're staying in the hotel across the street tonight. You should talk to them. A week of hiking without a pack will take a lot of stress off your knees," I say.

Dig looks a little disappointed at the possibility of losing his hiking companions, and Unemployed notices this.

"Um, I'm not sure. I'll see how I hold up," Unemployed says, for Dig's sake.

"No, go do it," Dig interrupts. "If walking without a pack for a week will let you heal enough to finish the trail, then do it. Don't worry about me. Save yourselves some pain and I'll meet up with you on the other side of the Whites."

"Okay, I think we'll go find them and see if we can slack-pack too. This will relieve a lot of worries," Homeless says, and Unemployed smiles at the thought of no pack for a week. They head over to the hotel to find Rocky and Bedouin.

At 10:00 P.M. Teresa, Rufus and I walk half a mile down to the combination gas station, Dunkin' Donuts and bus station, and right on time the bus arrives. My dad steps out carrying a huge duffel bag, looking in great shape. I can tell he's been training for this. I introduce Dad to Teresa and we walk back to the lodge. He flew into Boston this morning and took a bus out here, so it's been a long, tiring day for him.

Back at the room we sneak Rufus upstairs, and Dad rolls out his sleeping pad and bag on the floor. Teresa and I go through his pack and find he has done an incredible job of packing. We manage to find only a couple of items he doesn't need, including a stick of deodorant.

"You don't need this, Dad, we all stink. It's an extra couple of ounces you'll be carrying," I say, ready to toss it into the garbage.

"No way, boy! You're not letting me take much else, but I want the deodorant. I'll carry that," he says, snatching it out of my hand. Oh well, he deserves a luxury item. Still, I decide to introduce him to the hiker stink early. I hold my nylon watch band — the one I've been wearing since Pearisburg, the one that smells like a rotting corpse — up to my nose.

"Wow, that's really weird. I must have rubbed my watch on some plants. It smells like mint. Check it out, Dad." I say, sniffing intently.

"I don't want to smell your watch," he says suspiciously.

"Don't smell it, Dennis, it's a trick," Teresa warns.

"No really, it smells like mint, check it out. It's weird." I toss my watch over to Dad. He holds it up to his nose and inhales deeply. Instantly, he gags on the putrid stench. He sits up coughing and rubbing his nose, trying to get the funk out of it while I roll in the bed laughing. Teresa smacks me on the arm.

"That wasn't very nice," she says, trying to hide a smile.

"That was gross, Kevin. I should have known you were up to no good," Dad says, giving a little chuckle.

"Just think, even with the deodorant that's how you're going to be smelling in ten days. Have a good night."

It's Dad's first hiking day, and though the rain has stopped, it is still cloudy. We rise early, get Rufus back down on the patio and pack up all our stuff. The cranky old owner comes out on the porch and eyes Dad several times.

"You sleep here last night?" he asks, pointing at Dad.

"No, he just came in this morning," I say, knowing what the owner is going to say next. But my dad is too honest.

"Yes, I came in late last night and slept on their floor. Is that okay?"

"No, it's not okay. It's $18 a person to sleep here, no matter if you have your own room or if you are sharing," Cranky says stubbornly.

"So we should have woken you up at midnight last night so you could have checked him into his own room? You would have preferred that to letting him sleep on our floor?" I ask. This guy is incredible. He runs a crappy place and still nickels and dimes hikers for everything he can get.

"That's right. You spend the night, it costs $18."

Dad hands him a twenty, not wanting to argue, as Cranky is our ride back to the trail. I would have refused to pay and found another ride. We load our stuff into the 1970 wood paneled station wagon and are getting in when Cranky walks up to inform us that it'll be nine dollars for the three of us — when earlier he'd driven Teresa for nothing — and even then he drops us at a trailhead a mile from the A.T., to avoid his having to drive another six miles to the next spot where he can turn his van around. I start the day pissed off, but Dad doesn't care about the money or extra mile of walking. After months of training he's finally hiking with his son in the White Mountains of New Hampshire, and he heads down the trail with a smile adorning his face. I put Cranky behind me and start down the trail after him.

10

New Hampshire Brings Dad, but Takes Rufus

The White Mountains of New Hampshire are often compared to the Smokies, but the Smokies consist of one long ridgeline with deep valleys and small spur ridges branching off. The White Mountains are made up of multiple mountain ridges running north to south. Roads pass through all the valleys, called notches here, making the Whites a very popular tourist destination. The Whites boast forty-eight peaks over 4,000 feet and hundreds of miles of trail above tree line. The A.T. runs for seventy-five miles through the mountains and crosses over a dozen 4,000-foot peaks including Mt. Washington, the highest peak in New England. The plan is to hike with my Dad all seventy-five miles to Gorham, New Hampshire, a small town on the northern end of the Whites and just shy of Maine. Gorham offers daily bus service to Boston, so Dad will be able to get back to the airport.

The White Mountains see millions of visitors a year, and like the national parks, have very strict camping restrictions. We cannot camp closer than 200 feet to any trail, within a quarter mile of a hut or designated campsite, or within half a mile of a road when below tree line. Camping above tree line is only allowed at designated campsites. That doesn't sound so bad, except that most of the trail through the Whites is above tree line, and the sections that are below are either too close to a road or in brush so thick it's impossible to set up a tent.

The Whites don't have shelters like the rest of the trail; instead they have a hut system. Run by the Appalachian Mountain Club (AMC, informally known as the Appalachian Money Club) the huts are enclosed cabins with bunk rooms, meals cooked by a staff, a fireplace, and other luxuries one would expect to receive when paying $50 a night for the "wilderness experience." Since most hikers can't afford to sleep in the huts, and camping close to them is not allowed, the other option is the designated campsites. These campsites are nothing more than primitive camping areas, with elevated tent platforms and a caretaker, for a mere $6.00 a night per person. Six bucks to set up my tent on a piece of plywood.

There isn't anywhere in the Whites to camp for free, and this late in the trip money is real tight so we will have to stealth camp. There are about a dozen places to stealth camp in the Whites. The location of the hidden trails that lead to small, cleared areas in the undergrowth big enough for a tent or two is passed on by word of mouth.

The trail coming out of North Woodstock is hard and steep, and I am glad Dad took his training seriously. For the last three months he has been hiking up a 1,000-foot mountain three times a week. He slowly increased his pack weight and distance until right before the trip he was hiking twelve miles round trip with a thirty-pound pack. Now it pays off as we climb 3,000 feet towards Franconia Ridge. Franconia Ridge runs for ten miles above the tree line, crossing several peaks, the highest being 5,249-foot Mt. Lafayette. I look up at the dark swirling clouds engulfing Mt. Lafayette, occasionally showing small patches of blue sky before closing back up. The weather is unpredictable in the Whites. The clouds can pass by leaving us bathed in sunshine, or rip the mountain apart with bolts of lightning and gale-driven rain. With no way to control the weather, we keep hiking past tree line and reach the rocky, windswept ridge.

"Wow, this is hard. Kevin, why didn't you tell me these mountains were so steep?" Dad says, sitting down to take a breather. "If I had known it was this hard I would have brought a donkey to ride."

"Keep chugging, old man, that was the easy climb," I say in encouragement.

"What do we do if it storms and lightning starts striking?" Dad asks.

"We run."

"We run? Where do we run to? There's nothing up here!" Apparently he disapproves of my answer.

"Simple, Dad. We run to where the lightning isn't. Welcome to hiking."

As we reach the summit of Mt. Lafayette the clouds relax their threat and open up, giving us amazing views of the steep peaks and deep valleys. The contrast between the lush green valleys and naked brown ridges is remarkable. It looks like someone took a giant pencil and drew a wavy horizontal line on the slopes. Taking advantage of the sun break, we stop for lunch, and I head down the side of the mountain towards a spring for water, but it's dry.

"Dad, just how thirsty are you?" I ask when I return to the summit.

"Is this a trick question, Kevin? Because I'm not smelling your watch again," he says. I don't know why he's so defensive.

"No trick. The spring is dry. Our only other water source is these," I say, pointing to small puddles of water on the rocks. It rained last night so the water should be fresh, and we don't have any other choice. Teresa and I take turns spooning the water out of various puddles, filtering it through a bandanna and treating it with bleach. Rufus, not sure what we are doing, walks over to a puddle, takes a drink, then pees in it. I wonder if any of the other puddles have been "enhanced."

10. New Hampshire Brings Dad, but Takes Rufus 187

August 21, 2001. 1797 from Springer, 370 to Katahdin. ***Top:*** Teresa and Dad heading towards the summit of Mt. Lafayette, New Hampshire. ***Above:*** Rufus and I headed up Mt. Lafayette.

It's hard to find a place large enough for three people to stealth camp, but as dusk approaches we manage to find one off the trail and hidden from view. Dad has done a lot of camping and introduced my brother and me to the woods when we were young, but he has never done anything as intense as this. Tired from a long day of hiking, he eats his bowl of noodles and is asleep before the day's lingering light is gone.

The next two days are as different as New York and New Jersey. We wake to a thick fog and constant drizzle, and it takes us eight hours to walk 5.6 miles. Steep muddy hills, slick mossy rocks, and slippery roots slow Rufus and Dad down to a crawl. Teresa and I have had five months to figure out how to balance on wet rocks, but Dad hasn't, so we slow to a pace he is comfortable with. We come across several portions of trail so steep we have to dig our hands in the muddy slope to keep from sliding. Rufus, even with his four feet, can't get any traction in the mud and refuses to walk down these parts. I have to go down first; then Teresa pushes Rufus from behind and he slips and slides down the trail until I catch him. I don't think Rufus enjoys that. Finally we find a small clearing off the trail. Wet, muddy and exhausted, we set up camp for the night.

The next day is warm and sunny without a cloud in the sky, and we are able to see for miles into Maine, Canada and Vermont. The rocks dry out and we walk the whole day on the fairly flat ridge line with near vertical drops on both sides. A little after noon we reach Zealand Hut, built next to a series of cascading falls. The AMC huts allow the first two thru-hikers who ask each day a work-for-stay opportunity. The work is minimal, and in return hikers can eat leftovers and sleep on the covered porch. With such a gorgeous day, and nowhere better to stay for the next five miles, we decide to stay here. Teresa tells Dad and me to go work together and spend some quality time, so we wander through the hut and find the manager in the kitchen.

"Hey, have any thru-hikers already asked to work-for-stay for the night?" I ask her.

"You're a hiker? You don't look like a thru-hiker," she says, so I quickly jump to Dad's defense.

"He took some time off from the trail and just got back on in North Woodstock," I say.

"No, not him. He looks like a hiker. You don't. You're not dressed right to be a hiker," she says, pointing to my cotton T-shirt and nylon shorts.

"Ma'am, I have two months of beard on my face, my shirt has holes from where my pack rubs, and I haven't used deodorant since March. If that doesn't say thru-hiker I don't know how to convince you."

She decides, though reluctantly, that I am a hiker and lets me work-for-stay with my Dad.

The Whites are notorious for unpredictable and ever-changing weather. People have frozen to death in August, and hikers are advised to be prepared for any type of weather at any time, but being prepared simply means having warm clothing with you, not wearing it all the time. I look around and see that most of the tourists staying in the hut are dressed in North Face down jackets and fleece pants. Some are wearing so much arctic clothing that they should be following Sir Edmund Hillary up Mt. Everest, not staying in a heated log hut at 3,000 feet. Apparently that's how the hut manager thinks I should be dressed.

While only two hikers can work, the rules allow two more hikers to pay $15 to sleep on the porch, without leftover privileges. Dad pays for Teresa to stay with us. Rufus is considered wildlife and gets to sleep for free. The manager explains our chores: setting up for dinner and cleaning afterwards. Since dinner isn't for another couple of hours we have some time to kill.

"Hey, Dad, want to watch some TV?" I ask, having nothing else to do and not wanting to go on one of the several "nature hikes" around the hut.

"It's such a beautiful day, Kevin. I didn't come all the way out here to sit inside and watch TV. If you want to, go right ahead."

"Hiker TV, Dad. Come, I'll introduce you to it." I sit down on the front porch and motion him to do the same.

"So what do we do?" Dad asks as he sits next to me.

"We're doing it. We relax and watch. Like right there. Look at that." At the bottom of the porch steps, about ten feet away from us, is a fat squirrel trying desperately to get into a food bag someone left lying next to a brand new backpack. The squirrel takes the nylon bag in his mouth and starts chewing.

"Shouldn't we do something? That squirrel is going to ruin the food," Dad asks as the squirrel gets into the nylon bag and pulls out a large plastic bag of trail mix.

"No, Dad, we don't do anything. This is TV. We sit back and watch."

The squirrel eats half of the bag before wobbling off to tell his friends about the incredible find. A few minutes later a woman with her two small kids walks out of the hut to the pack and now-ruined trail mix. The woman picks up the pack and stares at the ruined bag with awe before exclaiming to her kids, "Wow, there are animals out here!" Now that's good TV.

In the morning, after a breakfast of leftover pancakes and bacon, the staff tells us a storm is expected in a couple of days. Not wanting to summit Mt. Washington during a storm, we decide to push long and hard today so we can summit tomorrow in good weather. For the first half of the day we make great time down to Crawford Notch, the gap separating Franconia Ridge from the Presidential Range. The climb out of the notch proves to be much tougher than the descent and requires hand-over-hand climbing at times, which means I have the joy of lifting Rufus up and over my head repeatedly to get him onto the dozens of ledges along the trail. Rufus isn't able to help much as his feet have been bothering him. The trail through the Whites has been mostly rocks and is wearing down Rufus' pads. Since Pennsylvania the trail has been very rocky with only a few grassy sections, never giving his pads much time to heal, and they are now red and tender, and he walks in pain. Dad, on the other hand, is doing incredibly well, and as night falls, we have hiked 16 miles to Nauman Tentsites where we fork over $6.00 a person to sleep on a wooden platform.

We awake early to a crystal clear sky accompanied by a morning chill. After a few minutes of hiking, Mt. Washington comes into sight, the summit wrapped in a swirl of white, wispy clouds.

"Don't worry about those clouds," Dad tells me. "They'll burn off by the time we get there. We are going to have a great day today."

The trail becomes increasingly rocky as we reach Lake of the Clouds Hut. Built in 1915, this stone lodge is huge, capable of sleeping up to 90 guests. True to its name, the hut sits at 5,000 feet next to two small lakes, which really should be called ponds, but Pond of the Clouds Hut doesn't sound as romantic. The summit of Mt. Washington, a mere 1.4 miles away, stands majestically against the blue sky without a single cloud near its summit, just like Dad said.

"Ready for the last climb to the top, Dad?" I ask.

"Boy, I've been training for months for this. I'm ready," he says and starts up the mountain in front of us.

The trail up to the summit is composed entirely of the sharp granite rocks that make up the White Mountains, and Rufus is starting to walk with a discernible limp. He has several deep cracks in his paws, and I'm worried about him. So is Teresa.

August 24, 2001. Mt. Washington looming before us. Note the cog train bellowing black smoke as it chugs up the ridge.

10. New Hampshire Brings Dad, but Takes Rufus

"Hey, Kevin, what are we going to do about Rufus? He can barely walk. There's no way he can make it another 300 miles without a week of rest," Teresa says as we take a break, Dad twenty yards away snapping pictures of butterflies.

"I know, I've been thinking about that. You remember Achilles, right?"

"Of course I do. What about him?"

"Well, Achilles lives in Maine, and way back at Kincora he gave me his phone number, saying if I needed anything when I reached Maine to give him a call. When we get to Gorham I'm going to call him and see if I can pay him to pick up Rufus and watch him until we finish."

"We can try that, but what if he can't? Then what?"

"I don't know. We'll have to see how bad his pads are when we reach Gorham."

We get back on the trail, and an hour later we reach the summit of mighty Mt. Washington, 6,288 feet above sea level and the second highest peak on the trail (Clingmans Dome in the Smokies is 355 feet higher). Though all of the Whites have a reputation for nasty weather, Mt. Washington has the worst. Three weather systems, one coming down from Canada, one coming off the Atlantic, and one coming up from the East Coast, all converge at Mt. Washington, making its weather unpredictable and deadly.

Mt. Washington has claimed the lives of 135 people, more than 14,441-foot Mt. Rainier in Washington State (92 deaths) or the feared 20,320-foot Mt. McKinley in Alaska (approximately 100 deaths), making this peak the deadliest mountain in North America. What makes this mountain so dangerous is that the storms come in fast. Snow, ice storms and 100 mph winds can happen in any month, and the weather can change from 80 degrees and sunshine to 35 degrees and fog in less than an hour, catching people unprepared. The summit is often in the clouds, making it impossible to see an approaching storm, and it has an average summer temperature of 52 degrees. Winter is much worse, with an average daily temperature of 15 degrees and over 21 feet of snow a year. In February of 1969 over nine feet of snow fell on the mountain in two days. The incredible snowfall is great for skiing in the winter, but also causes dozens of avalanches. Every winter a hiker or climber is buried.

What secures its title for the worst weather isn't the snowstorms or the temperature; it's the wind. The winds are often very strong, and the wind-chill can turn a rainy 45-degree day into a hypothermic situation. It often reaches speeds of 100 mph, but on a cold spring day in 1934 the wind was howling like never seen before. The two scientists stationed in the summit weather observatory tied ropes around their waists and went outside to measure the wind speed. The measuring device calculated the wind at 231 mph before it broke. With nothing else to do, the scientists pulled their way back inside and watched the wind intensify, but without their device, they had to settle for a world record surface wind speed of 231 mph. It hasn't been broken.

Once only the hardiest of hikers equipped to handle the changing weather could reach the top of the mountain, but in 1853 a daring entrepreneur decided to build a hotel on the summit. Needing a way for his clientele to get to the top, he also started building a road. By 1861 the Mount Washington Carriage Road was complete, allowing anyone with a horse and buggy to ascend the mountain. The eight mile road took all day to travel, and the road was hard on both horses and equipment, but it was easier and safer than hiking.

At the same time that the road was being built, Sylvester Marsh and a friend started hiking up the mountain on a warm August day. Just as they climbed above tree line, a storm hit with gale-force winds and freezing rain. Somehow they stumbled into the summit house hours later, exhausted and frozen. Marsh knew there had to be a better way up the mountain and envisioned a steam train powering people to the top. After years of planning and several financial setbacks, he began construction in 1866 and by 1869 the three-mile Mt. Washington Cog Railroad was completed, carrying tourists to the top in just over an hour.

A cog train operates differently from a standard train. A standard train would slide backwards on the steep grade, never making it out of the train station. Between the tracks is a cog rack, basically a device that looks like a horizontal ladder. The engines have large cogs, or gears, underneath them that fit into the cog rack and propel the train up the hill. The wheels on the locomotives are only there to support and guide the train on the rails and are not motor-driven. All the power is accomplished by the cog gear meshing with the rack as the locomotive proceeds up the mountain cog tooth by cog tooth.

Between the railroad, the auto road and hiking, over a quarter million people reach the summit every year. The hotel has long since closed (and is now being used as storage) but the summit is still covered by buildings: scientific laboratories, weather stations, and a huge cafeteria and gift shop. Dad, Teresa and I walk into the cafeteria, which is already half-full at ten in the morning, and buy a couple of overpriced chilidogs before heading outside into the chilly morning air to eat. We watch car after car filling the parking lot and great billowing plumes of black smoke puffing out of the trains as they chug up the mountain. Apparently driving to the summit must be a terrifying ordeal as one out of every ten people sports a new T-shirt reading "I survived Mt. Washington!" or my favorite, "I conquered Mt. Washington!" I may be old fashioned, but I don't think of driving a car or riding in a train to the top of a mountain as "conquering" it.

The actual summit pinnacle is a ten-foot pile of rocks outside the cafeteria doors, adorned by a "Mt. Washington Summit 6288" sign. The summit pile resembles an anthill with throngs of people clambering over it for a summit picture next to the sign. Having spent the last two days hiking to get here, Dad, Teresa and I do not need a picture to prove our claim. Instead we admire the view we worked so hard to attain, and it's one of the best on the entire trail. Behind us we can see across Franconia Ridge and Mt. Lafayette all the way to

10. New Hampshire Brings Dad, but Takes Rufus

the Green Mountains of Vermont. In front of us is the northern Presidential Range back-dropped by the remote mountains of Maine. The northern Presidential Range consists of three more peaks: Jefferson, Adams, and Madison. Each is really nothing more than a huge pile of rocks jutting a thousand feet above the ridgeline, and together they give the ridge a serpentine look with Mt. Washington at the snake's head.

Having seen enough of the overpopulated and overbuilt top, we leave the summit for the rocky pile called Mt. Jefferson. Dad, Teresa and Rufus follow a trail around Jefferson, but I scramble up to the top. Two miles later I stand completely alone on Mt. Jefferson and watch the scurrying mass of tourists on Mt. Washington, none daring to walk this far from their security blanket of buildings and vehicles. I drop down the other side and meet up with Dad, Teresa and Rufus, and we find a place to stealth camp among some scrub trees.

Today is gray and overcast, threatening rain. The storm has moved in, and I'm glad we reached Mt. Washington yesterday. We climb the rocks to the summit of Mt. Adams and watch the day's first cog train belch its black smoke as it hauls tourists up Mt. Washington. Ready to leave the Presidents, we descend down Adams. Rufus has to jump from boulder to boulder, which rips his feet even more. Once down we follow the A.T. along the ridge to Mt. Madi-

August 25, 2001. 1831 from Springer, 336 to Katahdin. The Presidential Range (Jefferson, Adams and Madison) from the summit of Mt. Washington.

August 25, 2001. Dad and Teresa crossing the Presidential Range.

son, a pile of rocks identical to Adams and Jefferson, and the last mountain before we can descend off the Presidential Range.

"Hey, Kevin, my knees are sore and my feet hurt. I have no desire to climb up another pile of rocks," Dad says.

"Me neither, and I know Rufus doesn't want to," Teresa adds. "Is there a way we can bypass it?"

"Probably. Let's take a look," I say, pulling out the map. "The Parapet Trail skips the mountain and follows a ravine off the ridge, meeting back up with the A.T. in four miles. How about if you guys take Rufus and go that way while I scamper over Madison and meet you where the two trails connect?" For some reason I enjoy climbing these mountains and I don't want to skip this one.

"Okay, we'll meet you there," Dad says, and they take Rufus down the Parapet Trail.

Without having to lift Rufus over every large rock I make great time and quickly reach the summit. It starts raining as I begin the descent down the other side, making the rocks slick and treacherous. I'm glad Rufus and Dad took the other way down because this is dangerous. I reach our rendezvous point expecting to see them already here since the Parapet Trail is two miles shorter than my way, but no Dad, Teresa, or Rufus anywhere. They must be taking their time, snapping pictures along the way.

An hour and a half later they still haven't arrived and I'm starting to worry. No way it should have taken them this long to hike a couple of miles. What if Dad had a heart attack? What if Teresa slipped and broke a leg? What if Rufus ... oh, I'm sure Rufus is fine. Not wanting to wait any longer, I drop my pack and head up the trail to find them. After a mile I run into Dad, red-faced and breathing hard. He looks exhausted.

"Dad! Are you all right? What happened?" I ask, not seeing Teresa.

"The trail you sent us on turned into a series of cliffs, then the rain came down and turned the cliffs into waterfalls. Rufus wasn't able to get down so we've been lifting him down each set of cliffs, but then your dog sat down and refused to move. We couldn't drag or push him close enough to the edge to lift him down. When we ran out of strength I came down here to get you. Teresa is about a mile up with Rufus."

"Okay. I'll head up there and find them. I stashed my pack a mile down the trail where it crosses a stream. Head on down and take a break. We'll meet you there."

Dad hikes down and I hike up. Within half an hour I see Teresa dragging a limping Rufus by his leash. Her face is red with a scowl that could snap a tree in half.

"Kevin, I hate your stupid dog! Take your mutt! He didn't want to move so I had to lift and drag him down the rocks! He's been fighting me and twice we almost went tumbling down the mountain. I was so close to just pushing him off," she rages, throwing the leash at me and storming down the trail. Rufus is cowering and not sure why he is being yelled at. He only knows that his feet hurt. I comfort him for a few minutes before hurrying down the trail to catch Teresa.

"Just leave me alone for now. I don't want to talk to you and I don't want to talk to Rufus," she says as I approach.

I keep my distance until we reach Dad, and then we hike on, planning to stop for the night at the first place we find to set up camp. But the undergrowth is too thick; we can't find a single place that can accommodate three tents, so we end up hiking four more miles in the rain to Pinkham Notch. Dad and Teresa are already exhausted from dealing with Rufus, and the four miles drain the last of their strength. At the notch we set up our tents behind a maintenance shed, out of view of the road and the White Mountains Visitor Center a hundred yards away. Teresa retires to her tent without saying a word, but Dad, who hasn't quite acclimated to hiker life, heads over to the visitor center to see if the showers are still open. Half an hour later he emerges, clean, with three Snickers bars and a huge grin.

"Hey, Kevin. Even though today was hard for me I still enjoy being out here. Thanks for inviting me. Think Teresa wants a Snickers?" Dad asks, handing me one of the candy bars. A resounding "No!" coming from her tent answers that question. Best just to let her calm down and sleep it off.

"Thanks for coming out, Dad," I say. "I'm glad you like it. So, you up for taking a day off tomorrow?"

"Oh god, yes. This old body isn't used to hiking for a week straight. What's your plan?"

I tell him about Achilles and how I hope he can come down and pick up Rufus. The road running through Pinkham Notch heads towards Gorham, but the A.T. continues through the notch and up Wildcat Ridge, running for twenty-one miles before dropping down into Gorham. That would take us several days to hike, and both Dad and Rufus need a break. I suggest that for now we hitch a ride into Gorham. There are a couple of hostels there and we can stay at one of them for a day off. Two new experiences for Dad: a zero day and a hostel.

In the morning, after a delicious all-you-can-eat breakfast buffet at the visitor center, we pack up in the rain and try to catch a ride. Teresa is very sore but back to her normal happy self, and she makes amends with Rufus. Like most of the tourist places we have been at so far, this is a tough spot to hitch, especially now that we have three people and a dog. After an hour we finally get to the Hiker's Paradise hostel in Gorham. The other hostel is called The Barn, and from the rumors I've heard, The Barn is the place to be because the Hiker's Paradise rules are too strict. But we're here now, so we find Bruno, the proprietor.

"You guys wanting to stay in hostel?" he asks in a gruff Polish accent.

"Yes, the three of us and my dog," I say.

"Okay, twelve dollars a night per person, dog is free. Here are rules. No alcohol on premise, quiet hours by 10:00 P.M. and if you want breakfast from the restaurant, the grill's open between 7:00 and 9:00 A.M. After 9:00, you'll have to go elsewhere for food. If your dog makes mess, clean up after him and make sure he don't bother other hikers."

That's all of his rules. The place is clean and has several kitchenettes, a washer and dryer, and bicycles for rent for a dollar. I'm not sure what all the bitching is about because this place is fine as long as you don't want to stay up all night partying. Some nights I like to party, but when under someone else's roof I can follow the rules. After stowing my pack I jump on the phone and call Achilles. I'm in luck: he's home.

I tell him about Rufus' feet and ask the gigantic favor of him: watching Rufus for three weeks while Teresa and I finish the trail. He tells me he would gladly watch Rufus, but since he sold his car he has to ask his mom if he can borrow hers. He puts down the phone and comes back a few minutes later with great news. He can be down tomorrow night to pick up Rufus! I thank him profusely before hanging up.

That is the epitome of hikers looking out for one another. I hiked with Achilles for only a few days and split a motel room with him for two nights. Four months later he is willing to drive halfway across Maine to pick up my dog and watch him for three weeks. There are a few bad apples on the trail but for the most part we take care of one another, and I am thankful for that.

While we sit on the porch and read books, Patch Monkey, Jiffy Pop, Thumper, Assface, Hemlock and Tabasco (Moss went home), Preacher and Squirrel arrive throughout the day. Homeless and Unemployed also walk in carrying little day packs.

"MaryAnn! What are you guys doing here?" Teresa says.

"We're slack-packing. This is the place Rocky and Bedouin were talking about. Every evening at five a big guy named Bruce holds a meeting in the restaurant and sets up an itinerary of who wants to be picked up and dropped off where. It has been great hiking without a pack and my knees have healed a lot. I think I can make it through Maine now. And his prices are amazingly cheap," Homeless tells Teresa. That gives me an idea.

"Hey, Dad, you want skip the rest of the Whites and hike to Maine?" I ask him. "We might be able to set it up for Bruce to pick you up from one of the forest roads in Maine and bring you back here. It looks like easier hiking for the next few days if we skip Wildcat Ridge. You up for Maine?" I say.

"Kev, I'm here to hike with you. I'm up for anything, especially if it means easier hiking. You sure you want to skip part of the trail, though?"

"Tomorrow Teresa and I can slack-pack Wildcat Ridge and be back here by evening to meet Achilles. We'll head out the day after that. You want to slack-pack the twenty-one miles tomorrow with us?" I ask, already knowing the answer.

"Um, twenty-one miles in one day? Are you nuts? You two go. I have no problem sitting here reading my book and resting for another day. Then I'll be ready for Maine."

At 5:00 P.M. we meet up with Bruce, a very large but soft spoken man. We tell him our situation and he pores over his maps. He finds a forest road about twenty trail miles away from here. A side trail, the Mahoosuc Notch Trail, connects the road to the A.T. The Mahoosuc Notch is reportedly the hardest mile of the A.T., but Dad won't have to hike it as his escape trail is on the southern end of the notch. With this plan, we will have three days to hike an easy twenty miles and get Dad out to the road to meet Bruce. The price for Bruce to drive thirty miles to pick Dad up, ten of it on a country dirt road, and thirty miles back? Ten dollars.

In the morning Bruce takes Teresa and me back to Pinkham Notch, free of charge, and we start the climb up Wildcat Ridge, which proves to be like the rest of the Whites: hard, long, and steep.

"Hey, Kevin, sorry about the other day when I was mad at you and Rufus. I was just so tired and frustrated. You forgive me?" she asks as we trudge up the near vertical mountain.

"Absolutely, babe. I don't blame you for being mad. Remember all the times I was fed up with Rufus? I understand how you felt."

"Thanks for understanding. You know what? I was so mad I was ready to leave Rufus on the cliffs and just keep hiking to Gorham," she says while we pause to catch our breath.

"You were going to leave Rufus?"

"Not just Rufus. I was going to leave you, too. I was ready to hike to Maine and let you catch up to me after your dad left. I'm glad I didn't. I would have missed you."

"Me too. The trail wouldn't be the same without you," I say, letting my emotions show.

The trail somehow becomes even steeper, and we have to quit talking to save the oxygen for the exertion. Three miles from the notch we make it to the summit of Wildcat Mountain. A gondola runs from the summit to the notch and operates year 'round, in winter for skiers and in the summer for hikers and mountain bikers. Teresa decides she's had enough hiking for today and takes the gondola back down to civilization, but I keep hiking.

Six miles later I realize there is no way I can do twelve more miles before dark, so I take a side trail down off the ridge and hitch back to Gorham. I could have pushed on and completed the whole ridge, but it would have been very late by the time I made it back to Gorham, and I would have missed Achilles completely. It's not right to ask him for such a huge favor and then not even be there when he shows up. I make it back to the hostel just as he and his mom

August 30, 2001. 1880 from Springer, 287 to Katahdin. Dad and Teresa overlooking the town of Gorham, New Hampshire.

pull into the parking lot. Teresa is already in the parking lot with Rufus. I drop my pack and walk over to the car as Achilles and his mom step out.

"Mom, here's the man who loaned me his sleeping bag when I was freezing my butt off," Achilles says, giving me a quick hug.

"So ... did you do it?" Teresa asks in an excited voice. Achilles and I exchange confused looks.

"Do what? What are you talking about?" Achilles asks. I have no idea either.

"Propose to your girlfriend! That's what you said you were going to do when you reached Maine." Wow, Teresa has one heck of a memory. I have trouble remembering if I'm wearing clean underwear, while Teresa can remember a conversation five months ago.

"No. It's a long story, but the short version is we broke up a couple of months ago. It just wasn't meant to be," he says.

"That's sad to hear. Now what are you going to do?" I ask.

"Right now I'm working construction until I can save up some money. Then, well, I have no idea. I'd like to hike the Pacific Crest Trail, but we'll see," he says.

We chat for a few more minutes, but Achilles and his mom have a long drive home and need to leave. I load Rufus into the back seat, shut the door, and Achilles and his mom get back into the vehicle. Rufus, not understanding why he is in a car without me, puts his paws on the windowsill and looks out the window as they drive away. It's hard to watch. We have hiked almost 1,900 miles together, sharing everything from a sleeping bag to a bagel. Now I'm without my buddy and already I miss him. I know it's for the best and in three weeks I'll see Rufus again: fat, still dumb, and happy.

For two days Dad, Teresa, and I hike over small mountains and fairly level land, and on the last day of August we reach a tree with a small sign on it. It simply says, "Welcome to Maine." Our last state. Teresa and I have 1,887 miles under our boots and a mere 280 miles left before the end of our journey.

"Congratulations, Dad. We made it to Maine."

"Son, I must say, this is Mainificent." He never has been very good with puns.

"Dad, that was bad. A good attempt, but Mainly terrible. I would think you could do better for something of this Mainitude."

"Yes, I know, but it's hard to Maintain such a high level of wit at all times," he replies.

"Any time you two Maingy hikers want to quit thinking you're funny, we still have some miles to do," groans Teresa, bringing us back to the reality of walking.

We stop for the night at Full Goose Shelter, and the name fits. Twenty-four students from nearby Colby College out for a weekend class are staying here. After staking our claim in the shelter, we start dinner and Dad turns to us.

"Hey you two, feel like watching some TV while the food cooks?" he asks. Flipping on the hiker "tube," we pick the group of students closest to us who are trying to set up a large tent. They lay out the poles in various angles, toss the stakes around like darts, move the entire thing several times, and make comedic attempts to properly erect the tent. Fifteen minutes later the group stands back and looks at what their hard work accomplished: something resembling a tablecloth thrown over a pair of fighting pitbulls. Unfazed, the students rip the tent down and start over. With help from several more students, they finally erect it correctly.

We watch and talk to the students until it's time for us to sleep. The students stay up talking a bit longer but are courteous and keep the noise level down. Come morning, we hike a leisurely 1.5 miles to the Mahoosuc Notch Trail–Appalachian Trail intersection. The Mahoosuc Notch is nothing like the White Mountain notches, which are wide and level enough to run a highway through. This 100-yard-wide notch runs for a mile between two very steep cliffs that have been dropping house- and car-sized boulders since the last ice age.

August 31, 2001. Dad playing among the boulders on the Mahoosic Notch, his last day on the A.T.

10. New Hampshire Brings Dad, but Takes Rufus

What lies before us is a jungle gym of rocks to climb over, around, and under, following no real trail. Dad, Teresa, and I drop our packs and charge into the notch to play on the rocks. It's fun and easy without our packs on, but after half an hour we are only a couple hundred yards into the notch. There is no way I would want to bring Rufus through this. It would take all day to lift and lower him over every boulder.

"Hey, guys, it's almost time to meet Bruce," Dad says as Teresa and I start to explore a small cave under one of the boulders.

"Okay, we'll walk you down to the road," I say. We scramble out of the notch and hike with Dad two miles out to the road. Right on time, Bruce shows up in his rusty blue pickup truck.

"Hope you haven't been waiting long. That road has gotten worse since I last drove it. There's a cooler in the back with sodas in it. Help yourself," Bruce says, and I pick out a root beer. Bruce takes some pictures of the three of us together, but then it's time for Dad to head back to Gorham and end his trip.

"Bruce, here's a twenty. I know we agreed on ten, but take it for the sodas and the rough road," Dad says.

"No sir, can't do that. We agreed on ten, and that's all I'm taking. Come on now, got to get back 'cause I have some hikers that'll be waiting for me coming off of Washington."

Teresa and I give Dad one last hug before he's bouncing down the road heading for home. I hope he had fun in his ten days of hiking with us. He was able to see a complete view of trail life in the eighty miles he hiked: a rude owner of a crappy lodge, a friendly owner of a good hostel, a work-for-stay, some stealth camping, shelter life, and hiking in the wind, rain and sun. I'm glad my dad decided to come out and partake in part of my adventure.

Teresa and I walk back to the notch, but neither of us feels like tackling it this late in the afternoon. I set up my tent and we both lay out our sleeping bags inside it. Teresa sent her tent home with Dad, who will mail it to her house. I also gave him my heavy, but comfortable, sleeping pad to take home. We each manage to drop our pack weight by three pounds, allowing us to travel a little bit faster. Our plan is to stay in shelters as much as possible for the last 280 miles and use the tent only when necessary. Tonight is one of those times. Squishing two people into a one-man tent isn't very comfortable but we manage to fall asleep, until 2:00 A.M. when a storm rolls in. Lightning cracks the sky so close we can't tell if the BOOM is from thunder or rocks being blown off the mountains. It rains hard, the water flowing around my tent like an island in a river. The moisture slowly saturates the tent walls and seeps into our sleeping bags. It's too cold and dark to start hiking, so we lie side by side in our damp sleeping bags, listening to the rain until dawn.

The notch, hard yesterday, is treacherous today now that the rocks are wet and slick. We drag, push, lower, and lift our packs through most of it as the gaps between rocks are too narrow to squeeze through and the rocks are too slick to descend with a full pack. After three exhausting hours we emerge from the mile-long gap and continue on as the temperature drops.

The next couple of days are as cold as we've seen since the south, and though it's only the first week of September, it's obvious that winter isn't very far off. Maine in the fall is beautiful and is unlike any other part of the trail. The drought hasn't hit Maine too hard, so the springs and rivers are running strong. The forests are mostly spruce and pine with the few deciduous stands awash in color. Many of the steep mountain summits are above tree line, giving 360-degree views of the surrounding forests and dozens of dark blue ponds.

While the trail in Maine is remote, we are again in the midst of a large group. It's unlikely that the trail will thin out as everyone is intent on getting to Katahdin while the weather is still good. Park rangers officially close Katahdin to hikers on October 15, but the weather often closes the mountain earlier than that.

Walking across the summit meadow of Baldpate Mountain, we come across a huge tent with a tiny figure next to it cooking breakfast. As we approach I recognize the person. It's Packman! We stop to chat for an hour. Turns out Packman made it to Connecticut when he realized he would never get to Katahdin before winter, so he "flip-flopped," meaning he took a bus to Katahdin and is hiking south to Connecticut where he left off. He has a lighter pack now, having dropped a lot of heavy stuff, but he has picked up a guitar. We listen to him play as he tells us his new trail name is Patch, earned from spending three days on the summit of Max Patch watching sunsets and playing the guitar.

We leave Patch strumming his guitar and head down the trail. I'm glad to see that he is still on the trail. When he started out he was only hiking five miles a day. Packman, now Patch, proves that anyone with the will can hike the trail.

A couple hours later we descend into a county park at Grafton Notch and find dozens of people out enjoying the cold, clear day. The parking lot is packed with cars, children are running around playing, and a couple of dogs are barking frantically, wanting to join in the fun. We walk into the small park and sit down next to the road to eat lunch.

A huge red SUV comes blasting up the road, stopping next to us. A young blond girl hangs her head out the passenger-side window.

"Hey, you know of anyplace we can get some water? We're going hiking today and need to get some," she asks us.

"There's a really great stream about a mile up the trail. It's clean, cold, and tastes great," I say, thinking I'm being helpful.

A confused look comes over her face, as if I'm speaking gibberish.

"No, we need real water. Is there a store or gas station around here where we can buy some?"

After we tell her that we are hiking and have no idea about any stores, she flips us the finger and the SUV speeds down the road. Obviously she thinks we're trying to pull some kind of prank on her. Our worlds are different. She would never dream of drinking out of a stream when stores sell water, while I can't imagine paying for water when the streams are running full. Laughing, Teresa and I finish our lunch and keep hiking.

The weather warms, and we walk in perfect comfort under the autumn sun. The bugs are gone, the heat is gone, there is water, and I'm hiking with Teresa, which makes everything more enjoyable. When bored or tired we wade in the creeks and sing songs to each other. On one particularly hard day we sit down next to a fast-flowing stream and race stick 'boats' before sinking them with rocks. I have fallen in love with her, but haven't expressed it yet out of fear. In a short couple of weeks we will be finished hiking. Then what? So on our sixth day in Maine it is time to ask the big one.

Dropping to one knee, after stubbing my toe on a rather big rock, I look up to her and ask, "Hey Teresa, do you want to go into town?"

"Oh yes, Kevin! I'd love to. I've been waiting for you to ask for the last two days!" she replies, yanking me up off the ground and planting a kiss on my lips.

What did you expect me to ask? Marriage? Heck no, I'm still wary from my divorce, and besides, it's been six days since our last resupply and we're almost out of food. We stop at Maine Road 17 where it takes us an hour to hitch into the tiny logging town of Oquossoc and get dropped off at a gas station offering very limited supplies.

"No bagels, no bread, and not much in the way of noodles," I say, looking over the meager shelves.

"Kevin, look at this!" I walk out to the front porch where Teresa is pointing to a bulletin board. Pinned to it is a business card for Gull Pond Bed and Breakfast at a rate of $15 a person. It's located in Rangeley, a town about ten miles away. The price seems reasonable but the hook, line and sinker is the fine print at the bottom of the card that reads, "Free pickup. Just call."

"Come on, let's stay there! We can sleep in a bed, take a shower, and maybe he will take us to a real grocery store," Teresa says, and I'm sold.

We call the number and talk to the owner. Fifteen minutes later a car pulls up and the driver gets out, introduces himself as Bob and drives us to his B&B, a simple two-story cabin that sits on the shores of Rangeley Lake and has its own little beach. The upstairs rooms have been converted into bunk rooms, and the downstairs has a kitchen and a comfortable common area with big cushy chairs, a TV, and lots of magazines to peruse. A canoe sits near the beach, free to use, and Bob owns a very playful black lab that loves to run around and chase any thrown object.

Gull Pond is one of the top places on the trail to stay. With the large yard and comfortable common area, it feels like I'm spending a weekend at a friend's lake cabin. I take the dog out for a swim, and then throw a stick into the water until my arm is sore. The dog isn't even panting. I love Rufus, but he doesn't play, fetch, swim, run, or do anything other than sleep and eat. Someday I'll have to get a real dog that likes to play. Teresa and I round out the day with a long canoe ride, then fall asleep on the very cozy bunks.

In the morning, Bob has coffee, juice, doughnuts, bagels, and fresh fruit set up for breakfast, and afterwards he shuttles us, again free of charge, back to the trail. It would have been nice to take a zero day here, but we are on a schedule. Teresa's parents are going to pick us up on September 21 in Millinocket, a small town near Mt. Katahdin. That means we have to hike 17 miles a day for the next two weeks to make it on time. No time for a zero.

Fueled by breakfast, we eagerly march down the trail towards the looming 4,120-foot peak of Saddleback Mountain. There's no denying it: Maine has some of the most rugged terrain on the trail. In the next thirty miles we will climb almost 10,000 vertical feet over half a dozen peaks.

Luckily, we have motivation. For the last several days we have seen signs posted in the shelters and at road crossings about a huge trail magic event on September 9. The gathering, named *The Best Trail Magic Ever!*, is at a road called East Flagstaff Road, fifty miles away. Fifty miles in three days for free food? No problem.

Crossing over Saddleback Mountain we get our first sighting of Katahdin, our magic destination. It's just a huge hazy bump 140 air miles away, but it's

September 6, 2001. Crossing one of the many peaks in Maine.

10. New Hampshire Brings Dad, but Takes Rufus

September 9, 2001. 1992 from Springer, 175 to Katahdin. Best trail magic ever!

there. Now that I can see the end of my hike, I really need to start planning my life after the trail and see if Teresa wants to fit into it. I've been half-joking lately about her moving out to Washington once I've landed a job, and she's hinted that she might come out. Time will tell.

We cover our fifty miles up and down the mountains and reach the road at noon of the third day. *The Best Trail Magic Ever!* is set up just off the road in a small meadow, right next to a lake. True to its claim, it is the best. The trail magic is courtesy of half a dozen trail-maintainers and previous thru-hikers. They brought cooler upon cooler of food, drinks, water, and a very big barbecue. There is chicken, burgers, beer, pop, lots and lots of fruit, yogurt, chips, homemade cookies and brownies, corn-on-the-cob, and much more. They also brought basic supplies such as thread and needles, different types of stove fuel, first-aid supplies, toiletries, and other odds and ends.

There are already two dozen hikers here, and by nightfall there will be a lot more. Every hiker several days ahead of us slowed down and every hiker several days behind sped up to get here, so we will have over a week's worth of hikers here today. Homeless and Unemployed, Dig, Wood Nymph, Shambala, The Four Horsemen, Tabasco and Hemlock are here. There is also a foursome called the Hula-Gang. Each member of this group has a section of a large hula-hoop that snaps together to make one big hoop. After a couple of beers I give it a try, but only succeed in making myself dizzy and falling down.

Failing at hula-hooping, I dive into an event I know I'm good at: eating. Beer in one hand and chicken leg in the other, sitting under eighty-degree sunshine — life doesn't get any better.

"Another beer, Fruit Pie?" asks Thumper, tossing me a can. "There's a ton here and these guys say they don't want to have to take anything back, so drink up!"

"I got to pace myself, man. It's still early. I don't want to be looking like Patch Monkey there." Patch Monkey is asleep in his chair with strands of drool stringing from his lips.

After eating three times, I join Tabasco, Hemlock, and Thumper at the lake for a swim. As the chilly night air creeps in we build a driftwood fire on the beach underneath the stars.

"Hey guys, check this out," Hemlock shouts, banging a piece of driftwood onto a large drift log. "It sounds really cool, like a funky snare drum." He picks up another piece and starts rattling the log. It does sound like a mangled snare drum, and I pick up a couple of sticks and bang as well.

"Man, that's really cool. We got a percussion session going," shouts Tabasco, picking up two fairly flat pieces of wood and banging them together like cymbals. Thumper grabs some wood and also joins in the driftwood thumping. The echo reverberates across the lake and back, doubling our cacophony. Luckily there isn't a house within a mile of us or they would have thought a stampede of rabid moose were rampaging across Maine.

"What the hell is all this noise about?" yells Teresa as she and Wood Nymph come down to the beach.

"Music, baby. Just good music!" Hemlock answers. Teresa and Wood Nymph look at the four of us, sitting bare-chested around a fire, banging pieces of wood together. Hemlock and Thumper have streaks of black soot running across their faces and Tabasco, for some unknown reason, has his shirt draped over his head.

"You guys look like the Beatles meet the Neanderthals!" giggles Wood Nymph.

"Must be a testosterone thing. Let's go back to the normal people," says Teresa, and the girls head back to camp. We pound away until our arms are tired and the beer is gone, then stagger back to camp to sleep wherever we happen to fall down.

Breakfast consists of hot coffee, pancakes, eggs, bacon, and sausage. *The Best Trail Magic Ever!* plans on staying another day to benefit more hikers, but Teresa and I have a deadline, so my hangover will have to hike with me. Luckily our benefactors thought of everything and have plenty of Gatorade and aspirin for the morning recovery.

Most of the people hike out today and the trail is crowded, much like it was in Georgia. The difference this time is that we are a mere 170 miles from the end. We reach the 2,000-mile mark an hour out of camp. Two thousand miles hiked. I remember back in the Smokies when I crossed the 170-mile mark, leaving me with only 2,000 miles go. It seems so long ago. Everybody was new to hiking, filled with ambitious energy and learning what works and what doesn't. Now each person has his or her system down and hiking is as natural as breathing. The excitement of starting out on the trail has been replaced with the anticipation and regret of finishing. I, along with everyone else, want to finish the trail to get back to soft beds, water always within an arm's reach, and a sturdy roof overhead to keep out the bugs, wind and rain. At the same time, though, that means returning to the fast-paced world of work and responsibilities where everybody is always in a rush and no one takes the time to look at a sunset, listen to a bird sing, or smell the proverbial roses.

11

Mainly Beautiful

The 2,000-mile marker is a paved road with "2,000 miles" painted across the middle of it. It takes on a different meaning depending on if you're hiking northbound or southbound. For us it's a place to sit down and celebrate our milestone. Hemlock and Tabasco open a can of beer they carried from the trail magic for this moment, and Shambala lets Wood Nymph paint his foot. She creates a small face on his foot and 'Footy' proceeds to tell us the story behind his stench. Shambala and Wood Nymph have been flirting for the last few weeks, but both are afraid to start any type of relationship with only a couple of weeks left before having to go separate ways. They are content to hike together until the finish.

The heat and humidity return, but we pass three ponds today and I take advantage of each one to cool off. Teresa joins me at the first two, but when we reach Pierce Pond Shelter at dusk I jump in the water alone. Teresa decides not to swim because there is no sunshine to dry out under. The swim helps with the sweat but not with my chafing, the first time I've had any in several months. I ran out of Gold Bond a few days back, and today's heat and humidity has turned my inner thighs into bright red patches of tender skin. Out of the twenty hikers here tonight, somebody has to have some Gold Bond I can borrow. Dig's tent is closest, so I ask him. He says he has something better than Gold Bond and hands me a small tube of Desitin, the diaper rash cream. I give Dig a quizzical look, but he assures me that it is good stuff, so I rub it on my inner thighs and the stuff works. The pain disappears within minutes and an hour later my skin is back to a rosy flesh color. I try to give the tube back but Dig tells me to keep it, so in the morning I apply another dose for luck and start hiking.

Today the endless hills are monotonous. We don't pass any ponds, none of the hills have views, and it is hot again. I don't feel like talking to anyone so I pull out my little radio to pass the time. Maine doesn't seem to have a lot of radio stations. After dialing through all the frequencies twice I finally pick up a male voice.

"...and our preliminary report is a plane just flew into one of the towers. Unknown the extent of the damage, casualties, or what type of plane it was. Again, our preliminary report is that a plane just flew into the World Trade

11. Mainly Beautiful

Centers in New York City. Witnesses think ... stshshshshshhhhhh." The radio turns to static as I drop down into a valley.

"Holy shit! Teresa, get out your radio and listen. It sounds like a plane flew into one of the World Trade Center towers!" I say. She digs out her radio and puts it on. As we climb out of the valley my station comes back.

"...plane smashed into the tower. Several witnesses say it was a small commuter type plane. Unknown if it had mechanical malfunction or if it was deliberate. Stay tuned to WDSI 1200 for the latest updates as we receive them."

"You find a radio station, Teresa?" I ask her.

"Yeah, I found one. They say planes have crashed into both towers and — shhhh, they're back on."

We continue listening to our radios. My station hasn't mentioned anything about the second tower yet, and so far my newsman is repeating what he has already said. It's a half mile before there is any new information.

"This just in. Apparently both towers have been hit by aircraft and both buildings are currently burning. Right now we have no idea how many people have been killed or hurt but rescue crews are all over the scene doing what they can. We also have a report of a plane hitting the Pentagon in Washington, D.C.," my newsman blurts out.

"What do you think is going to happen, Kevin? What's to burn in the buildings? Aren't they mostly glass and steel?" asks Teresa.

"Yeah, the structure is glass and steel but there's still all the paper, desks, carpets, flooring, and stuff like that. I heard that it was a small plane. Can't imagine a small plane doing that much damage to the building."

"I heard that it was two passenger planes. The big ones. Would those do a lot of damage?"

"Those would. They carry a whole lot of fuel, not to mention passengers."

The radio reports are slow in coming, and we walk another mile before anything new comes out. Finally I get an update.

"...all flights have been grounded across the nation. All planes are being told to land and so far there are several planes still unaccounted for. New reports have come in about a plane crashing into a field in southwest Pennsylvania, and a federal building in Boston has also been hit."

"You hear that, Teresa? A building in Boston was hit."

"No, I didn't hear that — Oh my god! The radio said one of the towers just collapsed!" Teresa says in shock.

"The whole building? That can't be what they meant. Maybe the guy meant the huge radio tower on top of the building fell off," I say.

"No, he said the whole tower collapsed. Those were his exact words, that the whole tower fell."

"I can't believe that happening, not from a plane. He must have meant the radio tower," I tell her, trying mostly to convince myself the newsman is wrong. The whole building collapsing? All one hundred floors? That would kill thousands and thousands of people. I dial through the radio stations but I can still only get the one station. Teresa's radio is stronger and she is able to pick up several stations. Ten minutes later as we climb out of a valley my station confirms the worst.

"...again, about ten minutes ago one tower collapsed onto itself, the whole building went down in flames. The second tower is still standing but floors 65–80 are engulfed in flame. It is estimated that 100,000 people work in the two towers so I'm not even going to try to guess at the number of casualties. If you haven't already, turn on the TV for live footage of this tragic event." I wish I had a TV to see what is really going on, but so far we are relegated to the airwaves. Tomorrow we will be in the little town of Monsoon and I can catch the TV news there.

"...the second tower just fell! Oh my god! The second tower has just collapsed into a huge ball of smoke and flame. No one can survive that! There must have been thousands of people inside. Holy shit!" The air is quiet for a few seconds before my newsman comes back on, his voice trembling as he tries to control his emotions.

"Sorry about that outburst, this scene is so horrific that I can't describe it over the radio. Both towers have now collapsed. We have no estimate of casualties at this time."

Still listening to the radio, Teresa and I reach Bald Mountain Brook Shelter. The Horsemen are here eating lunch, unaware of what is happening outside our little trail world.

"Guys, any of you have a radio? You might want to turn in on and listen. Two planes smashed into the World Trade Center towers and both buildings have collapsed. I've also heard that a plane crashed in Pennsylvania, a plane hit the Pentagon, and a plane hit a federal building in Boston. Also, there are two planes still unaccounted for," I say.

The group goes silent as Patch Monkey and Thumper dig in their packs, pulling out little radios. For the next half hour we listen to various stations and give updates of what we hear.

"I heard a plane did hit the Pentagon, but the FAA says all the planes are now accounted for," says Patch.

"I haven't heard anything about the federal building in Boston either," Teresa says.

"The station I'm listening to has said four planes have been hijacked. The two that hit the towers, the Pentagon plane, and the plane that crashed. Nothing about the federal building either," adds Thumper. It looks like the federal building was a mistake by my emotional newsman. I don't blame him for making a mistake. He wanted to get out as much news as possible with the little information he must have had.

We sit in the shelter in silence, only talking to give the latest update, of which there are few. One station ventures a casualty count of 20,000 people.

11. Mainly Beautiful

The rest of the day Teresa and I hike in silence, the peace and tranquility of the woods shattered by these events. We are ripped from our isolated community and shoved back into the world, all the more real as in two weeks we will rejoin that world.

I fall asleep listening to the radio and the latest death toll is down to 5,000 people. A lot less than what it could have been, but 5,000 people too many.

"Ready to hit our last town, baby?" I ask Teresa as we wake to the cloudless blue skies and the crisp fall air. "A mere 15 miles and we will be in Monsoon."

"Wheeee! Our last town, Kevin! Isn't that exciting! One last hot shower before Katahdin," Teresa exclaims, donning her pack.

This section of trail is some of the best we've seen, flat and fast. Maine is weird that way. One day we hike up and down mountains on rocks and roots, then the next day it is completely flat for twenty miles without a rock or root to be seen. Today is one of those easy days and we make great time into Monsoon where we check into the Shaw's Hiker Hostel. Pat and Keith Shaw have been taking in hikers since 1977 and boast to have hosted over 33,000 hikers. We plan on staying the night here, and apparently about forty other hikers do too. I have no idea where most of these people have come from as thirty of them are new faces.

The first thing I do is head up to the room and turn on the TV while Teresa takes a shower. I finally see the images the rest of the country has seen over and over: the two towers collapsing, the still smoking, ruined section of the Pentagon, the charred hole in Pennsylvania. For an hour I watch the news and learn the death toll is down to 4,000. I'm truly amazed so few people died. It could have been a whole lot worse. I also watch the speech from President Bush vowing to bring justice to the cowards who did this. That means using the military, and if it becomes a full-scale war, I might be called back up.

I call my folks, my last phone call home from the trail. My mom picks up the phone on the first ring.

"Kevin! I'm so glad you called. I've been worried about you since the attacks yesterday!"

"Worried, Mom? I'm hundreds of miles from New York City. Why would you be worried about me?"

"Because I heard that some of the terrorists came down through Maine. What if they were hiking down the trail and you ran into them?"

"Mom, the terrorists are not going to hike 500 miles to New York. They'd take a car, it's a whole lot faster," I say, laughing to myself.

"Oh, I know. I'm still your mother so I worry. Wait until you have kids, Kevin, you'll never stop worrying about them." Good ol' moms, always worrying and thinking the worst.

My dad isn't home, so I finish up my conversation while waiting for my turn in the shower. Homeless, Unemployed and Dig are here when I get out. Unemployed's knees are bothering her, so they are taking a zero day before the last push to Katahdin. Teresa is pretty bummed because she really wanted to finish with them, but our schedule doesn't allow us to take a zero day. While Teresa and Unemployed sit in the common room and partake in girl talk, I explore the town of Monsoon, which takes five minutes. A couple of gas stations and one pathetic general store make up the whole town. The store has just enough in it to scrape together enough meals for the next week.

Walking back to the hostel I take a different route and pass a house with a twenty-foot banner wrapped around the porch proclaiming, "God Bless America." I get goose bumps looking at it. In this tiny town that sees no traffic other than hikers and locals, these people still have enough pride and love for their country to hang this banner. Only a handful of people will see it and it will never be on TV or in the papers. They hung the banner with no other motivation than to show their love for this nation.

At the hostel the conversation drifts between yesterday's terrorists attacks and the end of the trail. We place our orders for the morning's breakfast as requested by the Shaws. Knowing how many hikers to feed dictates how early they have to start cooking. The Shaws have a great business going. It's very affordable and very comfortable, and it is also the first hostel southbound hikers see and the last hostel for northbounders.

After a huge, delicious breakfast Mr. Shaw shuttles us to the trailhead, marked by a weathered wooden sign stating, "100-Mile Wilderness. No supply for the next 100 miles." It warns hikers to carry ten days' worth of food. Now that's just silly. I haven't carried ten days of food yet and I don't plan to start now. If we can't get through this stretch in less than six days I'll eat my shoes.

"This is it, baby, last section of Maine," I tell Teresa.

"I know. I have butterflies in my tummy," she says, and we leave the road to venture into the forest.

The sign lied to us. This section of trail is anything but wild. We cross three roads, pass four day hikers, and walk by two groups of car campers in the first ten miles. I also see three moose, but they don't count. They're supposed to be out here.

We are the first hikers at Long Pond Stream Shelter but within two hours twenty other hikers surround us, mostly new faces. It's crowded here and shelter spots are at a premium.

"Teresa, you want to get ahead of this group a little bit?" I ask her, looking at the maps.

"Not if it means walking twenty-five miles tomorrow, I don't."

"That's not my plan. Coming off of West Chairback Pond six miles from here is a trail leading to some logging roads. Looks like we can take the logging roads around the next mountain range and make some great time. You up for it?"

"Sure, why not? Sounds like an adventure!" Teresa replies. That is part of the reason why I love her: her willingness to try something new. I study the map a bit longer and plan our route.

When morning comes we quickly walk the six miles to the side trail and begin a very daunting blue-blaze. We soon discover that there have been several more logging roads built since the map was printed in 1996. Using my compass (I had my dad bring it out after the fiasco on Mt. Moosilauke), we are able to pick the right roads until we come to a four-way intersection where my map shows there should only be one road.

"Which way, Kevin?" Teresa asks.

"I don't know. These roads all curve once they leave the junction here so I'm not sure which one is the original road. Give me a minute to think." I sit down with the map and study it for a few minutes, then pick a road.

"This one, babe."

"You sure this is the right way?"

"No, but the only way to tell is to follow it. We have two choices: follow the road until we figure out where we are, or turn around and hike back to the A.T."

"I don't want to hike backwards. I'm going to trust your judgment, Kevin, so let's keep going," Teresa says.

Three hours later we cross a stream that's on the map and I'm able to pinpoint where we are. We are right where we want to be. It turns dark before we reach the A.T. so we set up camp next to a stream, our first blue-blazing camping experience.

Our trail leaves the road and continues up the side of White Cap Mountain, where it connects with the A.T. It's a great trail, and the trees have old white blazes on them that have been painted over. This used to be the A.T. Once again the old A.T. is easy walking with amazing views and better scenery. We hop across several small streams and pass an old homestead before reaching the cold summit of White Cap Mountain. Fall is here, and the cool air means lower humidity, allowing us to see for miles.

"There she is, Kevin. Katahdin. I'd never thought I'd be so happy and sad at the same time to see a mountain," Teresa says to me as we huddle together on the summit. Katahdin stands in a picturesque pose before us, thirty air miles away. It looks extremely steep and appears to have several faces that require technical climbing. I'm hoping the A.T. route is easier than it looks, because right now it looks real hard.

White Cap is the last peak rising over 2,000 feet until Mt. Katahdin, and once off the mountain the trail becomes relatively flat. Teresa and I stop for lunch at Antlers Campsite on the shores of Jo-Mary Lake, with soft spruce needles covering the forest floor and towering spruce trees rising overhead. It is a very peaceful spot and I wouldn't mind staying here for several days, but time doesn't permit it.

September 15, 2001. Mighty Mt. Katahdin.

"Come check this out, Kevin! There's clams in the lake!" Teresa yells over to me from the shore. Sure enough, small white clams are scattered along the pond floor. I don't know how these got here, as none of the other ponds have clams in them.

"You think they're any good to eat?" I ask her. I like clams.

"I don't know. I'm not going to eat one, but go ahead."

I collect half a dozen clams and steam them in my pot.

"Here goes, wish me luck," I tell her as I pluck one out and pop it in my mouth. The riveting flavors of vomit, feces, and spoiled meat swirl in my mouth as I bite down on the bi-valve.

"Ugh! What the hell was that! It tasted like it's been fried in sewer juice," I exclaim, spitting the half-chewed clam out.

"Not so good? Well, maybe you just picked a bad one. Be brave and try another," Teresa goads me. Be brave? I don't see her trying one. Still, I like clams and have my hopes set for a feast. Maybe I did pick a bad one.

"Okay, I'll try one more. Here goes," and I pop another one in my mouth. This time the vomit I taste is my own as I empty the contents of my stomach, and the clam, onto the beach.

"My god, that was bad! What the hell are these things?" I say, tossing the rest of the cooked clams into the woods. I wouldn't even wish these upon my ex-wife.

"Hahaha, that bad, huh?" Teresa manages to say as she laughs at my misfortune. "See, that's why I don't eat clams. They're disgusting."

"Clams are usually not this bad," I say, thinking it over. "Hmm, they might have been a little better with butter, though."

We don our packs and I step over my puddle of vomit, leaving the clams for someone else to try.

The 100-mile Wilderness is actually the 70-mile Wilderness now that Bill Ware has opened up his White House Wilderness Camp to hikers. Once predominantly used by hunters in the fall and snowmobilers in the winter, the camp is located across Pemadumcook Lake with no reasonable access to it from the A.T. Bill has fixed that problem by hanging an air horn on a tree. Teresa blasts the horn and twenty minutes later Bill comes across the lake in a small motorboat.

Bill welcomes us into his boat and asks if we are staying the night, or just coming over for the day. We explain that we are here just for the day and have a mail drop to pick up. Bill reminds us that it is $15 to pick up a mail drop, just like our book says. When I ask why it costs so much, Bill explains that the nearest post office is several hours away, and that the only way to his cabin is by boat or a twenty-mile dirt road that he maintains himself. We reach his camp, and he gets our box and tells us to make ourselves at home.

The camp itself consists of the main house, a bunkhouse, and several smaller cottages that offer private rooms. Everything runs off propane, solar power, or a gas generator. There isn't any electricity or phone service out here. Bill does have a few supplies for sale, but they are all double what it would cost in town. Right above the grill is a huge sign stating all of the costs, saving hikers the embarrassment of eating a $2.00 candy bar or ordering a $6.00 cheeseburger and not realizing the price. It's simple supply and demand. I want a cheeseburger, he has one, and I'm willing to spend the money. It proves to be a damn fine cheeseburger.

After the burgers Bill takes us back across the lake, and we walk along the rocky shore for an hour before setting up camp next to a small inlet. Just as I finish setting up the tent, a huge crashing sound comes from the other side of the inlet.

"Oh my god, what is that? Kevin, go look!" Teresa whispers to me.

"Why do I have to look? What if it's a starving bear? You would make a better meal," I say, and quickly receive a smack to the arm. I walk down to the inlet and on the other side of the inlet, with less than thirty feet of water between us, is a gigantic bull moose. He has antlers that I could hang a Jeep on and legs that would make a Rockette jealous.

"Teresa, get down here!" I whisper, and she joins me. The moose looks up at us for a minute, then goes back to chewing on tasty morsels of nasty-looking seaweed. After half an hour of munching on seaweed (the moose, not me) he turns around and leaves, crashing through the forest behind him.

"Wow, that was amazing. But what if he comes over here, Kevin?" Teresa asks.

"Well, first off, you don't look like a big gloop of green seaweed so I'd say you're fairly safe. Second, if he does want to come attack us, not a damn thing we can do about it, so no reason to worry." I don't think I eased her apprehension, but Teresa's a tough woman and before long she's asleep.

After two easy days of hiking, Teresa and I leave the 100-mile Wilderness and enter Baxter State Park, home of Mt. Katahdin and the last fifteen miles of our trip. Baxter Park is an anomaly when it comes to a state park. In 1921, millionaire Percival Baxter was elected governor of Maine, and he fought to make Katahdin a state park to protect it from loggers and developers. The Maine legislature refused, so Baxter started buying the land himself. In 1931 he had accumulated five thousand acres of land, which he donated to the people of Maine for the formation of a park. He continued to be a political force and finally got the legislature to approve the park. Over the next thirty years it was expanded to over 200,000 acres, mostly because of Percival Baxter's efforts.

The park is now funded by a trust fund and is administered separately from the rest of the state parks in Maine. The purpose of the trust is to keep the park as natural as possible, so there are no paved roads, electricity, stores or telephones within the park, and camping restrictions are extremely strict. Luckily, the park has an agreement with the Appalachian Trail Conference and reserves twelve spots a night for thru-hikers at Katahdin Stream Campground, the closest campground to the mountain.

This late in the season the park is relatively empty, and Teresa and I arrive at noon with the campground to ourselves. Other hikers slowly trickle in and by evening the twelve reserved spots are full. The spots are actually three four-person shelters, and we double up with a couple named Foots-A-Flame and Walkitoff. Foots-A-Flame is a lanky 6'4" man with a beard almost as scraggly as mine. His wife, Walkitoff, is a young woman and a full foot shorter than her husband. We share a campfire and have a great last night on the trail. I wouldn't have minded meeting these two several months ago and hiking with them.

Morning comes and a dreary gray sky meets us for our last day on the trail. I hope it clears up. We walk over to the ranger station because all hikers are required to sign in before attempting the summit. We are numbers 292 and 293 so far this year, almost the same as Harpers Ferry. We are coming down the same trail we'll hike up, so there is no reason to carry our heavy packs, and the rangers have a supply of tattered day packs for hikers to borrow. Armed with our ten-pound day packs, we head up Mt. Katahdin.

On the way up we meet the Hula-Gang, all carrying their full packs and hula-hoop sections. The Hula-Gang are going to descend down a trail on the backside of the mountain where one of their parents will pick the group up.

With our light packs we outpace the Hula-Gang, but not by much. Katahdin is the hardest climb of the whole trail, rising 4,200 feet in five miles up a long rocky ridge, and we are constantly scrambling over huge boulders, some with iron bars drilled into them to assist in climbing. It's like the

Mahoosuc Notch, only vertical. Our excitement and adrenaline power us up the ridge, and soon Teresa and I are standing on a huge plateau called The Table with the summit a mile away, a long ridge rising out of the plateau. The dreary gray skies have turned into a random mass of swirling clouds that give the whole experience a sublime feeling. One moment we can see from Canada to New Hampshire, and then the dark clouds are whipping past looking like a tornado may form, only to open up again with the magnificent views. It is cold and windy, and if it drops a few degrees it could snow.

Staring at the summit, I take Teresa's hand in mine.

"That's it, babe, ready to do this?" I ask her.

"We've hiked 2,166 miles for this. Let's go get to the top!"

We walk hand in hand until the rough trail forces us to walk single file the rest of the way to the summit cairn. Foots-A-Flame and Walkitoff have already arrived and are taking pictures of themselves next to the huge wooden sign marking the northern terminus of the Appalachian Trail, 2,167 miles away from Springer Mountain, Georgia.

The Hula-Gang arrives shortly after, and they put together the hula-hoop. After practicing with it at *The Best Trail Magic Ever!* I'm ready. Standing on the summit of Mt. Katahdin among the swirling clouds, I hula-hoop, swaying my hips in perfect rhythm.

"Nice hips, Kevin! Way to move them!" cheers Teresa as I master the plastic ring. She walks over to me, knocks the hoop to the ground, and gives me a

September 19, 2001. 2167 miles from Springer. The summit, and the end.

September 19, 2001. Hula-hooping on the top of the world.

huge hug. She leans her head against mine and gently asks, "Do you still want me to move out west with you?"

"Absolutely I do. Teresa, I love you and I don't want the end of the trail to mean the end of our relationship," I say, opening my heart to her.

"I've been giving it a lot of thought, and if you could stand living with me I want to come out. I need to take a couple more classes, but in six months I would be able to come out. Will that work?" she asks tentatively.

I sweep her off her feet and answer her with a kiss.

"Put me down, you big oaf! You're going to make us fall and break something the last day hiking!"

I put her down, and it's time to descend before the weather decides to go from mesmerizing to dangerous. We hike in silence, happy and depressed at the same time now that the hike is over. During these last six months of hiking I have gone through a tremendous change. I've healed completely from my divorce, made the transition from Marine to civilian, met the woman of my dreams, and fallen in love. I'm ready to take on the rest of my life with Teresa at my side.

Epilogue

Teresa and I came off of Katahdin and met her parents in Millinocket. They drove us to Achilles' place. Rufus was fat! He had gained twenty pounds in three weeks. Though Rufus was happy to see me, bounding over into my arms, he was reluctant to leave. He didn't want to go hiking again. I stayed with Teresa at her parents' house for a week, then flew home to Spokane. (The events of September 11 were over and all the airlines were flying normal schedules again.)

Several months later I moved to Seattle and found a job. Teresa stayed in Rochester for six months to take several classes, then moved out to Seattle with me. We are still together.

Homeless and Unemployed summited Katahdin the day after we did. It was cold, raining and miserable for them. Keystone returned after his bout with Giardia and rejoined with Tubesteak. They both finished in mid-October. Marcus, Webb, Sticks and Patches, Shambala and Wood Nymph also finished sometime after we did. I never did hear anything more about the Outlaws, nor do I know what happened to Arkon. The last time I saw him was in North Carolina. The ATC estimates 2,655 hikers attempted the trail in 2001, with 439 finishing. Teresa and I are proud to be in that group.

Teresa, Rufus and I still hike, but now it is mostly day hikes. Full-time jobs limited our ability to get into the woods. We would love to do another long-distance hike, either the A.T. again or the Pacific Crest Trail, but I don't know if we ever will. Six months off was a luxury most people don't have, and I don't know if I will have it again until I am retired. Someday, hopefully, I can have another great adventure.

Index

Achilles 20–23, 25, 26, 64–67, 178–179, 191, 196–199, 220
Amicalola Falls State Park 3, 6, 9, 53
aqua blaze 107, 109, 111
Arkon 8–11, 16, 26, 220
Assface 100, 118, 119, 121, 122, 197
ATC 7, 8, 10, 11, 19, 104, 112, 116, 220

Baxter 216
bear 9, 10, 30, 34–36, 39, 72, 105–107, 120, 126–127
Bear Bait 126–128, 133, 157, 159, 174
Blood Mountain 17, 18, 21
blue blaze 3, 8, 124, 169, 173, 213
Blue Ridge Mountains 102, 115, 123
Bob *see* Homeless

Clingmans Dome 37, 160, 191
Connecticut 8, 146, 147, 151, 152, 161, 173, 202
Cookie Lady 157, 158
cow 60, 61, 68, 77–78, 86

Dad 183–201, 203, 205, 207
Damascus 68–71, 80, 91, 100, 148
Dartmouth 173, 175, 176, 180
Debbie 20, 22, 26, 96, 98, 101
deer 34, 35, 84, 85, 102, 104, 106
Dig 33, 82, 149, 151, 182, 183, 205, 208, 212
Dover Oak 146
Doyle 120–124
Duncannon 120, 122

Fontana 29–33, 47, 53, 75
Four Horsemen 100, 118–119, 121, 205, 210

Georgia 1, 3, 7, 8, 11, 17, 18, 26, 38, 62, 75, 95, 96, 100, 119, 124, 126, 162, 207, 217
Gnome 177, 178
Gorham 185, 191, 196, 198, 201
Grayson Highlands 71
Great Barrington 154, 165
Great Smoky Mountains 29–31, 34–38, 40, 64, 85, 102–104, 141, 185, 191, 207
Green Mountains 162, 172, 193
gypsy moth 93, 94, 104

Hanover 173–176
Harpers Ferry 107, 111, 115, 120, 126, 147, 159, 216
Hemlock 158, 159, 171, 172, 182, 197, 205, 206, 208
Hiawassee 22, 24, 25, 27, 49, 53, 64
Homeless 36, 37, 82, 99, 103, 106, 107, 141, 149, 151, 164–166, 182, 183, 197, 205, 212, 220
Horsemen *see* Four Horsemen
Hot Springs 46, 47, 50, 52, 54, 55, 64
Hula-Gang 205, 216, 217

Jason *see* Achilles
Jiffy Pop 100, 121, 122, 142, 197

Katahdin 3, 7, 21, 24, 35, 44, 45, 50, 58, 65, 69, 71, 76, 83, 108, 118, 122, 132, 135, 137, 140, 152, 157, 161, 162, 171, 176, 177, 187, 193, 198, 202, 204, 205, 211–214, 216, 217, 220
Keffer Oak 87, 146
Kent 147–149
Keystone 62, 63, 68, 70–72, 74–76, 100, 220
Kincora Hostel 61, 63, 64, 80, 93, 135, 191

Lightning 1, 39, 40, 81, 87, 117, 166, 186
Long Trail 161–163, 167, 169, 172
Loren 4, 5, 10, 11, 16, 53

MacKaye, Benton 7
Mahoosuc 197, 200, 217
Maine 1, 3, 7, 21, 24, 30, 36, 38, 47, 49, 57, 63, 68, 95, 96, 99, 119, 121, 124, 126, 135, 145, 165, 169, 182, 185, 188, 191, 193, 196–199, 202–204, 206, 208, 211, 212, 216
Marcus 27, 29, 33, 63, 70, 74, 75, 77, 78, 81–83, 89–92, 99, 174, 220
Marine Corps 1, 3–5, 24, 49, 92, 114, 115, 125, 127, 133, 147, 148, 178, 219
MaryAnn *see* Unemployment
Massachusetts 94, 151, 154, 156, 158, 161
Max Patch 44–47, 202
moose 162, 206, 212, 215
Moosilauke 177, 179, 180, 213
mosquitoes 138, 143, 150

Index

Mt. Greylock 154, 159–161
Mt. Lafayette 186, 187, 192
Mt. Washington 7, 176, 185, 190–193
Mouth 74, 75, 98, 99

Nantahala 27
Neels Gap 18, 21
New England 7, 146, 147, 173, 185
New Hampshire 7, 30, 57, 107, 133, 137, 159, 173, 176, 184, 185, 187, 189, 191, 193, 195, 197–199, 201, 203, 205, 207, 217
New Jersey 130–143, 145, 188
New York 24, 63, 91, 99, 110, 120, 125, 130, 133–135, 138, 142–145, 159, 177, 188, 209, 211
North Carolina 7, 26, 45, 54, 57, 58, 60, 80, 94, 119, 160, 162, 220
North Woodstock 137, 146, 181, 186

Othra 75, 76, 80, 81, 95, 96, 98–100, 106, 107, 109, 110, 112, 114, 120–122, 124, 172, 174
Outlaws 41, 42, 44, 46, 100

Packman 13, 14, 20, 21, 202
Patch *see* Packman
Patch Monkey 64, 65, 100, 119, 197, 206, 210
Pennsylvania 5, 7, 51, 85, 112, 116–123, 126–128, 130, 132, 135, 136, 189, 209–211
Preacher 126, 128, 133, 165, 172, 197

Ripplin' Water Kennels 31
Roan Mountain 57–59, 62

Satellite 113–115
Shaffer, Earl 7
Shambala 159, 174, 205, 208, 220
Shaw's Hostel 211
Shenandoah National Park 101, 102, 104–107, 109, 115, 159
Shennies *see* Shenandoah National Park
Shiggy 27, 29, 33, 63, 70, 71, 74, 75, 78, 81, 89, 99

Slatington 130, 132
Smokies *see* Great Smokey Mountains
snake 28, 97, 128, 129
Spokane 3, 4, 28, 92, 125, 128, 220
Springer Mountain 6–8, 12–13, 18, 97, 98, 118, 127, 177, 178, 217
Squirrel 126–128, 133, 165, 197

Tabard 174, 175
Tabasco 158, 159, 171, 182, 197, 205, 206, 208
Tennessee 30, 40, 54, 57, 58, 60, 64
Thumper 35, 37–40, 64, 65, 100, 118, 119, 121, 142, 197, 206, 210
Trail angels 1, 79, 98, 124, 158, 173
Trail magic 1, 60, 98, 158, 204–206, 217
Travis 51–53, 56
Tubesteak 62, 63, 68, 70, 72, 74–76, 100, 220

Unemployment 36, 37, 82, 99, 103, 104, 106, 107, 141, 142, 149, 164–166, 182, 183, 197, 205, 212, 220

Vermont 161–163, 165, 169, 171, 173, 176, 178, 188, 193
Vernon 137, 140–142, 146

Walasi-Yi 18, 21, 26
Waynesboro 47, 98, 99, 103
Webb 40, 42, 46–50, 52, 57, 82, 220
West Virginia 19, 107, 112
White blaze 8, 124, 169, 213
White Mountains 107, 176, 179–181, 183, 184–186, 188, 189, 190, 191, 195, 197
Whites *see* White Mountains
wolves 84, 85, 104
Wood Nymph 103, 106, 174, 205, 206, 208, 220
World Trade Center 208–210